CORYATS CRUDITIES: SELECTIONS

CORYATS CRUDITIES: SELECTIONS

Thomas Coryate

a *Broadview Anthology of British Literature* edition

Contributing Editor, *Coryats Crudities: Selections*
Philip S. Palmer, UCLA

General Editors,
The Broadview Anthology of British Literature:
Joseph Black, University of Massachusetts, Amherst
Leonard Conolly, Trent University
Kate Flint, University of Southern California
Isobel Grundy, University of Alberta
Don LePan, Broadview Press
Roy Liuzza, University of Tennessee
Jerome J. McGann, University of Virginia
Anne Lake Prescott, Barnard College
Barry V. Qualls, Rutgers University
Claire Waters, University of California, Davis

broadview press

BROADVIEW PRESS – www.broadviewpress.com
Peterborough, Ontario, Canada

Founded in 1985, Broadview Press remains a wholly independent publishing house. Broadview's focus is on academic publishing: our titles are accessible to university and college students as well as scholars and general readers. With over 600 titles in print, Broadview has become a leading international publisher in the humanities, with world-wide distribution. Broadview is committed to environmentally responsible publishing and fair business practices.

The interior of this book is printed on 100% recycled paper.

© 2017 Broadview Press

Library and Archives Canada Cataloguing in Publication

Coryate, Thomas, approximately 1577–1617
[Crudities. Selections]
    Coryats Crudities : selections / Thomas Coryate ; contributing editor, Philip S. Palmer, UCLA.

(A Broadview anthology of British literature edition)
ISBN 978-1-55481-323-0 (softcover)

    1. Europe—Description and travel—Early works to 1800.   2. Coryate, Thomas, approximately 1577–1617. Coryat's crudities—Poetry.   I. Palmer, Philip S., 1983–, editor II. Title.   III. Series: Broadview anthology of British literature (Series)

D915.C67 2017   914.04'23   C2016-907445-5

Broadview Press handles its own distribution in North America
PO Box 1243, Peterborough, Ontario, Canada K9J 7H5, Canada
555 Riverwalk Parkway, Tonawanda, NY 14150, USA
Tel: (705) 743-8990; Fax: (705) 743-8353
email: customerservice@broadviewpress.com

Distribution is handled by Eurospan Group in the UK, Europe, Central Asia, Middle East, Africa, India, Southeast Asia, Central America, and the Caribbean. Distribution is handled by Footprint Books in Australia and New Zealand.

Broadview Press acknowledges the financial support of the Government of Canada through the Canada Book Fund for our publishing activities.

Canada

Developmental Editors: Laura Buzzard, Jennifer McCue
Cover Designer: Lisa Brawn
Typesetter: Alexandria Stuart

PRINTED IN CANADA

Contents

Introduction

Thomas Coryate
(1577?–1617)

"He is an engine, wholly consisting of extremes, a head, fingers, and toes. For what his industrious toes have trod, his ready fingers have written, his subtle head dictating." Thus begins the poet Ben Jonson's "Character of the famous *Odcombian*," a satirical portrait of the early seventeenth-century traveler Thomas Coryate, known today for his five-month tour of Western Europe. This tour, which according to popular legend was completed entirely on foot, culminated in one of the strangest travelogues published in early modern England: *Coryats Crudities* (1611), a more than nine hundred-page book blending detailed "observations" of churches, palaces, and local customs (including the first account of forks in English) with lengthy historical digressions and lively accounts of personal misadventure. Coryate, who had strong connections to the political, legal, and literary circles of early modern England, became a figure well known for his eccentricity and odd style, though he was also respected for his antiquarian scholarship and facility with foreign languages.

An engaging raconteur open to new experiences and fascinated by foreign cultures, Coryate has one of the most unique travel-writing voices ever known in English letters. From his first appearance in print to the modern day, his narrative voice and persona have been the subject of numerous reprints, imitations, allusions, and appropriations, from the eighteenth-century traveler who dubbed himself "Coryate Junior" to modern iterations such as the Thomas Coryate Twitter account and Tim Moore's *Continental Drifter* (2001), a comic travelogue in which the author retraces Coryate's steps.

The first publication of Crudities occasioned a minor literary sensation when dozens of nobleman and literati (including the poets Ben Jonson and John Donne) contributed mock commendatory poems to the volume, resulting in over one hundred pages of experimental verses that ridicule Coryate's European journey. (Coryate was in on the joke, however, and carefully curated the comic persona emerging from those verses.) Much of this material can be described as Menippean satire, which encouraged the miscellaneous compilation of disparate genres, languages, and forms in inventive ways. His creative and self-deprecating use of media culture to gain personal celebrity—apparent most notably in the satirical verses and engraved illustrations appended to Crudities—further shape Coryate as remarkably modern in both his writing style and sense of public self-fashioning.

Thomas Coryate was born around 1577 to George Coryate (d. 1607) and his wife Gertrude (d. 1645), who lived in the small village of Odcombe, Somerset. As well as a rector of Odcombe Church, George Coryate was a minor Latin poet and fellow of New College, Oxford. Thomas studied at Winchester School before proceeding to Gloucester Hall, Oxford, where he stayed for three years before leaving without a degree. Through family connections, Coryate secured a post in the household of Henry Frederick (1594–1612), Prince of Wales and son of King James I. According to contemporary allusions, Coryate may have played the role of Prince Henry's informal jester; in any case, it is clear he was a source of entertainment and the butt of jokes for gentlemen at Henry's court.

The travels for which he would become famous commenced in May 1608, when Coryate journeyed from England into France. After landing in Calais, he traveled south, passing through several towns in Picardy on his way to Paris, where he viewed Notre-Dame Cathedral and the "pompous ceremonies" of Catholics on Corpus Christi Day. Coryate proceeded to the royal palace at Fontainebleau, which he admired for its statues, gardens, and birds, and then traveled south to Lyons, where he arrived in early June. During his stay at the Three Kings Inn in Lyons, Coryate would have his first of many religious disputes with non-Christians—in this case a Turkish scholar. From Lyons Coryate made his way through the Alps into Northern Italy, stopping at Turin, Milan, Cremona, and Mantua before making his way to Venice on 24 June. Coryate remained in Venice, a city he termed "the richest paragon and queen of Christendom," for six weeks, visiting the typical tourist sites of St. Mark's Square and Church, the Doge's Palace, and the Rialto, while also observing the customs of Venetian gondoliers, actors, mountebanks, and courtesans. As in Lyons, Coryate once again attempted to proselytize non-Christians, this time a group of Jews in the Venetian ghetto; the episode nearly ended in violence, but Coryate escaped in the nick of time through the opportune arrival of Sir Henry Wotton, English ambassador to Venice, on a passing gondola.

From Venice Coryate journeyed to Vicenza and Verona, where he saw the great Roman amphitheater, before entering Switzerland and viewing the city of Zurich. He regarded the baths of Baden, especially the co-ed bathing customs of the Swiss, with particular interest. Entering Germany, Coryate traveled to Basel, Strasbourg, and Heidelberg, visiting the Great Tun of wine kept in the latter city's palace. After drinking a bit too much in Heidelberg, Coryate continued down the Rhine to Worms, Mainz, Frankfurt am Main, and Cologne, viewing the shrine of the Magi in Cologne's cathedral church. Coryate finished his five-month tour in the Netherlands, traveling through Nijmegen, Dordrecht, Middelburg, and Flushing before leaving Europe and entering London on 3 October. Upon returning to his family home in Odcombe, Coryate hung up his traveling shoes in the parish church for public display.

In 1611 Coryate would publish an eccentric book relating his travel observations. The publication of *Coryats Crudities hastily gobbled up in five months travels ... Newly digested in the hungry air of Odcombe in the County of Somerset, & now dispersed to the nourishment of the travelling Members of this Kingdom* was presumably funded out of Coryate's own pocket, using money he earned from a shrewd wager placed before leaving England. Coryate made this bet with the linen-draper Joseph Starre, a resident of Yeovil, Somerset (not far from Odcombe): if Coryate returned alive, Starre would pay Coryate 200 marks (around £133); if he did not return, Starre could keep the £40 Coryate initially paid before he left England. After much legal wrangling upon his return, it seems Coryate eventually secured the 200 marks from a reluctant Starre.

A few years later Coryate set out on a more ambitious journey, this time to the Middle East and India. He left England in the autumn of 1612 on a sea voyage to Constantinople, where he stayed for ten months. Before arriving in the Ottoman capital city, Coryate visited the presumed site of the ancient city of Troy. In 1614 he traveled by sea from Constantinople to Aleppo and then journeyed by caravan towards Jerusalem, where he sojourned for Easter before returning to

Aleppo. Determined at this point to walk from Aleppo to the Mughal Empire in India, Coryate set out in February 1615 and arrived in Ajmer, at that time the seat of the Mughal Emperor Jahangir, in mid-July. At Ajmer Coryate fell in with English East India Company merchants, including Sir Thomas Roe, an ambassador to Jahangir's court. He also learned several eastern and middle-eastern languages (Turkish, Arabic, Persian, and Hindi-Urdu), and delivered an oration in Persian to Jahangir. In the autumn of 1616 Coryate parted ways with Jahangir and the English, traveling solo until he met up again with Roe (and his chaplain Edward Terry) in late summer 1617.

After moving on that autumn to Surat and its East India Company factory, Coryate apparently became a profligate drinker with the English merchants and died of dysentery in December 1617. The whereabouts of his burial place are unknown. Accounts of Coryate's Asian travels have survived in fragments only—his journey to Constantinople being printed in Samuel Purchas's *Purchas his Pilgrimes* (1625) and a portion of his Indian travels appearing in two letter-pamphlets, *Thomas Coriate Traveller for the English Wits: Greeting. From the Court of the Great Mogul* (1616) and *Mr Thomas Coriat to his friends in England sendeth greeting: From Agra the Capitall City of the Dominion of the Great Mogoll in the Easterne India* (1618). The full travel journal, which Sir Thomas Roe described as "too great for portage," has been lost.

English Travel and Travel Writing, c. 1550–1650

At the time *Coryats Crudities* was published, England occupied a relatively marginal political position (on a world stage dominated by the Spanish and Ottoman Empires) and struggled to gain footholds in foreign commercial markets; it also imported many of its travelogues and geographies from the Continent. The English travelogue as a form would not fully come into its own until the long eighteenth century—the age of British naval supremacy and of the custom of Grand Tours of Europe—when the popularity of the travel genre exploded and themes of travel permeated all aspects of literary culture. What came before was often experimental in both its form and content. Certainly English travel writing in the Tudor and early Stuart periods anticipates the imperial and colonial power Britain would later wield. But these were not the travel writers of the British Empire the world would come to know a century later; rather, it was a group of enterprising (and often eccentric) individuals driven by the pursuit of knowledge and hope of financial reward, whose experiences as travelers and travel writers were often marked by anxiety, envy, experimentation, and failure.

The Age of Overseas Expansion

England played a relatively minor role in the fabled age of exploration that swept Europe in the fifteenth and sixteenth centuries. While Portugal and Spain were the major players in transatlantic navigation, travel, commerce, and colonialism, England participated in a smaller series of oceanic voyages, sponsored by both the crown and private investors. These voyages were the subject of written narratives in both print and manuscript.

One of the earliest English voyagers to appear in print (1569) was John Hawkins, the first English slave trader, who wrote and published a first-hand account of his third voyage (the first two were published anonymously and written in the third person). The famous circumnavigations of Sir Francis Drake (1577–80) and Thomas Cavendish (1586–88) were also reported in print narratives, none of which were written by the explorers themselves but rather pilots and other crew-members. These accounts played a central role in the first anthology of English voyage narratives, Richard Hakluyt's *Principal Navigations of the English Nation* (1589). Purporting to compile edited versions of the most important narratives of English overseas commerce and travel from the Middle Ages to the present day, Hakluyt's *Principal Navigations* concludes with a section of English voyages to the "West," with the Drake and Cavendish voyages prominently featured. The second, expanded edition of Hakluyt's *Principal Navigations* (1598–1600) presented a more balanced view of English voyaging in the period, including alongside the success stories of Drake and Cavendish scores of failed voyage narratives. Attempts at colonizing North America proved to have similarly mixed results; while the Jamestown settlement, for example, became permanent, others were not so long-lasting (one well-known example is the Roanoke colony, whose inhabitants mysteriously disappeared). The most famous early English account of the New World, Sir Walter Raleigh's *Discovery of Guiana* (1596), blends emotions of wonder and admiration with frustrated accounts of the search for El Dorado. The celebrated—and unexpected—victory over the Spanish Armada in 1588 was certainly a high point in early English naval history, but the period as the whole is marked by a number of high-profile failures, not the least of which were several vain attempts to discover the Northwest Passage. As an anthology of this period's travel narratives, Hakluyt's *Principal Navigations* registers both the triumphs and shortcomings of early modern English voyaging.

A few decades later, *Principal Navigations* would be succeeded by another large collection of English travel narratives, based in part on Hakluyt's unpublished manuscripts: Samuel Purchas's *Hakluytus posthumus or Purchas his Pilgrimes* (1625). Purchas's anthology features several voyages to the Middle East, India, and East Asia, including an abridged portion of the lost travelogue of Thomas Coryate's Asian travels. Purchas's *Pilgrimes* would be the last major collection of travel narratives to appear in English until the eighteenth century.

The Multicultural Mediterranean

In the past twenty years, scholars of early modern travel and travel writing have started to shift their attention away from voyages of exploration and discovery to the complex cultural exchanges enacted in the Mediterranean Sea. The blending of ethnicities, languages, religions, and governments in the early modern Mediterranean established a rich cross-cultural setting for the travels of various types of people, including merchants, pirates, pilgrims, ambassadors, soldiers, and galley slaves.

Most importantly, the early modern Mediterranean world was dominated by the Ottoman Empire, whose power encompassed Northern Africa, Egypt and the Sinai Peninsula, the Balkans, Turkey, and the Middle East. Ottoman supremacy in the region provoked feelings of both anxiety and envy from English travel writers of the period—anxiety over increasing territorial expansion and the possibility of conversion to Islam, envy over their imperial ambitions and sophisticated military. Anxieties regarding Islam are most notably felt in English conversion and captivity narratives, which typically feature a European anti-hero, sometimes a pirate, who is captured by the Ottoman Turks, converts to Islam, and never returns to England. Philip Massinger's tragicomedy *The Renegado* (1624) and Roger Daborne's *A Christian Turned Turk* (1610) offer excellent examples from imaginative literature, while John Rawlins's *The Famous and Wonderful Recovery of a Ship of Bristol* (1622) is more typical of the period's non-fiction prose captivity narratives.

The period abounds with other types of English travel narratives set in the Ottoman Near East. George Sandys's *A Relation of a Journey* (1615), reprinted several times in the seventeenth century, views the contemporary Mediterranean and Middle East through the lens of classical antiquity and its great literary works, often as a way to bemoan the faded glory of Greece or Egypt under their new Ottoman overlords. Henry Blount's *A Voyage into the Levant* (1636), William Lithgow's *A most delectable, and true discourse, of an admired and painefull peregrination* (1614), and the manuscript narratives of Thomas Dallam and Peter Mundy illustrate other English approaches to describing Turkey and the Ottoman Empire.

The Proto Grand Tour

Historians typically date the heyday of the European Grand Tour—the journey through western Europe customarily undertaken by upper-class young men—from 1660 to the early 1800s. However, travel by Europeans in Europe, for the purpose of education, art, or leisure, existed in a prototypical form from the sixteenth century onwards. The Protestant Reformation and Catholic Counter-Reformation made this sort of travel difficult for much of the sixteenth century (it was, for example, unsafe for the Protestant English to travel into Italy because of the threat of physical violence from Catholics), and there was much ink spilled in England warning travelers of becoming blasphemous, morally dissolute "Italianate Englishmen." But in 1598 the Edict of Nantes relaxed tensions enough to make pan-European travel possible once again, and English travelers began to write down and print their experiences. This is not to suggest, however, that English audiences were no longer anxious over the potentially malevolent influence of travel in Catholic countries. In *Coryats Crudities*, for instance, the author's discussion of his visit to a Venetian courtesan prompts a host of defensive rhetorical maneuvers, necessary to appease an English readership who firmly believed in the corrupting power of Italy. Yet Italy was also the source of classical culture, the home of awe-inspiring art, and, with the rest of Europe, the site of world-class educational institutions. Sons of the nobility conducted one- to two-year European tours, usually with an appointed tutor, as a kind of finishing school near the end of university study. Other English students traveled to European universities, such as the nearby University of Leiden, or to Padua for its famous medical school. Still other travelers were motivated by a love of art, such as Thomas Howard, fourteenth Earl of Arundel (1585–1646), who compiled a famous collection of paintings and statuary during his forays on the Continent. As a model for the traveling connoisseur, Arundel anticipated the concerns and practices of later-seventeenth-century Europeans on the Grand Tour.

A Note on the Text

This edition excerpts a large portion of *Coryats Crudities*, which in its original edition of 1611 runs to over nine hundred pages. As this is an edition intended for teaching, not for critical scholarly research, I have made numerous cuts to the original text. The following types of content have for the most part been omitted: 1) Coryate's epigraphical transcriptions copied from tombs and monuments; 2) Coryate's long digressions regarding past battles, the founding of cities, and other historical events; 3) Joseph Justus Scaliger's Latin verses on European cities (prefixed to Coryate's account of each major European city he visited); 4) George Coryate's Latin poetry, appended to the end of the volume; and 5) many of Coryate's longer architectural descriptions. Nonetheless, I have for various reasons included many architectural descriptions and a few epigraphical transcriptions in the current text, such as the architectural descriptions of Venice (due to readers' perennial interest in the Venice sections of *Crudities*), as well as the inscriptions found on the famous clock of Strasbourg, which is one of the book's showpiece scenes.

In my selection of passages to include in this edition, I have incorporated episodes from all parts of Coryate's journey rather than focusing entirely on the Venice section, as has been common with other editions of excerpts from *Crudities*. I have included every major episode in the travelogue, including each scene depicted on the engraved title page and the book's engraved plates, famous passages discussed in scholarship on *Crudities* (descriptions of Venice, especially the courtesans, mountebanks, theaters, and Jewish ghetto; Coryate's crossing of the Alps; Coryate's descriptions of forks, umbrellas, Venetian glass, and parmesan cheese; Coryate's observation of a Corpus Christi celebration in Paris), and passages frequently marked or annotated by early readers of the text. (In my research on early readers of *Crudities* I have inspected over seventy surviving copies of the 1611 edition for contemporary marks and marginalia.) Outside of these major episodes, I have focused on including Coryate's observations and experiences as a traveler rather than his accumulation of historical material, which in many cases was copied (as he admits) from books by François Schott and Sebastian Münster. It has also been necessary to cut most of the "Panegyricke Verses," though I have retained the "Introduction" to those verses as well as six of the verses themselves (in the "In Context" materials of this edition). I have also included in the "In Context" section other paratextual materials that were gathered at the front of the 1611 edition, including the distichs of Laurence Whitaker and Ben Jonson, Coryate's dedication to Prince Henry, and Coryate's "Epistle to the Reader," as well as Ben Jonson's "Character of the Author" and acrostic on Coryate's name.

As with other editions in this Broadview series, spelling and capitalization have been modernized. For the most part I have retained original punctuation, except in cases where it may cause confusion for the reader. I have also retained Coryate's italicization of section titles and non-English words and phrases, excluding proper names. I have modernized the spelling of toponyms if Coryate's original is only slightly misspelled, but if the toponym appears in a highly variant form or an Anglicized spelling/translation I have supplied a note with the modern place name. I have not glossed proper names belonging to obscure and/or unidentifiable persons. I have provided notes with English translations for passages written in foreign languages except when Coryate himself provides an in-text translation. Finally, this edition incorporates Coryate's holograph corrections to the presentation copy of *Crudities* given to Prince Henry Frederick, now held in the British Library (shelf-mark G.6750).

Philip S. Palmer

Coryats Crudities

To the high and mighty prince, Henry,[1] Prince of Wales, Duke of Cornwall and Rothsay, Earl of Chester, Knight of the most noble Order of the Garter, &c.

Though I am very confidently persuaded (most gracious Prince the orient pearl[2] of the Christian world) that I shall expose myself to the severe censure at the least, if not the scandalous calumniations of diverse carping critics, for presuming to dedicate to your highness the green fruits[3] of my short travels, especially since I am no scholar, but a man altogether unworthy to be dignified with so laudable a title: yet there are some few reasons that have emboldened and encouraged me to present these my silly[4] observations unto your highness, whereof these two are the chiefest. First, that if your highness will deign to protect them with your favourable and gracious patronage, as it were with the seven-fold shield of Ajax, or the aegis of Pallas (a favour that I most humbly crave at your highness's hands) against the envious cavillations of such critical Momi[5] as are wont to traduce the labours of other men; it may perhaps yield some little encouragement to many noble and generous young gallants that follow your highness's court, and give attendance upon your peerless person, to travel into foreign countries, and enrich themselves partly with the observations, and partly with the languages of outlandish regions, the principal means (in my poor opinion) to grace and adorn those courtly gentlemen, whose noble parentage, ingenuous[6] education,

---

1   *Henry* Henry Frederick, Prince of Wales (1594–1612), the promising heir to King James I's throne who died prematurely in 1612. Coryate was employed in Prince Henry's household in some capacity, perhaps at times as a sort of jester.

2   *orient pearl* Shining, precious pearl.

3   *calumniations* Slanders; *green fruits* Immature and unfinished works: the image expresses the affected modesty trope, which is common in early modern dedicatory epistles.

4   *silly* Unrefined (another expression of affected modesty).

5   *seven-fold shield of Ajax* Shield of the famed Greek hero of the Trojan War—made from seven leather hides; *aegis of Pallas* Protective shield of Pallas Athena, goddess of wisdom; *cavillations* Pedantic criticisms; *Momi* More than one Momus, who was the Greek god of censure.

6   *outlandish* Foreign; *ingenuous* Befitting their (noble) rank, high-class.

and virtuous conversation have made worthy to be admitted into your highness court: seeing thereby they will be made fit to do your highness and their country the better service when opportunity shall require. For the description of many beautiful cities, magnificent palaces, and other memorable matters that I have observed in my travels, may infuse (I hope) a desire to them to travel into transmarine[1] nations, and to garnish their understanding with the experience of other countries. Secondly, because amongst other things that I exhibit in this my journal to your princely view, that most glorious, renowned, and virgin city of Venice, the Queen of the Christian world, that diamond set in the ring of the Adriatic gulf, and the most resplendent mirror of Europe,[2] I have more particularly described, than it has been ever done before in our English tongue. The description of which famous city (were it done with such a curious and elegant style as it does deserve) I dare boldly say is a subject worthy for the greatest monarch in the world to read over. But for mine own part I am no scholar (as I have already said) and therefore unable to delineate & paint out the singular beauty thereof in her genuine colours with such an exquisite pencil as an eloquent historiographer ought to do. Notwithstanding those observations that I gathered thereof during the time of my abode there (which was about the space of six weeks) I have written though not as eloquently as a learned traveller would have done, yet as faithfully and truly as any man whatsoever; being often holpen both by the discourse of learned men, and certain Latin books that I found in Italy,[3] wherehence (I confess) I derived many principal notes, with which I have beautified the description of many other Italian cities.

But methinks I seem to hear some Momus objecting unto me now I speak thus of Venice, that this is *Crambe bis cocta*,[4] as it is in the proverb. For we have the history of Venice (he will perhaps say) already translated out of Italian into English. Therefore what need we more descriptions of that city? Truly I confess that Cardinal

---

1   *transmarine* Overseas.

2   *mirror of Europe* Paragon of Europe.

3   *holpen* Helped; *Latin books ... Italy* Of the books Coryate used as references, the one he relied on most heavily was François Schott's *Itinerarii Italiae* (1600).

4   *Crambe bis cocta* Latin: cabbage twice cooked; that is, reused material presented once again to the reading public.

Contarene's[1] *Commonwealth of Venice* has been so elegantly translated into English, that any judicious reader may by the reading thereof much instruct himself with the form of the Venetian government. But that book reports not half so many remarkable matters as mine does (*absit dicto invidia*[2]) of the antiquities and monuments of that famous city, together with the description of palaces, churches, the Piazza of S. Mark, which is one of the most beautiful places (I believe) that ever was built in any city whatsoever of the whole world, and other memorable things of no mean importance. Howbeit were this true that the history of Venice has been more than once divulged in our mother tongue, yet I hope your highness will not miscensure[3] me for communicating to my country new notes of this noble city, with a corollary of observations that (I am sure) were never before printed in England, seeing (according to the old speech) δις καὶ τρὶς τὰ καλὰ.[4]

Howsoever, if the curious reader that is wholly addicted unto novelties, will not so well accept my notes of Venice, for that the history of the Venetian commonwealth has been already printed in our language: nevertheless I conceive some hope that the descriptions of other cities which I surveyed in diverse countries in my travels, as in France, Italy, Switzerland, and some parts of high Germany, will yield more matter of news unto him, because none of these cities have been described in our language that I could ever hear of. And whereas I have written more copiously of the Italian, Helvetical,[5] and German cities, than of the French, that is to be attributed partly to my industry (whatsoever the same was) which I used more in Italy, Switzerland, and Germany by many degrees than in France; being often dissuaded by some of my fellow travellers from gathering any observations at all till I came into Italy: and partly to the helps of books which I found in Italy and Germany, wherewith I have something enlarged the descriptions of those cities.[6] For seeing I made very short abode in diverse fair Italian cities, as Cremona, Mantua, &c. (where I desired to have

---

1   *Cardinal Contarene* Gasparo Contarini. *The Commonwealth and Government of Venice* (London, 1599) is an English translation of an Italian version translated from his Latin original.
2   *absit dicto invidia* Latin: to be said without boasting.
3   *miscensure* Unfairly censure.
4   δις καὶ τρὶς τὰ καλὰ Greek: twice and thrice the beautiful.
5   *Helvetical* Swiss.
6   *books ... descriptions of those cities* François Schott's *Itinerarii Italiae* (1600) and (for Germany) Sebastian Münster's *Cosmographia universalis* (1544).

observed all the principal matters thereof) and thereby was barred of opportunity to note such things at large as were most memorable, I held it expedient to borrow some few notes from a certain Latin book printed in Italy, rather than to write so briefly of the same, as the shortness of time would not otherwise permit me. The like I did in Germany, being sometimes beholding to Munster for some special matter which neither by my own observations, nor by the discourse of learned men I could attain unto, especially about the institution of the bishoprics of certain cities through the which I passed.

I meant to have digressed into the praise of the excellency of travel into foreign countries, the more to stir up young gentlemen and every good spirit that favours learning, to so worthy an exercise; had I not prevented myself by translating those two elegant orations out of Latin into English, that were made by that learned German Hermannus Kirchnerus of Marpurg,[1] which I have inserted into my book; the one in commendation of travel in general, the other of Germany in particular; which are seasoned with such savoury Attic conceits, and adorned with those *flosculi & pigmenta eloquentiae*, that I may fitly apply unto them that pretty distich of the poet Lucilius:[2]

Quam lepide lexeis compostae, ut tesserulae, omnes
Arte pavimento, atque emblemate vermiculato.[3]

And surely for my own part I will say I never read any orations in all my life composed with a more terse and polished style (Tully's only excepted) though I have in my days perused some part of the orations of learned Melancthon, the phoenix of Germany, Antonie Muretus, my own rhetorical countryman Robert Turner,[4] &c. Therefore since these

---

1   *Hermannus … Marpurg* Hermann Kirchner (1562–1620), German author who wrote two essays on travel that Coryate translated and appended to the *Crudities*; they are not included in this edition.

2   *Attic conceits* Classically elegant expressions; *flosculi & pigmenta eloquentiae* Latin: flowerets and pigments of eloquence; *Lucilius* Roman satirist (second century BCE).

3   *Quam lepide … vermiculato* Latin: All his words as charmingly arranged as squares in a pavement of colored emblems (i.e., a mosaic pattern on a floor).

4   *Tully* Marcus Tullius Cicero (106–43 BCE), Roman politician and orator; *Melancthon* Philipp Melanchthon (1497–1560), German theologian; *Antonie Muretus* Marc Antoine Muret (1526–85), French Humanist known for his Latin prose style; *Robert Turner* English Catholic priest (d. 1599) known as a rhetorician and orator.

two orations do yield stronger motives, and more forceable arguments to animate the learned to travel into outlandish regions, than my poor invention can afford, I have thought fit to turn them into our mother tongue, according to my simple skill, and to present them also to your highness, together with the observations of my travels; both because I hope they will be very delectable to every reader that loves to hear of foreign affairs, and also for that they agree with the argument of my book.

As for these my observations in foreign countries, I was so far from presuming to dedicate them to your highness before the consummation of my future travels, that I resolved rather to conceal them from the world, and to bury them for a time in oblivion, if the importunity of some of my dear friends had not prevailed with me for divulging the same: whereof one amongst the rest, namely that right worshipful gentleman my most sincere and entire friend, M. Lionel Cranfield[1] was the original and principal animator of me; and another of my friends, even learned M. Laurence Whitaker, that elegant linguist and worthy traveller, now secretary to my illustrious *Mecoenas* Sir Edward Philips,[2] Master of the Rolls, has often urged unto me that proverbial verse:

Πολλὰ μεταξὺ πέλει κύλικος καὶ χέιλεος ἄκρου.[3]

By which he signified that many sinister accidents might happen unto me betwixt the time of my next going out of England, and my arrival again in my country; and so consequently my friends and country might be deprived of the fruits of my past travels, and of those to come: by these and such like persuasions of my friends I was animated to publish the observations of my travels much sooner than I thought to have done, and to address them to your excellent highness; not that I hold them worthy to undergo your highness censure, seeing

---

1   *M. Lionel Cranfield* Lionel Cranfield (1575–1645), merchant and first earl of Middlesex, also contributed to the "Panegyricke Verses."

2   *Mecoenas* Maecenas was a literary patron in the first century BCE whose name had become a byword for the generous patron; *Sir Edward Philips* Wealthy Somerset nobleman (c. 1555–1614) whose influence landed Coryate a position in Prince Henry Frederick's household.

3   [Coryate's Note] Many things do often slip twixt cup and lip.

many of them deserve rather *ad salsamantarios amandari*,[1] as learned Adrian Turnebus writes[2] of his *Adversaria*, and (as Horace says):

> *Deferri in vicum vendentem thus & odores,*
> *Et piper, & quicquid chartis amicitur ineptis.*[3]

But because they shall be an introduction (if your highness will vouchsafe to patronize them with your princely protection) to far more memorable writers that I determine by God's gracious indulgence to observe hereafter in most of the famous cities and prince's courts of Germany and Italy: as also in Constantinople, with diverse ancient cities of Greece, and the holy land, as Jerusalem, Jericho, Samaria, and other sacred places mentioned in the scriptures, and celebrated for the miracles done therein by our blessed saviour. Of which cities (if God shall grant me a prosperous issue to my designments[4]) I hope to write after a more particular manner than any of our English travellers have done before me. Wherefore most humbly beseeching your highness to pardon my presumption, I recommend your highness to the merciful clientele[5] of him whose throne is the heaven, whose footstool is the earth.

By him
That travels no less in all humble and
dutiful observance to your highness
than he did to Venice and the
parts above mentioned,

Your highness poor observer,
Thomas Coryate,
Peregrine[6] of Odcombe.

---

1   *ad salsamantarios amandari* Latin: to be sent away to delicatessens (that is, to be used as paper for packaging salted meats).

2   [Coryate's Note] In Epistola ad Hen. Memium. [Adrien Turnèbe was a French scholar whose *Adversia* (1564–65) Coryate mentions here. The citation refers to Turnèbe's letter to Heinrich Memm.]

3   [Coryate's Note] Horat. 2 lib. Epist. [Latin: to be carried into the street selling frankincense, spices, and pepper and whatever [else] is wrapped in foolish writings. Coryate's citation references the Epistles of Quintus Horatius Flaccus (65–8 BCE), Roman poet and satirist.]

4   *designments* Plans.

5   *clientele* Group of dependents, i.e., those dependent on God.

6   *Peregrine* Traveler.

Epistle to the Reader

Having lately considered in my serious meditations (candid reader) the unmeasurable abundance of books of all arts, sciences, and arguments whatsoever that are printed in this learned age wherein we now breathe, in so much that methinks we want rather readers for books than books for readers; my thoughts began to be much distracted like those of Aeneas, of whom Virgil speaks thus:

Atque animum, nunc huc celerem, nunc dividit illuc,
In partesque rapit varias, perque omnia versat.[1]

Yea I was plunged in an ocean of doubts, whether it were best that my observations gathered in foreign countries should be continually confined within the bounds of my poor study, and so at length *squalere situ, & cum tineis ac blattis rixari*;[2] or be presented to the view of my country, being (I confess) by so much the more doubtful to evulge the same, by how much the more I am no scholar, but only a superficial smatterer in learning, and therefore most unwilling to incur the censure of such severe Aristarchs as are wont ὀβελίζειν[3] and with their censorious rods do use to chastise the lucubrations of most kind of writers. But at length *post varias cogitationum fluctuationes*,[4] by the counsel of certain of my dear friends I put on a constant resolution, and determined to expose the abortive fruits of my travels to the sight of the world (after they had for the space of two whole years lurked in a kind of Cimmerian darkness[5]) which if they cannot endure, but will be dazzled with the least glimpse thereof, I wish the same of them that

---

1   [Coryate's Note] Aenei. 4. [Virgil, *Aeneid* 4.285–86; Latin: Flashing this way and that, his startled mind / Makes many a project and surveys them all.]
2   *squalere … rixari* Latin: to become dirty with disuse, and with moths and bookworms dispute.
3   *evulge* Make public; *Aristarchs* Harsh critics; ὀβελίζειν Greek: to annotate with an obelus (horizontal line marking a spurious passage).
4   *post … fluctuationes* Latin: after diverse vacillations of thought.
5   *Cimmerian darkness* Cimmeria was an ancient Nordic European region, its darkness proverbial for things unknown and obscure.

elegant Angelus Politianus[1] did of his Latin translation of Homer, even that I might *aut Thetidi aut Veneris largiri marito*.[2]

Since then I have thus far ventured with them, I will take occasion to speak a little of the thing which begat and produced these my observations, even of travel into foreign countries, whereby I may the better encourage gentlemen and lovers of travel to undertake journeys beyond the seas. Of all the pleasures in the world travel is (in my opinion) the sweetest and most delightful. For what can be more pleasant than to see passing variety of beautiful cities, kings' and princes' courts, gorgeous palaces, impregnable castles and fortresses, towers piercing in a manner up to the clouds, fertile territories replenished with a very cornucopia of all manner of commodities as it were with the horn of Amalthea,[3] tending both to pleasure and profit, that the heart of man can wish for: flourishing universities (whereof only Germany yields no less than three and twenty) furnished with store of learned men of all faculties, by whose conversation a learned traveller may much inform and augment his knowledge. What a singular and incomparable comfort is it to confer with those learned men in foreign universities and noble cities, whose excellent works we read in our private studies at home, as with Isaac Casaubonus the pearl of Paris; Paulus Aemylius in Padua; Rodolphus Hospinianus, Gasper Waserus, Henricus Bullingerus in Zurich; Amandus Polanus, Joannes Jacobus Gryneus in Basil; Janus Gruterus, David Pareus, Dionysius Gothofredus at Heidelberg; Joannes Piscator at Herborne; Bonaventura Vulcanius[4] at Leiden? Most of whom it was my good

---

1   [Coryate's Note] In Epistola ad Jacobum Cardinalem Papiensem. [Angelo Poliziano (1454–94) was an Italian humanist poet and scholar. Jacobum Cardinalem Papiensem refers to Jacopo Ammanati de' Piccolomini (1422–79), Cardinal of Pavia.]

2   *aut Thetidi ... marito* Latin: grant a gift either to Thetis [Greek sea goddess] or to Venus' spouse [Vulcan, Roman god of fire] (i.e., to cast into the sea or flames).

3   *horn of Amalthea* Cornucopia. Amalthea nursed the infant Zeus on Crete and gave him a goat's horn perpetually replenished with food.

4   *Isaac Casaubonus* Isaac Casaubon (1559–1614), French humanist scholar; *Paulus Aemylius* Paolo Emili (1460–1529), Italian historian; *Rodolphus Hospinianus* Rudolf Hospinianus (1547–1626), Swiss historian and theologian; *Gaspar Waserus* Kaspar Waser (1565–1625), Swiss theologian; *Henricus Bullingerus* Heinrich Bullinger (1534–83), Swiss theologian; *Amandus Polanus* Amandus Polanus von Polansdorf (1561–1610), Swiss Theologian; *Joannes Jacobus Gryneus* Johann Jacob Grynaeus (1540–1617), Swiss theologian; *Janus Gruterus* Jan Gruter (1560–1627), German philologist; *David Pareus* David Pareus (1548–1622), German theologian; *Dionysius Gothofredus* Denis Godefroy (1549–1621), Professor of Law at Heidelberg; *Joannes Piscator* Johannes Piscator (1546–1625), German

hap[1] not only to see in my travels, but also to my unspeakable solace to enjoy very copious and fruitful discourse with them. Again, what a contentment is it to a holy and religious Christian to visit the monuments and tombs of some of the ancient saints and fathers of the primitive church, as of S. Augustine in Pavia, S. Ambrose in Milan? &c. Also the ἐρείπια and ruins of the houses wherein those famous men lived, as Cicero, Varro, Virgil, Livy,[2] &c. that are to this day shown in sundry places of Italy, strike no small impression in the heart of an observative traveller. Likewise the places wherein diverse famous battles have been fought, so much celebrated partly by the ancient Roman historiographers, and partly by other neoteric[3] authors (many of which I exactly observed in my short voyage) when they are surveyed by a curious traveller, do seem to present to the eyes of his mind a certain idea of the bloody skirmishes themselves. Yea such is the exuberancy and superfluity[4] of these exotic pleasures, that for my own part I will most truly affirm, I reaped more entire and sweet comfort in five months travels of those seven countries mentioned in the front of my book, than I did all the days of my life before in England, which contained two and thirty years. Moreover the knowledge of foreign languages (which the shortness of time did not afford me) acquired by industrious travel, yields an ornament beyond all comparison the most precious and excellent that can be incident to a gentleman. For if the learning of two languages be commended by Ovid, who said:

> *Nec levis ingenuas pectus coluisse per artes*
> *Cura sit, & linguas edidicisse duas.*[5]

Much more praise does he deserve that by travelling in France, Italy, Spain, Alemannie,[6] and the Netherlands does learn the five languages

---

theologian; *Bonaventura Vulcanius* Bonaventura Vulcanius (1538–1614), Professor of Latin and Greek at Leiden.

1   *hap* Fortune.

2   ἐρείπια Greek: remnants, ruins; *Cicero ... Livy* Famous Roman authors.

3   *neoteric* Modern.

4   *exuberancy and superfluity* Overflowing amount and superabundance.

5   *Nec levis ... duas* Latin: Nor let it be a trivial concern to cultivate the mind through the liberal arts, and to study the two languages [i.e., Latin and Greek]. Ovid, *Ars amatoria* 2.121–22.

6   *Alemannie* Germany.

of those noble countries, which being added to his own mother tongue and the Latin, do answer the number of the seven liberal sciences. These certainly, and more, have been learned by famous travellers, as by Gulielmus Postellus[1] a Frenchman of excellent learning, who spoke twelve languages. Julius Caesar Scaliger[2] that incomparable scholar, nine. Joseph Scaliger[3] that died not long since in Leiden a university of Holland, spoke ten. Gaspar Waserus that ornament of Zurich, my kind friend, speaks eight. These are means that add much more grace and honour to an ingenuous gentleman, than he can purchase unto himself by all the exterior gifts of fortune. For though gentility be of itself gracious, yet it is much more excellent when it is adorned with the experience of foreign countries. Even as a gold ring of itself is fair and beautiful, but much more resplendent when it is decked with a rich diamond or some other precious stone. I will also illustrate this matter by some famous examples that I have noted in my poor[4] readings. The patriarch Jacob[5] travelled in his old age with his children out of the land of Canaan into Egypt. Very memorable is the travel of the Queen of the South mentioned in the holy scripture, who travelled out of her country of Sheba (which is a part of Arabia) to Jerusalem, to the end to hear Solomon's wisdom.[6] Pherecydes the master of Pythagoras[7] was a traveller. Also Pythagoras himself travelled out of his country of Samos into Italy. Polybius[8] that excellent historiographer travelled into many countries with Scipio Africanus whom he instructed in learning. Apollonius Tyaneus that famous Pythagorean philosopher, whose life Philostratus[9] has described in eight books, travelled for learning sake into Egypt, Persia,

---

1   *Gulielmus Postellus* Guillaume Postel (1510–81), French scholar and diplomat.

2   *Julius Caesar Scaliger* Italian physician and classical scholar (1484–1558).

3   *Joseph Scaliger* Joseph Justus Scaliger (1540–1609), French classical scholar and son of Julius Caesar Scaliger.

4   *poor* Lowly (an expression of affected modesty).

5   *patriarch Jacob* Son of Isaac, who traveled into Egypt as recounted in Genesis 45 and 46.

6   *Queen of the South ... wisdom* Queen of Sheba, who visits Solomon in 1 Kings.

7   *Pherecydes ... Pythagoras* Pherecydes of Syros (fl. 544 BCE), pre-Socratic philosopher said to be the teacher of Pythagoras (sixth century BCE), Greek philosopher and mathematician.

8   *Polybius* Greek historian (c. 200–c. 118 BCE) who taught Scipio Africanus Minor (185–129 BCE), Roman general and victor in the third Punic War.

9   *Apollonius Tyaneus* Apollonius of Tyana (first century CE), Greek philosopher from Asia Minor; *Philostratus* Lucius Flavius Philostratus (second–third century BCE), Greek sophist historian, who wrote *The Life of Apollonius of Tyana*.

India, Greece. Dionysius Areopagita[1] an Athenian born into Egypt also, and diverse other countries. Likewise Pliny the naturalist, and Cornelius Tacitus[2] the historiographer spent some time in travel. The like did S. Jerome[3] one of the four doctors of the west church. The emperor Hadrian[4] travelled over most of the provinces of the Roman Empire, and for a time made his residence in Athens for learning of knowledge. Him did the emperor Antoninus Bassianus Caracalla[5] imitate in the like action, though not with so good success. Also that eloquent orator Hermannus Kirchnerus in his two orations of travel which I have rudely translated out of Latin into English, and inserted into my observations, mentions these notable examples of travelling, namely Euclid, Plato, Aristotle, Anacharsis, Zamolxis, Lycurgus, Hippocrates, Cicero, Galen, and Dioscorides.[6] Moreover Vincentius Gonzaga[7] Duke of Mantua then travelled in diverse parts of Germany when I was abroad. All which from the first to the last (Jacob only excepted, who travelled for other causes) aimed at this main scope in their travels, as it were their helice and cynosura,[8] to purchase experience and wisdom, that they might be the better able to benefit their country and commonweal. In which they differed much from many of our English travellers, to whom I may very truly apply that memorable speech of Aeschines,[9] in his oration against Timarchus,

---

1 *Dionysius Areopagita* Dionysius the Areopagite (first century CE), Greek judge converted to Christianity by St. Paul.

2 *Pliny the naturalist* Gaius Plinius Secundus, or Pliny the Elder (23/24–79 CE), Roman writer known for his influential *Historia naturalis*; *Cornelius Tacitus* Cornelius Tacitus (c. 56–c. 120 CE), Roman historian.

3 *S. Jerome* St. Jerome (c. 345–420), church father and Latin translator of the bible.

4 *Hadrian* Fourteenth Roman emperor (76–138 CE).

5 *Antoninus Bassianus Caracalla* Caracella, or Marcus Aurelius Antoninus (188–217), twenty-second Roman emperor. Travel may be said to have killed him, as he was murdered on the return journey from visiting a temple.

6 *Euclid ... Dioscorides* Famous mathematicians, philosophers, physicians, and naturalists of antiquity.

7 *Vincentius Gonzaga* Vincenzo Gonzaga (1562–1612).

8 *helice* Figurative term for Ursa major, but also a word roughly synonymous with cynosure; *cynosura* Cynosure, a term that once referred to the constellation Ursa minor in addition to its modern meaning, a point of interest or attraction.

9 *Aeschines* (c. 397–322 BCE), Greek orator whose speech against Timarchus is known for its extensive references to Athenian law.

οὐ τὸν τρόπον ἀλλά τὸν τόπον μόνον μετήλλαξαν.[1] But I will proceed no further in this point, seeing the foresaid elegant orations of Kirchnerus do more artificially paint out the fruits of travel in their natural colours than I am able to do.

But now I will descend to speak something of my own travels. It has been oftentimes objected unto me since my coming home, by certain gentlemen of eminent note, and as it were laid in my dish as a choking pear,[2] that for the short time that I was abroad I observed more solid matters than any Englishman did in the like space this long time. For I copied out more inscriptions and epitaphs (said a certain knight that shall pass nameless)[3] that are written upon solid pieces of stone, than any judicious traveller would have done in many years. For which cause he branded me with the note of a tombstone traveller. Whereas it had been much more laudable (said he) to have observed the government of commonweals, and affairs of state. I answer him, that because I am a private man and no statist, matters of policy are impertinent unto me. For I observe that memorable distich:

Vive tibi, quantumque potes praelustria vita,
Saevum praelustri fulmen ab arce venit.[4]

Besides I have observed that in some places it is dangerous to pry very curiously into state matters, as diverse travellers have observed by their dear experience; a most tragic example whereof I heard to have been shown in the city of Strasbourg not long before my arrival there. Moreover I hope that every gentle reader that shall with a mild censure peruse my observations, will say it was impossible for me in

---

1 [Coryate's Note] This is answerable unto that in Horace. *Coelum non animum mutant qui trans mare currunt.* [Latin: They who travel across the seas change their skies, but not their spirits. See Horace, *Epistola* 1. The Greek translates to "not his habits but his place only does he change."]

2 *choking pear* Choke-pear, or a bitter, inedible pear, used figuratively as something difficult to "swallow" or get over.

3 *pass nameless* Though Coryate preserves the "certain knight's" anonymity here, the content of the poem titled "Incipit Robertus Phillips" (collected in the "Panegyricke Verses" printed at the front of *Coryats Crudities*) suggests it was Sir Robert Phillips who called Coryate a "tombstone traveller."

4 *Vive tibi ... venit* Latin: Live for yourself and, as much as you can, avoid renown; the lightning that comes from renown's citadel is cruel (Ovid, *Tristia* 3.4.5–6).

the space of five months to observe all these matters in descriptions of cities that I have handled, and politic affairs also. But because this objection shall not justly take hold upon me, that I am a tombstone traveller, if God shall grant me happy success in my next journey, I will so far wade into a few matters of policy for the better satisfaction of the reader, as I may with security of my life attain unto. Surely I do not a little wonder that the observing of inscriptions and epitaphs should be objected unto me by way of disgrace. For who that τὸν ἐγκέφαλον ἐν τοῖς κροτάφοις[1] (to use that sentence of Demosthenes) καὶ μή ἐν ταῖς πτέρναις καταπεπατημένον φορεῖ,[2] will deem it a vanity to write out those sweet elegancies that many epitaphs do present to the reader, whereof some few for example sake I will briefly recite. The epitaph of Pope Lucius the third, which I have mentioned in my notes of Verona, is so pretty, that I think it cannot but affect every learned reader.

Luca dedit lucem tibi Luci, Pontificatum
  Ostia, Papatum Roma, Verona mori.
Imo Verona dedit tibi vere vivere, Roma
  Exilium, curas Ostia, Luca mori.[3]

Also this witty epitaph that was given me by a learned man in my travels, was written upon the tomb of a grammarian in the city of Ghent.

Grammaticam scivi, multos docuique per annos,
  Declinare tamen non potui tumulum.[4]

---

1 [Coryate's Note] In Oratione de Haloneso, that is, who that hath his wit in his head, and not in his heels, &c. [Coryate refers to the ancient Greek orator Demosthenes (384–322 BCE), Oration on the Halonnesus 7.45.]

2 τὸν ἐγκέφαλον ... φορεῖ Greek: If you carry your brains in your heads and not trodden down in your heels.

3 *Luca dedit ... Luca mori* Latin: Lucca gave light to you Lucius, Bishop of Ostia, Pope of Rome, dead at Verona. More correctly, Verona allowed you to live in truth, Rome in exile, Ostia in care, Lucca in death.

4 *Grammaticam ... tumulum* Latin: I knew the grammar, and I taught for many years, but nonetheless I could not avoid the tomb (with a morbid grammatical pun on "declinare"/ decline, as in to decline a part of speech).

Who will not applaud that upon learned Joannes Picus Earl of Mirandula[1] in the city of Florence?

Joannes jacet hic Mirandula, caetera norunt
Et Tagus, & Ganges, forsan & Antipodes.[2]

And that upon Rodolphus Agricola in Heidelberg, composed by famous Hermolaus Barbarus,[3] as I have mentioned in my notes of that city.

Invida clauserunt hoc marmore fata Rodolphum
Agricolam, Frisii spemque decusque soli.
Scilicet hoc uno meruit Germania laudis
Quicquid habet Latium, Graecia quicquid habet.[4]

Let them therefore reprehend me as long as they list for the collection of those epitaphs and inscriptions in my book. For mine own part I am so far from thinking myself worthy of taxation for the same, that I rather fear I have ministered[5] just cause of reprehension to the learned for omitting so many notable epitaphs as I might have found in diverse famous cities of my travels, especially Paris, Milan, and Padua.

I suppose that diverse which will read my observations, will blame me for that I have not translated the Latin verses of Julius Caesar Scaliger, which I have prefixed before the description of certain of the nobler cities, and the epitaphs and inscriptions, into English, because many men that cannot understand them in Latin, would take some pleasure to read them in English. To this I answer, that if I should have turned them into English, many of them would have lost part of their grace by my improper translation. Because the Latin tongue has

---

1 *Joannes ... Mirandula* Giovanni Pico della Mirandola (1463–94), Italian humanist philosopher.
2 *Joannes ... Antipodes* Latin: Here lies John of Mirandola—[which] others know of, As [he is also known by] the Tagus and Ganges [Rivers], perhaps, and the Antipodes.
3 *Rodolphus Agricola* Rudolf Agricola (1443–85), Dutch humanist scholar; *Hermolaus Barbarus* Ermolao Barbaro (1453/54–93), Italian classical scholar.
4 *Invida ... habet* Latin: The envious fates shut up in this marble Rudolf Agricola, hope of Frisia and splendor of the throne. Certainly this one German deserves of praise everything Latium holds, everything Greece holds.
5 *ministered* Provided.

certain proper and peculiar elegancies, which when they are translated into another language, seem to leese something of that genuine *venustas*[1] that it has in her own original no otherwise than certain plants that being removed from their natural soil to a strange place, will not prosper as well as they did before. Therefore I thought good to labour but little in this business of translation, saving only in those two memorable things which I have translated for the benefit of the unlearned reader, the one, S. Bernard's epistle to the Bishop of Spira. The other the history of the three kings of Cologne.[2] Also whereas I understand that some have objected against me, that I deserve to be taxed for reporting certain things which I received only by tradition and report of other men, not by my own certain experience; I would have them know, that I am not the first that has grounded much of his matter upon the speeches of other men; for I have observed that Herodotus, Diodorus Siculus, Justin, Quintus Curtius,[3] and diverse other ancient historians, as well amongst the Greeks as Latins, have done the like, as they may easily observe that peruse their works. But I am sure I do very seldom depend upon the report of others, and when I trust to the tradition of them, they are men of such learning from whom I derive those matters, that I think a man need not doubt to allege them for authentic authors. As in Zurich learned Hospinian[4] told me that their city was founded in the time of Abraham. And the like notes I received from other learned men, whose testimonies I approve as much as the written authority of grave authors.

It remains now that I am to make one instant request unto thee (courteous reader) and with the same will shut up my epistle: even to desire thee whatsoever thou are (if thou should intend to translate my book into Latin in my absence, when I shall be abroad in my next travels) *manum de tabula tollere.*[5] Intermeddle not I entreat thee (gentle reader) with my book, neither thrust thy sickle into my harvest, except thou shall certainly understand by credible report that I have miscarried in my voyage. For if God shall grant me happy success in my next travels,

---

1   *leese* Lose; *venustas* Latin: charm, grace.
2   *S. Bernard's … Cologne* Coryate's lengthy English translations of these texts do not appear in the present edition.
3   *Herodotus … Curtius* Greek and Roman historians of antiquity.
4   *Hospinian* Rodolphus Hospinianus (1547–1626), Swiss historian and theologian.
5   *manum de tabula tollere* Latin: leave it alone (literally, remove [your] hand from the painting).

and a safe arrival in my country, I determine (Θεοῦ διδόντος)[1] to translate both these and my future observations into Latin for the benefit not only of my own country, but also of those countries where I have already travelled, and hereafter resolve to travel. Though truly I do ingenuously confess my Latin style is so barren and penurious, that it were much fitter for another man to perform it than myself. As for these observations which I now exhibit unto thy gentle censure, take them I pray thee in good part till I present better unto thee after my next travels, considering that it is not in my power to yield unto thee such exquisite notes of travel as great scholars gather in the course of their travels, since I neither profess myself a scholar, nor acknowledge myself worthy to be ranked amongst scholars of mean learning, but only wish to be accounted a poor well-willer of the Muses. Notwithstanding though my beggarly learning cannot aim at such weighty matters as are fit to be searched for by a learned traveller, yet I will promise thee (if thou will only wink at some light matters inserted into these my observations) to impart many such memorable things unto thee after the end of my next journey, as are oftentimes omitted by travellers of that learning, that I am not worthy to loose their shoe-latchet,[2] yea such as do as far excel me,

Ante alios quantum Pegasus ibat equos.[3]

Therefore in the meantime join with me in thy best wishes for happy success in my future travels; and so I commend thee to him whom I beseech to bless thee at home, and me abroad.

Thy benevolent itinerating[4] friend,
T.C.
The Odcombian Leg-stretcher

---

1   Θεοῦ διδόντος Greek: God willing.
2   *loose their shoe-latchet* Reference to a story of the famous Greek artist Apelles's encounter with a cobbler, who criticizes the artist's rendition of shoes. Overnight Apelles fixes the painting to satisfy his critic; at first the cobbler is pleased, but when he starts to criticize the painting again—this time finding a fault in the leg—a frustrated Apelles cuts him off, saying "Ne sutor ultra crepidam"—not above the shoe-latch, cobbler. Coryate here suggests that he is less worthy than even the cobbler and does not deserve to mend any part of the "painting" at all, not even the lowly shoe-latch.
3   *Ante alios … equos* Latin: so much as Pegasus walks before (all) other horses.
4   *itinerating* Traveling.

[...]

My observations of France

I was embarked at Dover about ten of the clock in the morning, the fourteenth of May, being Saturday and Whitsun-eve,[1] *Anno* 1608, and arrived in Calais (which Caesar calleth *Ictius portus*,[2] a maritime town of that part of Picardy, which is commonly called *le pai reconquis*, that is, the recovered province, inhabited in former times by the ancient Morini[3]) about five of the clock in the afternoon, after I had varnished the exterior parts of the ship with the excremental ebullitions[4] of my tumultuous stomach, desiring to satiate the gormandizing paunches of the hungry haddocks (according as I have hieroglyphically expressed it in the front of my book)[5] with that wherewith I had superfluously stuffed my self at land, having made my rumbling belly their capacious aumbry.[6]

Presently after my arrival, I was brought with the rest of my company to the deputy governor of the town, whose name was Monsieur de la Genet: the principal governor's name (whom we saw not) was Monsieur de Vic, who has one wooden leg. The deputy was a very worthy and gallant gentleman, and showed himself very affable unto us. For he asked us many questions, as about our king, and the news of Ireland, &c. and very courteously entreated us; and after this familiar parle[7] dismissed us to our lodging. For it is the custom of the town, that whensoever any strangers arrive there, they are brought before the deputy governor, to the end to be examined about the occasion of their coming thither, whither they travel, and to have their names enrolled before they go to their lodging. I lay in Calais Whitsun-eve and all Whitsunday, where I observed these particulars: a little on this side the town, when I was on the sea, I saw a thing which I much admired:

---

1   *Whitsun-eve* The evening before Whitsunday (i.e., Pentecost), held the seventh Sunday after Easter.

2   *Ictius portus* Latin: Struck harbor. Cf. Julius Caesar, De Bello Gallico 5.2.

3   [Coryate's Note] Of whom Virgil speaks thus, Extremique hominum Morini. Aenei. 8. [The Morini were a people of Northern Gaul conquered by Julius Caesar.]

4   *ebullitions* Agitated rushing forth of liquid, i.e., vomit.

5   *hieroglyphically ... book* Illustrated on the engraved title page (page 212, illustration "A").

6   *aumbry* Place of storage offering something in abundance.

7   *parle* Conversation.

the sands of Calais, which appeared so plain a great way off, that I thought they had not been covered with any water at all, but dry firm ground for me to walk on for recreation. The other sands on that part of the water that our ship sailed on, being not to be seen. These are such as we call in Latin *syrtes*, that is, quick sands. Sometimes at a low ebb they are all uncovered with water, insomuch that the people of the town do then walk upon them as upon firm land. But a certain Englishman within these few years, was deceived by those sands: for when he walked alone there, he was suddenly overtaken and over-whelmed with the waters; for a monument whereof, there are erected two wooden pillars in the water a little from the haven.

[…]

I departed from Calais about eleven of the clock in the morning on Whitsun-Monday, and came to Boulogne in Picardy, which was sixteen miles distant from it, about seven of the clock in the after-noon. Betwixt Calais and Boulogne I saw two churches grievously demolished, which was done in the time of the civil wars, and two monasteries extremely ruinated,[1] whereof one was situate in a solitary place on the left hand by the side of a wood.

[…]

I went from Boulogne about six of the clock the next morning, being Tuesday the seventeenth day of May, and came to Montreuil[2] a town of Picardy, which was sixteen miles beyond it, about four of the clock in the afternoon. Betwixt Boulogne and Montreuil I observed these things: a little beyond Boulogne there is a gallows, consisting of two goodly fair pillars of free-stone,[3] where there is no cross beam as upon our English gallows, but that cross beam is erected when any are hanged, and taken down again immediately after the execution. No offenders are hanged there, but only felons.[4] A little beyond that

---

1   *civil wars* French Wars of Religion (1562–98); *ruinated* Ruined.
2   *Montreuil* Montreuil-sur-Mer.
3   *free-stone* Sandstone or limestone.
4   *No offendors … felons* Only those who commit more serious felonies—not mere "offend-ers," guilty of less egregious infractions of the law—are hanged at these gallows.

there is a place of execution made of timber, at the top whereof there is a wheel, whereon the bodies of murderers only are tormented and broken in pieces with certain iron instruments, wherewith they break their arms first, then their legs and thighs, and after their breast: if they are favoured their breast is first broken. That blow on their breast is called the blow of mercy, because it doth quickly bereave them of their life. This torment of the wheel I find in Aristotle to have been used amongst the ancient Grecians also. Who in the seventh book of his Ethics[1] and third chapter, uses the word τροχίξευς,[2] which signifies to be tortured with the wheel. Again, a little beyond that place there is a little chapel made conduit-wise,[3] wherein is erected the picture of Christ and the Virgin Mary; there I saw three women and a man praying to that picture. This was the first of those kind of chapels that ever I saw, but afterward in Savoy, Piedmont, and some places of Lombardy, I saw very great store of them.

About eight miles beyond Boulogne I saw a very ruinous monastery, which belike was battered down in the civil wars. About two miles on this side Montreuil there was a Whitsuntide fool disguised[4] like a fool, wearing a long coat, wherein there were many several pieces of cloth of diverse colours, at the corners whereof there hanged the tails of squirrels; he bestowed a little piece of plate, wherein was expressed the effigies of the Virgin Mary, upon every one that gave him money: for he begged money of all travellers for the benefit of the parish church.

Montreuil is a strong walled town, situate on a hill, having a very strong fortification on the top thereof, environed with a strong wall. There are two gates at the entrance of the town, at each whereof there is a guard of soldiers that examined us before we came into the town. The principal church of the town is our Lady's church. Our hostess of Montreuil prayed the Virgin Mary to bless me, because she thought I was a papist,[5] but when she understood I was a Protestant, she seemed to pity me.

---

1   *Ethics* Aristotle's *Nichomachean Ethics* (350 BCE).
2   τροχίξευς Greek: trochixeus, to turn upon the wheel.
3   *chapel ... conduit-wise* Chapel with a fountain.
4   *disguised* Dressed ostentatiously.
5   *papist* Pejorative term for a Catholic.

I departed from Montreuil in a cart, according to the fashion of the country, which had three hoops over it, that were covered with a sheet of coarse canvas, about six of the clock the next day in the morning, being Wednesday, and the eighteenth day of May; and came to Abbeville about eleven of the clock that morning, betwixt Montreuil and Abbeville twenty miles. About ten miles on this side Abbeville we entered into a goodly forest called Veronne, which is reported to be forty miles in compass: at the entrance whereof a Frenchman that was in our company, spoke to us to take our swords in our hands, because sometimes there are false knaves in many places of the forest that lurk under trees and shrubs, and suddenly set upon travellers, and cut their throats, except the true men are too strong for them. Also there are wild boars and wild harts in that forest, but we saw none of them. About five miles on this side Abbeville there is a goodly park, environed with a fair brick wall, wherein there is deer: a little on this side Abbeville there is a stately gallows of four very high pillars of free-stone, which is joined together with two cross beams of stone, whereon the offenders are hanged.

[...]

I came to the goodly city of Amiens, which is the metropolitan and capital city of Picardy, about six of the clock a Thursday morning, being six miles distant from Picquigny. I remained there all that day, and the next day about two of the clock in the afternoon I took my journey there hence by coach towards Paris.

[...]

The fairest cage of birds that I saw in all France, was at the sign of the *Ave Maria* in Amiens, the workmanship whereof was very curious with gilt wires. In the same were four turtledoves, and many gold-finches, with other birds which are such as our hempseed birds[1] in England.

The first pilgrim that ever I saw was in Amiens, a very simple fellow, who spoke so bad Latin that a country scholar in England should be

---

1   *hempseed birds* Birds that consume hempseed.

whipped for speaking the like. He told me that he had lived two years at Compostela, a city and university of Galicia in Spain, where Saint James[1] is much worshipped, wherehence he then came, and was upon going to Rome. He had a long staff in his hand with a nobble[2] in the middle, according to the fashion of those pilgrims' staffs, a chain about his neck full of extraordinary great beads, and a box by his side, wherein was the picture of our Lady and Christ in her arms.

[...]

I took my journey from Amiens towards Paris in coach, the twentieth day of May being Friday, about two of the clock in the afternoon, and came that night by seven of the clock in the evening, to a village in the country fourteen miles therehence called Bretueil. In that space I observed only these two things, a village exceedingly ransacked and ruinated, by means of the civil wars, and about some few miles on this side Bretueil, certain vineyards which were the first that ever I saw.

I went from Bretueil on Saturday, being the one and twentieth of May, about five of the clock in the morning, and came about noon to a town in the province of Beauvoisis called Clermont, situate upon the top of a hill, being fourteen miles from Bretueil. This Clermont is a mean and ignoble place, having no memorable thing therein worthy the observation. Only I talked with a certain Franciscan[3] friar there, born in Ireland, who seemed to be a pretty scholar and a man of good parts. He was then travelling to Abbeville to preach there. I observed this in him, that he was as well able to discourse of all particular politic and state matters of England, as any man in our company: and he spoke passing good English. This also I observed in Clermont: in the midst of a street there was erected a gibbet with the picture of a certain fellow called Antony Peel, who was painted hanging on a gallows in the same picture. Under the which his offence was mentioned by way of a proclamation for apprehending of him. The reason why

---

1   *Compostela* Santiago de Compostela, Spain; *Saint James* St. James the Great (d. 44 CE), the Apostle, whose shrine at Santiago de Compostela had been attracting pilgrims since the ninth century.
2   *nobble* Knot.
3   *Franciscan* The Franciscan monastic order, founded by St. Francis of Assisi in the thirteenth century, emphasizes communal poverty.

his picture was set forth in that manner, was this: that as his picture was there hanged, so should he also if he might be apprehended. This custom is observed in many places of France.

[...]

The next morning being Trinity Sunday[1] about four of the clock, I was transported over a river called the Oise, which doth part Picardy from Île-de-France. That day I dined at a Parish called Saint Brixe, which was twelve miles beyond Saint Liew.[2] Betwixt Saint Liew and Saint Brixe I observed these things. An exceeding rich and fertile country, full of corn, especially rye, meadows, pastures, woods, many sweet rivers, a great multitude of goodly and sumptuous houses on both sides as we rode, most whereof were said to be the advocates[3] of Paris. Also many goodly rows of walnut trees, about three or four miles after we were entered into the Île, the fairest that ever I saw till then, about two hundred at the least in a row. About two miles on this side Saint Brixe, there is a most magnificent palace built of fair white free-stone with many lofty turrets on the top of a hill, in a beautiful park. The place is called Escovan. This place belongs to Monsieur Montmerency[4] the high constable of France, who has seventeen towns and parishes in the country belonging to it, which are very near bordering about it.

I went from St. Brixe about one of the clock in the afternoon, and came to Paris, which was eight miles therehence, about six of the clock that day.

[...]

My observations of Paris

This city is exceeding great, being no less than ten miles in circuit, very populous, and full of very goodly buildings, both public and private, whereof the greatest part are of fair white free-stone: wherewith

---

1 *Trinity Sunday* First Sunday after Pentecost.
2 *Saint Brixe* St. Brice; *Saint Liew* St. Leu.
3 *corn* Grain; *advocates* Lawyers.
4 *Monsieur Montmerency* Henri de Montmorency, lord of Damville (1534–1614).

it is naturally more plentifully furnished than any city of Christendom that ever I read or heard of. For the whole city, together with the suburbs, is situate upon a quarry of free-stone, which doth extend itself to a great part of the territory round about the city, and ministers that inexhausted[1] plenty of stone for their houses. It is round, and environed with very ancient stone walls that were built by Julius Caesar when he made his residence here in the midst of his French conquests;[2] from whom some have not doubted in former times to call it the city of Julius. In those walls it has at this time fourteen fair gates. As for her name of Paris, she has it (as some write) from Paris the eighteenth king of Gallia Celtica, whom some write to have been lineally descended from Japheth,[3] one of the three sons of Noah, and to have founded this city. [...] It is divided into three parts, the university, the city, and the town by the noble river Sequana, commonly called *la riviere de Seine*.

[...]

Besides there are three fair bridges more built upon this river, whereof the one is called the bridge of exchange, where the goldsmiths dwell, S. Michael's bridge,[4] and the bridge of birds, formerly called the millers' bridge. The reason why it is called the bridge of birds is because all the signs belonging unto shops on each side of the street are signs of birds.

The cathedral church[5] is dedicated to our Lady, which is nothing so fair as our Lady church of Amiens: for I could see no notable matter in it, saving the statue of St. Christopher[6] on the right hand at the coming in of the great gate, which indeed is very exquisitely done, all the rest being but ordinary, as I have seen in other churches. The street which is called *la rue de nostre Dame* (as I have before written) that is, our Lady street, is very fair, being of a great length, though not

---

1   *inexhausted* Unexhausted.
2   *his French conquests* Gallic Wars, waged between 58 and 51 BCE.
3   *Gallia Celtica* Ancient Roman name for central France; *Japheth* Son of Noah. According to legend, all Europeans descend from him.
4   *S. Michael's bridge* Pont Saint-Michel.
5   *cathedral church* Notre Dame de Paris.
6   *St. Christopher* Third-century Christian martyr.

so broad as our Cheapside[1] in London; but in one thing it exceeds any street in London. For such is the uniformity of almost all the houses of the same street which stand upon the bridge, that they are made alike both in proportion of workmanship and matter: so that they make the neatest show of all the houses in Paris.

The *Via Jacobaea*[2] is very full of booksellers that have fair shops most plentifully furnished with books.

I was at the palace[3] where there is the exchange, that is a place where the merchants do meet at those times of the day, as our merchants do in London. But it is nothing comparable to the place of our merchants meeting in London, being a plain pitched walk *sub dio,*[4] that is under the open air. As for their exchange where they sell many fine and curious things, there are two or three pretty walks in it, but neither for length, nor for the roof, nor the exquisite workmanship is it any way to be compared with ours in London. In this palace there are sundry fair buildings, whereof one is very spacious and broad, and of a great height, adorned with many goodly pillars of free-stone, wherein the advocates and civil lawyers with many others do walk; and it serves the Frenchmen in that manner as our Westminster Hall[5] doth us Englishmen.

[...]

I was also in a chamber wherein Queen Mary[6] does often lie, where I saw a certain kind of rail which encompasses the place where her bed is wont to be, having little pretty pillars richly gilt. After this I went into a place which for such a kind of room excels in my opinion, not only all those that are now in the world, but also all whatsoever that ever were since the creation thereof, even a gallery, a perfect description whereof will require a large volume. It is divided into three parts, two sides at both the ends, and one very large and spacious

---

1   *Cheapside* Market street in London.
2   *Via Jacobaea* Street of booksellers in Paris.
3   [Coryate's Note] Built by Philip the Fair, *Anno* 1313. [Philip the Fair (1268–1314) was King of France.]
4   *sub dio* Latin: under God.
5   *Westminster Hall* Administrative hub in seventeenth-century Westminster.
6   *Queen Mary* Marie de' Medici (1573–1642), Queen of France.

walk. One of the sides when I was there, was almost ended, having in it many goodly pictures of some of the kings and queens of France, made most exactly in wainscot, and drawn out very lively in oil works upon the same. The roof of most glittering and admirable beauty, wherein is much antique[1] work, with the picture of God and the angels, the sun, the moon, the stars, the planets, and other celestial signs. Yea so unspeakably fair it is, that a man can hardly comprehend it in his mind, that has not first seen it with his bodily eyes[....] The long gallery when I was there was imperfect, for there was but half of the walk boarded, and the roof very rude, the windows also and the partitions not a quarter finished. For it is reported that the whole long gallery shall be made correspondent to the first side that is almost ended. At the end of the long gallery there were two hundred masons working on free-stone every day when I was there, to make an end of that side which must answer the first side that is almost ended. Near to which side there is a goodly palace called the Tuileries, where the queen mother[2] was wont to lie and which was built by herself. This palace is called Tuileries because heretofore they used to burn tile there before the palace was built. For this French word Tuileries does signify in the French a place for burning of tile.

The six and twentieth day of May being Thursday and *Corpus Christi day*,[3] I went to the foresaid palace[....] There is a most pleasant prospect from that walk over the rails into the Tuileries garden, which is the fairest garden for length of delectable walks that ever I saw, but for variety of delicate fonts and springs, much inferior to the king's garden at Fontainebleau. There are two walks in this garden of an equal length, each being 700 paces long, whereof one is so artificially[4] roofed over with timber work, that the boughs of the maple trees, wherewith the walk is on both sides beset, do reach up to the top of the roof, and cover it clean over. This roofed walk has six fair arbours advanced to a great height like turrets. Also there is a long and

---

1   *oil works* Oil painting; *antique* Aged and esteemed.

2   *Tuileries* French royal palace built in the mid-fifteenth century; *queen mother* Catherine de' Medici (1519–89).

3   *Corpus Christi day* Held on the Thursday after Trinity Sunday, this liturgical solemnity celebrates belief in the "body of Christ" and its presence in the Eucharist.

4   *artificially* Skillfully.

spacious plot full of herbs and knots[1] trimly kept by many persons. In this garden there are two fonts[2] wherein are two ancient images of great antiquity made of stone. Also there is a fair pond made four square, and built all of stone together with the bottom, wherein there is not yet either fish or water, but shortly shall be replenished with both. There I saw great preparations of conduits of lead, wherein the water shall be conveyed to that pond. At the end of this garden there is an exceeding fine echo. For I heard a certain Frenchman who sung very melodiously with curious quavers,[3] sing with such admirable art, that upon the resounding of the echo there seemed three to sound together.

Seeing I have now mentioned *Corpus Christi* day, I will also make relation of those pompous ceremonies that were publicly solemnized that day in the streets of the city, according to their yearly custom: this day the Frenchmen call *Feste de Dieu*, that is, the feast of God.

[...]

About nine of the clock the same day in the morning, I went to the cathedral church which is dedicated to our Lady (as I have before written) to the end to observe the strange ceremonies of that day, which for novelty sake, but not for any hearty devotion (as the καρδιαγνώστης[4] God doth know) I was contented to behold, as being the first that ever I saw of that kind, and I heartily wish they may be the last. No sooner did I enter into the church but a great company of clergymen came forth singing, and so continued all the time of the procession till they returned unto the church again, some by couples, and some single. They walked partly in copes, whereof some were exceeding rich, being (in my estimation) worth at the least a hundred marks[5] apiece; and partly in surplices. Also in the same train there were many couples of little singing choristers, many of them not above eight or nine years old, and few above a dozen, which

---

1   *knots* Intricate garden plots.
2   *fonts* Fountains.
3   *quavers* Sung trills.
4   καρδιαγνώστης Greek: kardiagnostes, heart-knowing.
5   *copes* Cloak-like garments worn by Catholic churchmen; *marks* Monetary units used in early modern Europe, each equal to two-thirds of a pound sterling.

pretty innocent punies[1] were so egregiously deformed by those that had authority over them, that they could not choose but move great commiseration in any relenting spectator. For they had not a quarter so much hair left upon their heads as they brought with them into the world, out of their mother's wombs, being so clean shaved away round about their whole heads that a man could perceive no more than the very roots. A spectacle very pitiful (methinks) to behold, though the papists esteem it holy. The last man of the whole train was the Bishop of Paris, a proper and comely man as any I saw in all the city, of some five and thirty years old. He walked not *sub dio*, that is, under the open air as the rest did. But he had a rich canopy carried over him, supported with many little pillars on both sides. This did the priests carry: he himself was that day in his sumptuous pontificalities, wearing religious ornaments of great price, like a second Aaron, with his episcopal staff in his hand, bending round at the top, called by us Englishmen a crosier, and his miter[2] on his head of cloth of silver, with two long labels hanging down behind his neck. As for the streets of Paris they were more sumptuously adorned that day than any other day of the whole year, every street of special note being on both sides thereof, from the pentices[3] of their houses to the lower end of the wall hanged with rich cloth of arras, and the costliest tapestry that they could provide. The shows of our Lady street being so hyperbolical in pomp that day, that it exceeded the rest by many degrees. And for the greater addition of ornament to this feast of God, they garnished many of their streets with as rich cupboards of plate[4] as ever I saw in all my life. For they exposed upon their public tables exceeding costly goblets, and what not tending to pomp, that is called by the name of plate. Upon the midst of their tables stood their golden crucifixes, with diverse other gorgeous images. [...] Wherefore the foresaid sacred company, perambulating about some of the principal streets of Paris, especially our Lady street, were entertained with most divine honours. For whereas the

---

1   *punies* Young children.
2   *pontificalities* Robes related to the papacy; *Aaron* Moses's brother and the first high priest of Israel; *miter* Headdress worn by bishops and other religious officials.
3   *pentices* Sloped ledges on a wall offering protection from inclement weather.
4   *plate* Implements for eating and drinking made from silver or gold.

bishop carried the sacrament,[1] even his consecrated wafer cake, betwixt the images of two golden angels, whensoever he passed by any company, all the spectators prostrated themselves most humbly upon their knees, and elevated their hands with all possible reverence and religious behaviour, attributing as much divine adoration to the little wafer cake, which they call the sacrament of the altar, as they could do to Jesus Christ himself, if he were bodily present with them. If any godly Protestant that hates this superstition, should happen to be amongst them when they kneel, and forbear to worship the sacrament as they do, perhaps he may be presently stabbed or otherwise most shamefully abused, if there should be notice taken of him. After they had spent almost two hours in these pompous (I will not say theatrical) shows, they returned again to our Lady church, where was performed very long and tedious devotion for the space of two hours, with much excellent singing, and two or three solemn masses, acted by the bishop's own person.

[...]

I went to S. Denis, which is four miles from Paris the four and twentieth of May, being Tuesday, after dinner, where I saw many remarkable and memorable things. I passed through a cloister before I came into the church. These are the particulars that I saw: in a certain loft or higher room of the church I saw the images of many of the French kings, set in certain wooden cupboards, whereof some were made only to the middle with their crowns on their heads. But the image of the present king is made at length with his parliament robes, his gown lined with ermine,[2] and his crown on his head. There also I saw the crown wherewith the kings of France are crowned, and another wherewith the queens are crowned, being very rich and beset with many precious stones of exceeding worth; the gown faced with ermine, which they wear upon the day of their inauguration; their boots which they wear then also, being of watchet velvet, wherein many fleur-de-lis are curiously wrought; their spurs of beaten gold; a sword of King Solomon's, whose handle was massy gold; his drinking

---

1   *sacrament* Holy Eucharist.
2   *ermine* Fur of the ermine, a small mammal whose white winter coat was often used in clothing worn by royalty.

cup made of a rich kind of stone; a rich drinking cup of John of Gaunt[1] Duke of Lancaster; two crucifixes of inestimable worth, beset with wonderful variety of precious stones as carbuncles, rubies, diamonds, &c.; two sceptres of massy gold that the king and queen do carry in their hands at their coronation; a representation of our Lady church in Paris, made of silver, being a monument of exceeding value; for it contains the riches of our Lady church, as gold and jewels, &c. All these things I saw in that room.

[...]

The eight and twentieth day of May being Saturday, I rode in post from Paris about one of the clock in the afternoon to the king's stately palace of Fontainebleau,[2] which is eight and twenty miles from Paris, and came thither about eight of the clock in the morning: the king kept his court here at that time.

A little after I was past the last stage[3] saving one, where I took post-horse towards Fontainebleau, there happened this chance: my horse began to be so tired, that he would not stir one foot out of the way, though I did even excarnificate[4] his sides with my often spurring of him, except he were grievously whipped; whereupon a gentleman of my company, one Mr. J.H. took great pains with him to lash him: at last when he saw he was so dull that he could hardly make him go with whipping, he drew out his rapier and ran him into his buttock near to his fundament,[5] about a foot deep very near. The guide perceived not this before he came to the next stage, neither there, before we were going away. My friend lingered with me somewhat behind our company, and in a certain pool very diligently washed the horse's wound with his bare hands, thinking thereby to have stopped his bleeding, but he lost his labour, as much as he did that washed

---

1   *watchet* Light blue; *Solomon* Tenth-century BCE king of Israel who built the Temple of Jerusalem; *John of Gaunt* Member of the English royal family (1340–99). He was the son of Edward III and father of Henry IV.

2   *in post* Traveling by post-horse, a horse for hire; *Fontainebleau* Sixteenth-century royal palace commissioned by King Francis I (1494–1547).

3   *stage* Place at which travelers exchange their tired post-horses for rested ones.

4   *excarnificate* Torture.

5   *fundament* Anus.

the Ethiopian:[1] for the blood ran out a fresh notwithstanding all his laborious washing. Now when the guide perceived it, he grew so extreme choleric,[2] that he threatened Mr. J.H. he would go to Fontainebleau, and complain to the postmaster against him, except he would give him satisfaction; so that he posted very fast for a mile or two towards the court. In the end Mr. J.H. being much perplexed, and finding that there was no remedy but that he must needs grow to some composition with him, unless he would sustain some great disgrace, gave him six French crowns to stop his mouth.

This palace has his name from the fair springs and fountains, wherewith it is most abundantly watered, that I never saw so sweet a place before; neither do I think that all Christendom can yield the like for abundance of pleasant springs.

[...]

My observations of Fontainebleau

This palace is more pleasantly situate than any that ever I saw, even in a valley near to the forest on both sides. A little way off there are those rocky hills whereof I have already spoken. There are three or four goodly courts fairly paved with stone belonging to it. In the first there is an exquisite portraiture of a great horse made of white stone with a pretty covering over it, contrived with blue slate. The second is far fairer, wherein there is a gallery *sub dio*, railed with iron rails that are supported with many little iron pillars. In the third which leads to the fonts and walks are two sphinxes, very curiously carved in brass, and two images likewise of savage men carved in brass that are set in a hollow place of the wall near to those sphinxes. The poets write that there was a monster near the city of Thebes in Boeotia, in the time of King Oedipus,[3] which had the face of a maid, the body of a dog, the wings of a bird, the nails of a lion, and the tail of a dragon, which was called sphinx, according to which form these sphinxes were made. In this court there is a most sweet spring or fountain, in the midst

---

1 *he did ... Ethiopian* Reference to the idea of "washing an Ethiopian white," proverbial in this period for an impossible task.
2 *choleric* Angry.
3 *Oedipus* King Oedipus of Thebes, who solved the riddle of the sphinx.

whereof there is an artificial rock very excellently contrived, out of the which at four sides there does spout water incessantly through four little scallop shells, and from a little spout at the top of the rock. There are also some pretty distance from the corners of the rock four dolphins' heads made of brass, that do always spout out water as the other. Hard by[1] this font there is a pond of very goodly great carps, whereof there is wonderful plenty. The whole pond is very great, but that part of it which is derived towards this font is but little, being environed with a fair rail and little pillars of free-stone. In one of the gardens there is another stately font, in whose middle there is another excellent artificial rock with a representation of moss, and many such other things as pertain to a natural rock. At the top of it there is represented in brass the image of Romulus very largely made, lying sidelong & leaning upon one of his elbows. Under one of his legs is carved the she-wolf, with Romulus and Remus very little, like suck-lings, sucking at her teats.[2] Also at the four sides of this rock there are four swans made in brass, which do continually spout out water, and at the four corners of the font there are four curious scallop shells, made very largely, whereon the water does continually flow. This font also is environed with a fair enclosure of white stone. Also the statue of Hersilia, Romulus his wife[3] is made in brass, and lies a pretty way from that fountain under a part of the wall of one of the galleries. The knots of the garden are very well kept, but neither for the curiosity of the workmanship, nor for the matter whereof it is made, may it compare with many of our English gardens. For most of the borders of each knot is made of box,[4] cut very low, and kept in very good order. The walks about the gardens are many, whereof some are very long and of a convenient breadth, being fairly sanded, and kept very clean. One amongst the rest is enclosed with two very lofty hedges, most exquisitely made of filbird trees[5] and fine fruits, and many curi-ous arbours are made therein. By most of these walks there run very

---

1   *Hard by* Close to.
2   *Romulus … teats* Romulus and Remus, the mythical sibling-founders of Rome, are trad-itionally depicted suckling the she-wolf that rescued and nurtured them. Romulus would later kill his brother and become the first king of Rome.
3   *Hersilia, Romulus his wife* Wife of Romulus; she would become deified as Hora after her death; *Romulus his* Romulus's.
4   *box* Common box tree, also called boxwood.
5   *filbird trees* Filbert, or hazelnut trees.

pleasant rivers full of sundry delicate fishes. The principal spring of all which is called Fontainebleau, which feeds all the other springs and rivers, and wherehence the king's palace has his denomination, is but little, yet very fair.

[...]

Two things very worthy the observation I saw in two of the walks, even two beech trees, who were very admirable to behold not so much for the height, for I have seen higher in England, but for their greatness. For three men are hardly able to compass one of them with their arms stretched forth at length. Near unto a little stable of the king's horses, which was about the end of the walks, I was let in at a door to a fair green garden, where I saw pheasants of diverse sorts, unto which there do repair at some seasons such a multitude of wild pheasants from the forest, and woods, and groves thereabout, that it is thought there are not so few as a thousand of them. There I saw two or three birds that I never saw before, yet I have much read of admirable things of them in Aelianus the polyhistor,[1] and other historians, even storks, which do much haunt many cities and towns of the Netherlands, especially in the summer. For in Flushing a town of Zeeland[2] I saw some of them: those men esteeming themselves happy in whose houses they harbour, and those most unhappy whom they forsake. These birds are white, and have long legs and exceeding long beaks, being destitute of tongues as some write. We shall read that they were so much honoured in former times amongst the ancient Thessalians,[3] by reason that they destroyed the serpents of the country, that it was esteemed a very capital offence for any man to kill one of them: the like punishment being inflicted upon him that kills a stork, that was upon a murderer. It is written of them that when the old one is become so old that it is not able to help itself, the young one purveys food for it, and sometimes carries it about on his back; and if it sees it so destitute of meat, that it knows not where to get any sustenance, it casts out that which it has eaten the day before,

---

1   *Aelianus … polyhistor* Claudius Aelianus, Roman author of *De animalium natura* (*On the Nature of Animals*, third century).
2   *Flushing … Zeeland* Vlissingen, city in the far west province of Zeeland, Netherlands.
3   *Thessalians* People of Thessaly, in northern Greece.

to the end to feed his dam. This bird is called in Greek πέλαργος, wherehence comes the Greek word ἀντιπελαργεὲν,[1] which signifies to imitate the stork in cherishing our parents. Surely it is a notable example for children to follow in helping and comforting their decrepit parents, when they are not able to help themselves. Besides I saw there three ostriches, called in Latin *struthiocameli*,[2] which are such birds that (as historians do write of them) will eat iron, as a key or a horse shoe: one male and two female. Their necks are much longer than cranes, and pilled,[3] having none or little feathers about them. They advance themselves much higher than the tallest man that ever I saw. Also their feet and legs which are wonderful long, are pilled and bare: and their thighs together with their hinder parts are not only bare, but also seem very raw and red, as if they had taken some hurt, but indeed they are naturally so. Their heads are covered all with small stubbed feathers, their eyes great and black, their beaks short and sharp, their feet cloven not unlike to a hoof, and their nails formed in that manner, that I have read they will take up stones with them, and throw at their enemies that pursue them, and sometimes hurt them. The feathers of their wings and tails, but especially of their tails are very soft and fine, in respect whereof they are much used in the fans of gentlewomen. The authors do write that it is a very foolish bird: for whereas he doth sometimes hide his neck behind a bush, he thinks that nobody sees him, though indeed he be seen of everyone. Also he is said to be so forgetful that as soon as he has laid his eggs, he has clean forgotten them till his young ones are hatched.

[...]

A little without[4] one of the gates of the palace, there stood some of the king's guard orderly disposed and settled in their ranks with their muskets ready charged and set on their rests, who do the like always

---

1 πέλαργος Greek: pelargos, stork; ἀντιπελαργεὲν Greek: antipelargeen, mutual love or kindness, especially in the context of children's love for parents. The (now obsolete) English word "antipelargy" has the same meaning. In Ancient Greece Pelargonia was a law stipulating that adult children must care for their elderly parents.
2 *struthiocameli* From Greek στρουθός (strouthos; "sparrow") and κάμηλος (kamelos; "camel").
3 *pilled* Lacking feathers.
4 *without* Outside.

day and night. Many of their muskets were very fair, being inlaid with abundance of ivory and bone. Seeing I have now mentioned the guard, I will make some large relation thereof according as I informed myself partly at the French court, and partly by some conference that I have had since my arrival in England, with my worthy and learned friend Mr. Laurence Whitaker.[1]

The French guard consists partly of French, partly of Scots, and partly of Switzers.[2] [...] Of the Switzers, there is a regiment of five hundred, which wait before the gate by turns with the French regiment, and one hundred more who carry only halberds and wear swords, who wait in the hall of the king's house wheresoever he lies. [...] The Switzers wear no coats, but doublets and hose of panes,[3] intermingled with red and yellow, and some with blue, trimmed with long puffs of yellow and blue sarcenet rising up betwixt the panes, besides codpieces of the like colours, which codpiece because it is by that merry French writer Rabelais[4] styled the first and principal piece of armour, the Switzers do wear it as a significant symbol of the assured service they are to do to the French king in his wars, and of the main burden of the most laborious employments which lie upon them in time of peace, as old suresbyes[5] to serve for all turns. But the original of their wearing of codpieces and parti-coloured clothes grew from this; it is not found that they wore any until *Anno* 1476 at what time the Switzers took their revenge upon Charles Duke of Burgundy, for taking from them a town called Grandson within the Canton of Bern,[6] whom after they had defeated, and shamefully put to flight, together with all his forces, they found there great spoils that the duke left behind, to the value of three million, as it was said. But the Switzers being ignorant of the value of the richest things, tore in pieces the most sumptuous pavilions in the world, to make themselves coats and

---

1 *Mr. Laurence Whitaker* Laurence Whitaker (1577/78–1654), Coryate's best friend and a central figure in the "Panegyricke Verses." See Introduction and "In Context" Materials.

2 *Switzers* Swiss Guards, soldiers for hire from Switzerland.

3 *doublets* Form-fitting jackets worn by men; *hose of panes* Hose with differently colored strips of cloth.

4 *sarcenet* Fine silky material; *codpieces* Coverings worn over male genitals; *Rabelais* François Rabelais, author of *Gargantua and Pantagruel* (1532).

5 *suresbyes* Things that can be depended upon.

6 *Charles Duke of Burgundy* Charles the Bold (1433–77); *Grandson* Town in western Switzerland; *Canton of Bern* Switzerland is divided into administrative units known as cantons.

breeches; some of them sold silver dishes as cheap as pewter, for two pence half-penny a piece, and a great pearl hanging in a jewel of the duke's for twelve pence, in memory of which insipid simplicity, Louis the eleventh King of France,[1] who the next year after entertained them into his pension, caused them to be uncased of their rich clothes made of the Duke of Burgundy's pavilions, and ordained that they should ever after wear suites and codpieces of those variegated colours of red and yellow. I observed that all these Switzers do wear velvet caps with feathers in them, and I noted many of them to be very cluster-fisted lubbers.[2] As for their attire, it is made so fantastically, that a novice newly come to the court, who never saw any of them before, would half imagine, if he should see one of them alone without his weapon, he were the king's fool.

[...]

Also I saw a worthy and gallant gentleman of Germany, a Protestant, who has done the emperor great service in his wars against the Turk: he has been at our English court, where he has been very royally entertained by our king,[3] and knighted, and at his departure our king bestowed a very royal reward upon him, as an Irish gentleman told me at the French court. While he was in England he was a great tilter:[4] he went very richly at Fontainebleau. His cloak gorgeously beautified partly with silver lace, and partly with pearl. In his hat he wore a rich ruby, as big as my thumb at the least. Thus much of Fontainebleau.

[...]

At the town Montargis there is a very goodly castle of the Duke of Guise[5] strongly fortified, both by the nature of the place and by art: it has many fair turrets, and is situate in so eminent and conspicuous a part of the town, that it might be seen a great way off in the country.

---

1 *Louis ... France* King Louis XI (1423–83).
2 *cluster-fisted lubbers* Clumsy, stupid people.
3 *our king* King James VI/I of England, Ireland, and Scotland (1566–1625).
4 *tilter* Jouster.
5 *Duke of Guise* Presumably a reference to Charles de Lorraine, fourth Duke of Guise (1571–1640), not to his father Henry de Lorraine, third Duke of Guise (1550–88).

A little on this side Montargis I saw a very doleful and lamentable spectacle: the bones and ragged fragments of clothes of a certain murderer remaining on a wheel, whereon most murderers are executed: the bones were miserably broken asunder, and dispersed abroad upon the wheel in diverse places. Of this torment I have made mention before.

[...]

The windows in most places of France do very much differ from our English windows; for in the inside of the room it has timber leaves, joined together with certain little iron bolts, which being loosed, and the leaves opened, there comes in at the lower part of the window where there is no glass at all, the open air very pleasantly. The upper part of the window, which is most commonly shut, is made of glass or lattice.

The French guides otherwise called the postilions[1] have one most diabolical custom in their travelling upon the ways. Diabolical it may be well called: for whensoever their horses do a little anger them, they will say in their fury *Allons diable*, that is, Go thou devil. Also if they happen to be angry with a stranger upon the way upon any occasion, they will say to him *le diable t'emporte*, that is, The devil take thee. This I know by mine own experience.

[...]

I went from Moulins about three of the clock in the afternoon, and came to a place called St. Geran,[2] being sixteen miles from it, about half an hour after eight of the clock in the evening. In this space I saw nothing but one very rueful and tragic object: ten men hanging in their clothes upon a goodly gallows made of free-stone about a mile beyond Moulins, whose bodies were consumed to nothing, only their bones and the ragged fitters[3] of their clothes remained.

I saw the Alps within a few miles after I was passed beyond St. Geran: they appeared about forty miles before I came to them. Those

---

1 *postilions* Guides, sometimes associated with the post and/or post-horses.
2 *St. Geran* Saint-Gérand-de-Vaux.
3 *fitters* Pieces.

that divide Germany and Italy are by themselves, and they that divide France and Italy are by themselves: which Alps are sundered by the space of many miles the one from the other.

[…]

In Tarare I observed one thing that I much admired, a woman that had no hands but stumps instead thereof (whether she had this deformity naturally or accidentally I know not) did spin flax with a distaff as nimbly and readily, and drew out her thread as artificially with her stumps, as any woman that ever I saw spinning with her hands.

I went a Friday morning being the third day of June about six of the clock from Tarare in my boots, by reason of a certain accident, to a place about six miles therehence, where I took post horse, and came to Lyons about one of the clock in the afternoon. Betwixt the place where I took post and Lyons, it rained most extremely without any ceasing, that I was drooping wet to my very skin when I came to my inn. I passed three gates before I entered into the city. The second was a very fair gate, at one side whereof there is a very stately picture of a lion. When I came to the third gate I could not be suffered to pass into the city, before the porter having first examined me wherehence I came, and the occasion of my business, there gave me a little ticket under his hand as a kind of warrant for mine entertainment in mine inn. For without that ticket I should not have been admitted to lodge within the walls of the city.

My observations of Lyons […]

Lyons is a fair city being seated in that part of France which is called Lyonnois, and very ancient. […] It is fortified with a strong wall, and has seven gates, many fair streets, and goodly buildings, both public and private. Very populous, and is esteemed the principal emporium or mart town[1] of all France next to Paris. It is the seat of an archbishop, who is the primate and metropolitan[2] of France. The present

---

1   *mart town* Market town.
2   *primate* High-ranking bishop. "Primat des Gaules" was a title given to archbishops of Lyons; *metropolitan* Bishop with authority over other bishops in a region.

archbishop whose name is Bellievre[1] son to the Chancellor of France, is but young being not above thirty years old. Most of the buildings are of an exceeding height, six or seven stories high together with the vault under the ground. For they have vaults or cellars under most of their houses. I observed that most of their windows are made of white paper. In many places of the city the whole window is made of white paper only, in some partly of white paper as the lower part, and partly of glass as the higher part: almost all their houses are built with white free-stone.

[...]

There is in the south side of the town, near the rocky-hills, an exceeding high pair of stairs, which contains one hundred and fourteen stony greeses:[2] above these stairs there is a long stony walk at the least half a mile high, and very steep, which leads to the top of the hill where there are many old monuments, whereof one is the temple of Venus built on the very top of the hill, but now it is converted to a college of canon monks.[3] Also there are to be seen the ruins of that huge amphitheatre, wherein those constant servants of Jesus Christ willingly suffered many intolerable and bitter tortures for his sake: I call it a huge amphitheatre, because it is reported it contained at the least fifty thousand persons. As for those martyrs which suffered there, frequent mention of them does occur in most of the ancient ecclesiastical historians, especially Eusebius Bishop of Caesarea, who writes a no less tragic than copious history of the cruel sufferings of Attalus, Sanctus, Maturus, and the virtuous woman Blandina, all which were in this place most cruelly broiled in iron chairs for the faith of their redeemer, in the fourth persecution of the primitive church, under the Emperor Antoninus Verus.[4] He that will read the tragic and most pitiful history of their martyrdom, which I have often perused not without effusion of tears, let him read the epistle of the brethren of

---

1 *Bellievre* Claude de Bellièvre (d. 1612), Archbishop of Lyons.
2 *greeses* Steps.
3 *canon monks* Catholic priests leading semi-monastic lives under the rule of St. Augustine.
4 *Eusebius Bishop of Caesarea* Author of the *Historia Ecclesiastica* (fourth century); *Attalus ... Blandina* Early Christian martyrs; *Antoninus Verus* Antoninus Pius (86–161), emperor and strong proponent of Roman state religion.

Lyons and Vienna, to the brethren of Asia and Phrygia, in the fifth book and second epistle of Eusebius his Ecclesiastical History.

[...]

I spoke with a certain pilgrim upon the bridge over the Arar,[1] who told me that he had been at Compostela in Spain, and was now going to Rome, but he must needs take Avignon in his way, a French town which has these many years belonged to the pope. I had a long discourse with him in Latin, who told me he was a Roman born. I found him but a simple fellow, yet he had a little beggarly and coarse Latin, so much as a Priscianist[2] may have.

I lay at the sign of the three kings, which is the fairest inn in the whole city, and most frequented of all the inns in the town, and that by great persons. For the Earl of Essex[3] lay there with all his train before I came thither: he came thither the Saturday and went away the Thursday following, being the day immediately before I came in. At that time that I was there, a great nobleman of France Monsieur de Breves (who had lain lieger ambassador[4] many years in Constantinople) lay there with a great troupe of gallant gentleman, who was then taking his journey to Rome to lie there lieger. Amongst the rest of his company there were two Turks that he brought with him out of Turkey, whereof one was a black moor, who was his jester: a mad conceited fellow, and very merry. He wore no hat at all either in his journey (for he overtook us upon the way riding without a hat) or when he rested in any town, because his natural hair which was exceeding thick and curled, was so prettily elevated in height, that it served him always instead of a hat. The other Turk was a notable companion and a great scholar in his kind, for he spoke six or seven languages besides the Latin, which he spoke very well: he was born in Constantinople. I had a long discourse with him in Latin of many things, and amongst other questions I asked him whether he were ever baptized; he told me, no, and said he never would be. After that we fell into speeches

---

1   *Arar* Saône River.
2   *Priscianist* Grammarian, from Priscian (*fl.* c. 500–25), the Roman grammarian.
3   *Earl of Essex* Robert Devereux, third Earl of Essex (1591–1646), who in 1608 was in the midst of an extended tour through France and the Netherlands.
4   *lieger ambassador* Residential ambassador.

of Christ, whom he acknowledged for a great prophet, but not for the son of God, affirming that neither he nor any of his countrymen would worship him, but the only true God, creator of heaven and earth: and called us Christians idolaters, because we worshipped images; a most memorable speech if it be properly applied to those kind of Christians, which deserve that imputation of idolatry. At last I fell into some vehement argumentations with him in defence of Christ, whereupon being unwilling to answer me, he suddenly flung out of my company. He told me that the great Turk, whose name is Sultan Achomet,[1] is not above two and twenty years old, and that continually both in peace and war he does keep two hundred thousand soldiers in pay, for the defence of those countries in which they are resident: a matter certainly of incredible charge to the great Turk, in which I perceive that he far exceeds the ancient Roman emperors, that had both a larger empire and better means to defray the charge than himself. For they kept in all their provinces of Asia, Europe and Africa but five and twenty legions, each whereof contained six thousand and a hundred foot-men (according to the authority of Vegetius)[2] and seven hundred twenty six horse-men, besides twelve Praetorian and Urban cohorts[3] in the city of Rome, for the guard of the emperor's palace: whereof the first which was the principal of all, contained one thousand, one hundred and five foot-men, and one hundred thirty and two horse-men; the others equally five hundred and fifty foot-men and sixty-six horse-men, which number I find to fall short by more than thirty thousand of those that the Turk keeps this day in his garrisons. Many other memorable things besides these this learned Turk told me, which I will not now commit to writing.

At mine inn there lay the Saturday night, being the fourth of June, a worthy young nobleman of France of two and twenty years old, who was brother to the Duke of Guise and Knight of Malta.[4] He had passing fine music at supper, and after supper he and his companions

---

1   *Sultan Achomet* Ahmed I (1590–1617), Sultan of the Ottoman Empire.
2   *Vegetius* Roman author of a military treatise titled *Epitoma rei militaris* (4th century).
3   *Praetorian … cohorts* The Praetorian Guard was responsible for protecting the emperor in Ancient Rome. The *cohortes urbanae* served as Rome's police force.
4   *Knight of Malta* Also known as the Knights Hospitaller, the Knights of Malta were a military order originally established during the Crusades.

being gallant lusty gentlemen, danced corantoes and lavoltoes[1] in the court. He went therehence the Sunday after dinner, being the fifth day of June.

At the south side of the higher court of mine inn, which is hard by the hall (for there are two or three courts in that inn) there is written this pretty French poesy:[2] *On ne loge ceans à credit: car il est mort, les mauvais paieurs l'ont tue.* The English is this: Here is no lodging upon credit: for he is dead, ill payers have killed him. Also on the south side of the wall of another court, there was a very pretty and merry story painted, which was this: a certain peddler having a budget[3] full of small wares, fell asleep as he was travelling on the way, to whom there came a great multitude of apes, and robbed him of all his wares while he was asleep: some of those apes were painted with pouches or budgets at their backs, which they stole out of the peddler's fardle[4] climbing up to trees, some with spectacles on their noses, some with beads about their necks, some with touch-boxes and inkhorns in their hands, some with crosses and censer boxes, some with cards in their hands; all which things they stole out of the budget: and amongst the rest one putting down the peddler's breeches, and kissing his naked, &c. This pretty conceit seems to import some merry matter, but truly I know not the moral of it.

I saw a fellow whipped openly in the streets of Lyons that day that I departed therehence, being Monday the sixth day of June, who was so stout a fellow, that though he received many a bitter lash, he did not a jot relent at it.

At Lyons our bills of health[5] began: without the which we could not be received into any of these cities that lay in our way towards Italy. For the Italians are so curious and scrupulous in many of their cities, especially those that I passed through in Lombardy, that they will admit no stranger within the walls of their city, except he brings a bill of health from the last city he came from, to testify that he was free from all manner of contagious sickness when he came from the

---

1   *corantoes and lavoltoes* Fashionable dances.
2   *poesy* Short inscription.
3   *budget* Pouch.
4   *fardle* Pack.
5   *bills of health* Documents required of travelers arriving in cities, to prove they do not carry communicable diseases.

last city. But the Venetians are extraordinarily precise herein, insomuch that a man cannot be received into Venice without a bill of health, if he would give a thousand ducats. But the like strictness I did not observe in those cities of Lombardy, through the which I passed in my return to Venice homeward. For they received me into Vicenza, Verona, Brescia, Bergamo, &c. without any such bill.

He that will be thoroughly acquainted with the principal antiquities and memorables of this famous city, let him read a Latin tract of one Symphorianus Campegius[1] a Frenchman and a learned knight born in this city, who has both copiously and eloquently discoursed thereof. For it was my hap[2] to see his book in a learned gentleman's hands in this city, who very kindly communicated the same unto me for a little space: whereof I made so little use, or rather none at all, that I have often since much repented for it. Thus much of Lyons.

[...]

I went from La Tour-du-Pin about two of the clock in the afternoon, and came to a place called Pont-de-Beauvoisin about six of the clock. Betwixt these places there is six miles distance: at this Pont-de-Beauvoisin France and Savoy do meet, the bridge parting them both. When I was on this side the bridge I was in France, when beyond, in Savoy.

The end of my observations of France.

[...]

My observations of Savoy[3]

I went from Pont-de-Beauvoisin about half an hour after six of the clock in the morning, the eight day of June being Wednesday, and came to the foot of the mountain Aiguebelette which is the first Alp,

---

1   *Symphorianus Campegius* Symphorien Champier (1472–1539), French medical doctor and historian.
2   *hap* Fortune.
3   *Savoy* Mountainous region in Western Europe where southeastern France borders northwestern Italy.

about ten of the clock in the morning. A little on this side the mountain there is a poor village called Aiguebelle, where we stayed a little to refresh ourselves before we ascended the mountain. I observed an exceeding great standing pool a little on this side the mountain on the left hand thereof.

[...]

I ascended the mountain Aiguebelette about ten of the clock in the morning afoot, and came to the foot of the other side of it towards Chambery, about one of the clock. Betwixt which places I take it to be about some two miles, that is a mile and half to the top of the mountain, and from the top to the foot of the descent half a mile. I went up afoot, and delivered my horse to another to ride for me, because I thought it was more dangerous to ride than to go a foot, though indeed all my other companions did ride: but then this accident happened to me. Certain poor fellows which get their living especially by carrying men in chairs from the top of the hill to the foot thereof towards Chambery, made a bargain with some of my company, to carry them down in chairs, when they came to the top of the mountain, so that I kept them company towards the top. But they being desirous to get some money of me, lead me such an extreme pace towards the top, that how much soever I labored to keep them company, I could not possibly perform it: the reason why they lead such a pace, was, because they hoped that I would give them some consideration to be carried in a chair to the top, rather than I would lose their company, and so consequently my way also, which is almost impossible for a stranger to find alone by himself, by reason of the innumerable turnings and windings thereof, being on every side beset with infinite abundance of trees. So that at last finding that faintness in myself that I was not able to follow them any longer, though I would even break my heart with striving, I compounded with them for a cardekew,[1] which is eighteen pence English, to be carried to the top of the mountain,[2] which was at the least half a mile

---

1   *cardekew* Cardecu, French coin worth ¼ of an ecu or crown: a proverbially small amount of money.

2   *top of the mountain* See the illustrations on the engraved title page (page 212); this event is depicted in illustration "D."

from the place where I mounted on the chair. This was the manner of their carrying of me: they did put two slender poles through certain wooden rings, which were at the four corners of the chair, one before, and another behind. But such was the miserable pains that the poor slaves willingly undertook for the gain of that cardakew, that I would not have done the like for five hundred. The ways were exceeding difficult in regard of the steepness and hardness thereof, for they were all rocky, *petricosae & salebrosae*,[1] and so uneven that a man could hardly find any sure footing on them. When I had *tandem aliquando*[2] gotten up to the top, I said to myself with Aeneas in Virgil:

————*Forsan & haec olim meminisse juvabit.*[3]

then might I justly and truly say, that which I could never before, that I was above some of the clouds. For though that mountain be not by the sixth part so high as some others of them, yet certainly it was a great way above some of the clouds. For I saw many of them very plainly on the sides of the mountain beneath me.

[…]

In many places of Savoy I saw many fine and pleasant meadows, especially in some places betwixt Chambery and Aiguebelle on the left hand under the Alps, which is a thing very rare to be seen in diverse places of this country.

The worst ways that ever I travelled in all my life in the summer were those betwixt Chambery and Aiguebelle, which were as bad as the worst I ever rode in England in the midst of winter: insomuch that the ways of Savoy may be proverbially spoken of as the owls of Athens, the pears of Calabria, and the quails of Delos.[4]

I saw many chestnut-trees and walnut trees in Savoy, and pretty store of hemp.

---

1 *petricosae & salebrosae* Latin: rocky and rugged.
2 *tandem aliquando* Latin: at last.
3 *Forsan … juvabit* Latin: One day it will please us to remember even this. Cf. Virgil, *Aeneid* 1.203.
4 *owls … Delos* Each of these animals or plants was traditionally associated with the specific places mentioned: the owl was a symbol of Athens, Calabria (a region in Southern Italy) was known for its prickly pears, and according to legend, Delos (a Greek island) had a large quail population.

I commended Savoy a pretty while for the best place that ever I saw in my life, for abundance of pleasant springs, descending from the mountains, till at the last I considered the cause of those springs. For they are not fresh springs, as I conjectured at the first, but only little torrents of snow water, which distills from the top of those mountains, when the snow by the heat of the sun is dissolved into water. Of those torrents I think I saw at the least a thousand betwixt the foot of the ascent of the mountain Aiguebelette and Novalaise in Piedmont, at the descent of the mountain Senis,[1] which places are sixty-two miles asunder.

The swiftest and violentest lake that ever I saw is that which runs through Savoy, called Lezere, which is much swifter than the Rhone at Lyons, that by the poets is called *rapidissimus amnis*.[2] For this is so extreme swift, that no fish can possibly live in it, by reason that it will be carried away by the most violent source of the torrent, and dashed against those huge stones which are in most places of the lake. Yea there are many thousand stones in that lake much bigger than the stones of Stonehenge by the town of Amesbury in Wiltshire, or the exceeding great stone upon Hamdon Hill in Somersetshire, so famous for the quarry, which is within a mile of the parish of Odcombe my dear natalitial place.[3] These stones fell into this river, being broken from the high rocks of the Alps, which are on both sides of it. The cause of the extraordinary swiftness of this lake is the continual flux of the snow water descending from those mountains, which doth augment and multiply the lake in a thousand places. There is another thing also to be observed in this lake, the horrible and hideous noise thereof. For I think it keeps almost as terrible a noise as the river Cocytus in hell, which the poets do extol for the murmuring thereof, as having his name *Cocytus* from the old Greek word χωχύειν,[4] which signifies to keep a noise.

[...]

---

1 *Novalaise in Piedmont* Novalesa, a town in the Piedmont region of Northern Italy; *mountain Senis* Moncenisio.
2 *lake* Body of running water; *Lezere* River Isère; *rapidissimus amnis* Latin: swiftest river.
3 *Hamdon ... Odcombe* Ham Hill, known for its hamstone (a form of limestone) quarry, is situated close to Coryate's home village of Odcombe, Somerset; *natalitial place* Birthplace.
4 *Cocytus* In classical mythology, one of the four rivers of Hades; χωχύειν Greek: chochyein, to wail.

It seems very dangerous in diverse places to travel under the rocky mountains, because many of them are cloven and do seem at the very instant that a man is under them *minari ruinam*;[1] and by so much the more fearful a man may be, by how much the more he may see great multitudes of those stones fallen down in diverse places by the river, and the side of the way from the mountains themselves, & many of them four or five times greater than the great stone of Hamdon Hill before mentioned.

[...]

The country of Savoy is very cold, and much subject to rain, by reason of those clouds, that are continually hovering about the Alps, which being the receptacles of rain do there more distill their moisture, than in other countries.

I observed an admirable abundance of butterflies in many places of Savoy, by the hundreth part more than ever I saw in any country before, whereof many great swarms, which were (according to my estimation and conjecture) at the least two thousand, lay dead upon the highways as we travelled.

When I came to Aiguebelle I saw the effect of the common drinking of snow water in Savoy. For there I saw many men and women have exceeding great bunches or swellings in their throats, such as we call in Latin *strumas*,[2] as big as the two fists of a man, through the drinking of snow water, yea some of their bunches are almost as great as an ordinary football with us in England. These swellings are much to be seen amongst these Savoyards, neither are all the Piedmontanes free from them.

[...]

I noted one thing about six or seven miles before I came to Lasnebourg[3] that is not to be omitted. The ways on the sides of the mountains whereon I rode were so exceeding high, that if my horse had happened to stumble, he had fallen down with me four or five times

---

1   *minari ruinam* Latin: to threaten collapse.
2   *strumas* Goiters.
3   *Lasnebourg* Lanslebourg-Mont-Cenis, France.

as deep in some places as Paul's tower in London[1] is high. Therefore I very providently preventing the worst dismounted from my horse, and lead him in my hand for the space of a mile and half at the least, though my company too adventurously rode on, fearing nothing.

[...]

I observed an exceeding high mountain betwixt Lasnebourg and Novalaise, much higher than any that I saw before called Roch Melow:[2] it is said to be the highest mountain of all the Alps, saving one of those that part Italy and Germany. Some told it was fourteen miles high: it is covered with a very microcosm of clouds. Of this mountain there is no more than a little piece of the top to be seen, which seems a far off to be three or four little turrets or steeples in the air.

[...]

The descent of the mountain I found more wearisome and tedious than the ascent. For I rode all the way up being assisted with my guide of Lasnebourg, but down I was constrained to walk afoot for the space of seven miles. For so much it is betwixt the top and the foot of the mountain: in all which space I continually descended head-long. The ways were exceeding uneasy. For they were wonderful hard, all stony and full of windings and intricate turnings, where I think there were at the least two hundred before I came to the foot. Still I met many people ascending, and mules laden with carriage, and a great company of dun kine[3] driven up the hill with collars about their necks: in those ways I found many stones wherein I plainly perceived the metal of tin, whereof I saw a great multitude. One of them I took up in my hand, intending to carry it home into England, but one of my company to whom I delivered it to keep for me, lost it.

The end of my observations of Savoy.

---

1 *Paul's ... London* Tower of St. Paul's Cathedral, the tallest building in early-seventeenth-century London.
2 *Roch Melow* Mt. Roche-Melon.
3 *dun kine* Brown cows.

My observations of Italy [...]

I rode from St. Georges[1] about seven of the clock in the morning on Sunday, being the twelfth day of June, and came about twelve of the clock to a town in Piedmont called Rivoli, which is nineteen miles therehence.

[...]

In many places of Piedmont I observed most delicate straw hats, which both men and women use in most places of that province, but especially the women. For those that the women wear are very pretty, some of them having at the least a hundred seams made with silk, and some prettily woven in the seams with silver, and many flowers, borders, and branches very curiously wrought in them, in so much that some of them were valued at two ducatoons, that is, eleven shillings.

I rode from Rivoli about three of the clock in the afternoon that Sunday, and came to Turin which was four miles beyond it, about five of the clock.

[...]

There rode in our company a merry Italian one Antonio, that vaunted he was lineally descended from the famous Marcus Antonius of Rome the triumvir,[2] and would oftentimes cheer us with this sociable conceit *Courage, courage, le Diable est mort*. That is, be merry, for the devil is dead.

My observations of Turin [...]

I am sorry I can speak so little of so flourishing and beautiful a city. For during that little time that I was in the city, I found so great a

---

1 *St. Georges* San Giorio di Susa.
2 *Marcus ... triumvir* Mark Antony (c. 83–30 BCE), Roman general and member of the Second Triumvirate with Gaius Octavius and Marcus Aemilius Lepidus. He is famous for inciting the mob against Brutus and Cassius after Julius Caesar's assassination, and for warring with Cleopatra against Octavius.

distemperature[1] in my body, by drinking the sweet wines of Piedmont, that caused a grievous inflammation in my face and hands; so that I had but a small desire to walk much abroad in the streets. Therefore I would advise all Englishmen that intend to travel into Italy, to mingle their wine with water as soon as they come into the country, for fear of ensuing inconveniences.

[...]

Surely I observed it to be a fair city, having many stately buildings, both public and private: it is the capital city of Piedmont, situate in a plain, being in the east encompassed with hills, well walled, and has four fair gates, and a very strong citadel at the west end, exceeding well furnished with munition,[2] wherein there are five hundred pieces of ordinance. This city is built all with brick, and is of a square form. The river Duria[3] runs by it, and about a mile from the city the famous river Padus, which the Grecians called Eridanus, but the Italians at this day the Po.

[...]

Betwixt Turin and Sian[4] I was transported over a ferry. This Italian transporting was done after a pretty manner. For whereas there is a great long rope that reaches over the river, tied by certain instruments on both sides thereof, as soon as the horses and passengers are put into the boat, one of the boatmen that tarries at land turns a certain wheel about by means of that rope, by the motion of which wheel the boat is driven on to the other bank.

[...]

I observed a custom in many towns and cities of Italy, which did not a little displease me, that most of their roast meats which come to the table are sprinkled with cheese, which I love not so well as

---

1   *distemperature* Ailment.
2   *munition* Military equipment.
3   *Duria* Dora Riparia, a river near Turin and tributary of the Po.
4   *Sian* Cigliano, a town near Vercelli.

the Welshmen do,[1] whereby I was oftentimes constrained to lose my share of much good fare to my great discontentment.

In most of their inns they have white canopies and curtains, made of needlework, which are edged with very fair bone-lace.[2]

Here I will mention a thing that might have been spoken of before in discourse of the first Italian town. I observed a custom in all those Italian cities and towns through the which I passed, that is not used in any other country that I saw in my travels, neither do I think that any other nation of Christendom doth use it, but only Italy. The Italian and also most strangers that are commorant[3] in Italy, do always at their meals use a little fork when they cut their meat. For while with their knife which they hold in one hand they cut the meat out of the dish, they fasten their fork which they hold in their other hand upon the same dish, so that whatsoever he be that sitting in the company of any others at meal, should unadvisedly touch the dish of meat with his fingers from which all at the table do cut, he will give occasion of offence unto the company, as having transgressed the laws of good manners, in so much that for his error he shall be at the least brow-beaten, if not reprehended in words. This form of feeding I understand is generally used in all places of Italy, their forks being for the most part made of iron or steel, and some of silver, but those are used only by gentlemen. The reason of this their curiosity is, because the Italian cannot by any means endure to have his dish touched with fingers, seeing all men's fingers are not alike clean. Hereupon I myself thought good to imitate the Italian fashion by this forked cutting of meat, not only while I was in Italy, but also in Germany, and oftentimes in England since I came home: being once quipped for that frequent using of my fork, by a certain learned gentleman, a familiar friend of mine, one Mr. Laurence Whitaker, who in his merry humour doubted not to call me at table *furcifer*,[4] only for using a fork at feeding, but for no other cause.

[...]

---

1   *Welshmen do* The Welsh were (and still are) known for their cheeses.
2   *bone-lace* Linen lace. The name derives from the bone bobbins around which lace thread was wound.
3   *commorant* Resident.
4   *furcifer* Latin: scoundrel, but with a pun on "fork," in Latin *furca*.

My observations of Milan [...]

Many ancient monuments and worthy antiquities are to be seen in
this glorious city. The church wherein St. Ambrose Bishop of Milan
in the time of Theodosius the first was buried, which church he built
himself to the honour of the holy martyrs Gervasius and Protasius.[1]
This church is now called St. Ambrose's: it was the first Christian
temple in all the city, in the which the body of St. Ambrose lies interred under an altar in a deep cave of the ground, being supported
with four iron chains, and by his body there lies a certain book that
he wrote. This altar I saw.

[...]

The cathedral church is dedicated to our Lady, which John Galea-
tius Duke of Milan[2] caused to be built, anno 1386. [...] I ascended
almost to the top of the tower; wherehence I surveyed the whole city
round about, which yielded a most beautiful and delectable show.
There I observed the huge suburbs, which are as big as many a fair
town, and compassed about with ditches of water: there also I beheld a great part of Italy, together with the lofty Apennines; and
they showed me which way Rome, Venice, Naples, Florence, Genoa,
Ravenna, &c. lay. The territory of Lombardy, which I contemplated
round about from this tower, was so pleasant an object to mine eyes,
being replenished with such unspeakable variety of all things, both
for profit and pleasure, that it seems to me to be the very Elysian
fields, so much decantated and celebrated by the verses of poets, or
the Tempe or paradise of the world.[3] For it is the fairest plain, extended about some two hundred miles in length that ever I saw, or
ever shall if I should travel over the whole habitable world: insomuch

---

1 *St. Ambrose ... Milan* Church father (c. 339–97); *Theodosius the first* Roman Emperor
   (379–95); *Gervasius and Protasius* Second-century Christian martyrs whose remains and
   relics St. Ambrose preserved in the church, now called Basilica di Sant'Ambrogio.
2 *John ... Milan* Gian Galeazzo Visconti (1351–1402), first duke of Milan.
3 *Elysian ... world* Reference to different types of heaven or paradise. Dead heroes and war-
   riors of the classical world went to the Elysian Fields; Tempe was the reputed haunt of the
   Muses; and paradise suggests Christian Eden; *decantated* Sung repeatedly.

that I said to myself that this country was fitter to be an habitation for the immortal gods than for mortal men.

[...]

I rode in coach from Milan the sixteenth day of June being Thursday, about two of the clock in the afternoon, and came to the city of Lodi, being twenty miles therehence, about nine of the clock in the evening.

[...]

Here will I mention a thing, that although perhaps it will seem but frivolous to diverse readers that have already travelled in Italy; yet because unto many that neither have been there, nor ever intend to go thither while they live, it will be a mere novelty, I will not let it pass unmentioned. The first Italian fans that I saw in Italy did I observe in this space betwixt Pizighiton[1] and Cremona. But afterward I observed them common in most places of Italy where I travelled. These fans both men and women of the country do carry to cool themselves withal in the time of heat, by the often fanning of their faces. Most of them are very elegant and pretty things. For whereas the fan consists of a painted piece of paper and a little wooden handle, the paper which is fastened into the top is on both sides most curiously adorned with excellent pictures, either of amorous things tending to dalliance, having some witty Italian verses or fine emblems written under them, or of some notable Italian city with a brief description thereof added thereunto. These fans are of a mean price. For a man may buy one of the fairest of them for so much money as countervails our English groat.[2] Also many of them do carry other fine things of a far greater price that will cost at the least a ducat, which they commonly call in the Italian tongue *umbrellaes*, that is, things that minister shadow unto them for shelter against the scorching heat of the sun. These are made of leather something answerable to the form of a little canopy, & hooped in the inside with diverse little wooden hoops that extend

---

1   *Pizighiton* Pizzighettone.
2   *countervails ... groat* Equals a groat (four pence).

the *umbrella* in a pretty large compass. They are used especially by horsemen, who carry them in their hands when they ride, fastening the end of the handle upon one of their thighs, and they impart so large a shadow unto them, that it keeps the heat of the sun from the upper parts of their bodies.

[...]

My observations of Mantua [...]

The city of Mantua I take to be one of the ancientest cities of all Italy, ancienter than Rome by four hundred and thirty years.

[...]

Truly it is neither the long genealogy of the Tuscan kings, nor the magnificence of the ancient buildings nor the sweetness of the situation, nor any other ornament whatsoever that has half so much ennobled this delicate city, as the birth of that peerless and incomparable poet Virgil, in respect of whom the Mantuans have reason to be as proud as the Colophonians or Smyrnians in Greece were of their Homer.[1] I saw indeed the statue of Virgil made in stone as far as the girdle, which was erected in one of their marketplaces, but had I not been brought into such a narrow compass of time (for I came into the city about half an hour after seven of the clock in the evening, and rode therehence about eight of the clock the next morning) I would have seen the house at a place called Andes, a little mile from Mantua, wherein he was born and lived. For the ruins thereof are yet shown to the immortal glory of the Mantuans.

[...]

For they have such store of gardens about the city, that I think London which both for frequency of people, and multitude of houses doth thrice exceed it, is not better furnished with gardens. Besides

---

1   *Virgil* Roman epic poet (70–19 BCE), born in Mantua; *Colophonians ... Homer* Colophon and Smyrna were reputed birthplaces of Homer (eighth century BCE), epic poet of ancient Greece.

they have one more commodity which makes the city exceeding pleasant, even the fair river Mincius that flows out of the noble Lake Benacus,[1] of which Virgil speaks.

Hic viridis tenera praetexit arundine ripas
Mincius, &c.[2]

Withal they have abundance of delectable fruits growing about the city, whereof I saw great variety in the marketplace the Sunday morning when I departed therehence, and no small diversity of odoriferous flowers. Truly, the view of this most sweet paradise, this *domicilium Venerum & Charitum*[3] did even so ravish my senses, and tickle my spirits with such inward delight that I said unto myself, this is the city which of all other places in the world, I would wish to make my habitation in, and spend the remainder of my days in some divine meditations amongst the sacred muses, were it not for their gross idolatry and superstitious ceremonies which I detest, and the love of Odcombe in Somersetshire, which is so dear unto me that I prefer the very smoke thereof before the fire of all other places under the sun.

[…]

My observations of Padua […]

This city is seated in a very fertile and spacious plain that affords all manner of commodities, both for corn, vines, and fruits, necessary for man's sustentation.

[…]

The palace, in Latin *praetorium*, which serves for the Patavines as their council house, or as our Westminster Hall does us, for their public assemblies, and for the hearing and determining of controversies, is

---

1   *river Mincius* River Mincio;   *Lake Benacus* Lake Garda, in northern Italy.
2   [Coryate's Note] Georgi. 4. [The passage is not from Virgil's *Georgics*, but from his *Eclogues* 7.12–13. Latin: here Mincius with tender reeds fringed his verdant banks.]
3   *domicilium … Charitum* Latin: precious house of Venus.

(in my opinion) the fairest of all Christendom, at the least the fairest by many degrees that ever I saw.

[...]

At the west end of the hall near to one of the corners there is a very merry spectacle to be seen: there stands a round stone of some three feet high inserted into the floor, on the which if any bankrupt does sit with his naked buttocks three times in some public assembly, all his debts are *ipso facto*[1] remitted. Round about the stone are written these words in capital letters. *Lapis vituperii & cessationis bonorum.*[2] I believe this to be true, because many in the city reported it unto me. But belike there is a limitation of the sum that is owed; so that if the sum which the debtor owes be above the stint,[3] he shall not be released: otherwise it were great injustice of the Venetians to tolerate such a custom that honest creditors should be cozened and defrauded of the sum of thirty or forty thousand ducats by the impudent behaviour of some abject-minded varlet, who to acquit himself of his debt will most willingly expose his bare buttocks in that opprobrious and ignominious manner to the laughter of every spectator. Surely it is the strangest custom that ever I heard or read of, (though that which I have related of it be the very naked truth) whereof if some of our English bankrupts should have intelligence, I think they would heartily wish the like might be in force in England. For if such a custom were used with us, there is no doubt but that there would be more naked buttocks shown in the term time before the greatest nobility and judges of our land in Westminster Hall, than are of young punies in any grammar school of England to their *plagosi orbilii*, that is, their whipping and severely-censuring schoolmasters.

[...]

---

1   *ipso facto* Latin: by that deed.
2   *Lapis ... bonorum* Latin: The seat (literally "stone") of blame and surrendering of goods. Coryate's transcription diverges from most references to the phrase, which typically reads "cessionis" (surrendered, seized) instead of "cessationis" (relaxed).
3   *stint* Limit.

The church in the inside is richly garnished with sumptuous tapestry, and many other beautiful ornaments. Diverse monuments are to be seen in this church: but the fairest is that of St. Antony a Portuguese saint,[1] born in the city of Lisbon, from whom the church has his name. They told me that he lived in the time of S. Francis of Assisi,[2] and was canonized for a saint about the year 1241, by Pope Gregory the ninth. It is reported that his tomb has the virtue[3] to expel devils, which I do hardly believe. For I saw an experiment of it when I was in the church which came to no effect. For a certain demoniacal person prayed at the sepulchre upon his prostrate knees, who had another appointed to attend him, that he should not irreligiously behave himself at so religious a place. And a priest walked about the tomb while the demoniac was praying, to the end to help expel the devil with his exorcisms, but the effect thereof turned to nothing. For I left the fellow in as bad a case as I found him. The monument itself is very sumptuous, made all of marble, and adorned with most excellent imagery.

[...]

I saw the sumptuous and rich monastery of the Benedictine monks.[4] [...] In this church I saw many ancient monuments, as of Saint Luke the evangelist, near to which is hanged up a fair table, wherein his epitaph is written in Latin hexameter verses very elegantly. I have often repented since that time that I had not copied them: his bones were brought from Constantinople in an iron coffin which is enclosed in a great grate of iron that was likewise brought from Constantinople together with the coffin. That coffin I touched with my fingers, but with some difficulty: for it was so far within the grate that I could hardly convey the tops of my fingers to the coffin. [...] These Benedictines bestow exceeding bountiful alms twice every year upon the poor, as upon Justina's day, which with them is the seventh

---

1   *St. Antony ... saint* St. Antony of Padua (1195–1231), Augustinian friar.
2   *S. Francis of Assisi* Italian friar (1181/82–1226) and founder of the Franciscan Order.
3   *virtue* Miraculous power.
4   *Benedictine monks* Monks following the rule of St. Benedict (c. 480–c. 550), which encouraged a solitary life of prayer.

day of October, and upon Prosdocimus day[1] which is the seventh day of July. Their alms are twelve cart-loads of wine, and as many of bread upon each of those days. They have an exceeding fair garden to walk in for contemplation, wherein are many delectable walks, vaulted with pretty little rafters, over the which fair vines, and other green things do most pleasantly grow. These walks are both long and broad: in the knots and plots of this garden there grows admirable abundance of all commodious herbs and flowers. Also I saw two goodly fair rooms within the monastery abundantly furnished with passing variety of pleasant fine waters and apothecary drugs[2] that serve only for the monks. In the first of these rooms I saw the skin of a great crocodile hanged up at the roof, and another skin of a crocodile in the inner room. This crocodile is a beast of a most terrible shape fashioned something like a dragon, with wonderful hard scales upon his back. I observed that he has no tongue at all; his eyes are very little, and his teeth long and sharp. Also I noted the nails of his feet to be of a great length; he lives partly in the water, and partly in the land. For which cause the Grecians call him αμΦιβιον[3] that is, a beast that lives upon both those elements; and he lives for the most part in Nilus that famous river of Egypt, the Egyptians in former times being so superstitious that they worshipped him for a god, especially those people of Egypt that were called Ombitae, who consecrated certain days to the honour of him as the Grecians did their Olympia[4] to Jupiter; and if it happened that their children were at any time violently taken away by him, their parents would rejoice, thinking that they pleased the god in breeding that which served for his food.

[...]

---

1 *Justina's day* Feast day of St. Justina of Padua (d. 304 CE); *Prosdocimus day* Feast day of St. Prosdocimus (d. 100 CE), first bishop of Padua.
2 *apothecary drugs* Medicines.
3 αμΦιβιον Greek: amphibion, living in both.
4 *Ombitae* People of Kom Ombos, Egypt; *Olympia* Temple of Zeus at Olympia, home of the famous statue of Zeus (Jupiter), one of the seven wonders of the ancient world.

Also I saw a very pretty fruit which is esteemed far more excellent than apricots, or any other dainty fruit whatsoever growing in Italy. They call it *pistachi*,[1] a fruit much used in their dainty banquets.

[...]

In that I have written more copiously of Padua than of any other Italian city whatsoever saving Venice, I do thankfully attribute it to two English gentlemen that were then commorant in Padua when I was there, Mr. Moore Doctor of Physic, and Mr. Willoughby a learned student in the university, by whose directions and conducting of me to the principal places of the city, I ingenuously confess I saw much more than otherwise I should have done by mine own endeavours.

[...]

I made my abode in Padua three whole days, Tuesday being the eleventh of June, Wednesday and Thursday, and went away therehence in a bark[2] down the river Brenta the twenty-fourth of June being Friday, about seven of the clock in the morning, and came to Venice about two of the clock in the afternoon.

[...]

When I passed down the river to Venice I saw many goodly fair houses and palaces of pleasure on both sides of the river Brenta, which belong to the gentlemen of Venice.

When I came to the foresaid Lucie Fesina[3] I saw Venice, and not before, which yields the most glorious and heavenly show upon the water that ever any mortal eye beheld, such a show as did even ravish me both with delight and admiration. [...] At this Lucie Fesina I went out of my bark, and took a gondola which brought me to Venice.

[...]

---

1 *pistachi* Pistachios.
2 *bark* Boat.
3 *Lucie Fesina* Fusina, a port on the mainland near Venice.

The number of miles betwixt Odcombe, in Somersetshire, and Venice: in which account I name only a few principal cities.

Imprimis[1] betwixt Odcombe and London	106
Item[2] betwixt London and Dover	57
Item betwixt Dover and Calais	27
Item betwixt Calais and Paris	140
Item betwixt Paris and Lyons	240
Item betwixt Lyons and Turin	130
Item betwixt Turin and Milan	76
Item betwixt Milan and Padua	151
Item betwixt Padua and Venice	25
The total sum betwixt Odcombe and Venice is	952
Betwixt Calais and Venice	762

My observations of the most glorious, peerless, and maiden city of Venice: I call it maiden because it was never conquered. [...]

Though the incomparable and most decantated majesty of this city doth deserve a far more elegant and curious pencil to paint her out in her colours than mine. For I ingenuously confess mine own insufficiency and unworthiness, as being the unworthiest of ten thousand to describe so beautiful, so renowned, so glorious a virgin (for by that title does the world most deservedly style her) because my rude and unpolished pen may rather stain and eclipse the resplendent rays of her unparalleled beauty, than add any luster unto it: yet since I have hitherto continued this slender and naked narration of my observations of five months travels in foreign countries; this noble city does in a manner challenge this at my hands, that I should describe her also as well as the other cities I saw in my journey, partly because she gave me most loving and kind entertainment for the space of six weeks, which was the sweetest time (I must needs confess) for so much that ever I spent in my life; and partly for that she ministered unto me more variety of remarkable and delicious objects than mine eyes ever surveyed in any city before, or ever shall, if I should with

---

1   *Imprimis* First of all.
2   *Item* Also.

famous Sir John Mandeville our English Ulysses spend thirty whole years together in travelling over most places of the Christian and ethnic[1] world. Therefore omitting tedious introductions, I will descend to the description of this thrice worthy city: the fairest lady, yea the richest paragon and queen[2] of Christendom.

Such is the rareness of the situation of Venice, that it does even amaze and drive into admiration all strangers that upon their first arrival behold the same. For it is built altogether upon the water in the innermost gulf of the Adriatic Sea which is commonly called *Gulfo de Venetia*, and is distant from the main sea about the space of 3 miles. From the which it is divided by a certain great bank called *litto maggior*,[3] which is at the least fifty miles in length. This bank is so necessary a defence for the city, that it serves instead of a strong wall to repulse and reverberate the violence of the furious waves of the sea. For were not this bank interposed like a bulwark betwixt the city and the sea, the waves would utterly overwhelm and deface the city in a moment.

[...]

The city is divided in the midst by a goodly fair channel, which they call *Canal il grande*. The same is crooked, and made in the form of a Roman S. It is in length a thousand and three hundred paces, and in breadth at the least forty, in some places more. [...] Also both the sides of this channel are adorned with many sumptuous and magnificent palaces that stand very near to the water, and make a very glorious and beautiful show. For many of them are of a great height three or four stories high, most being built with brick, and some few with fair free-stone. Besides they are adorned with a great multitude of stately pillars made partly of white stone, and partly of

---

1   *Sir John Mandeville* Alleged English author of the *Voyages of John Mandeville*, a popular travelogue that first appeared in manuscript c. 1357 in France, but was later revealed to be plagiarized from several sources; *Ulysses* Roman name for Homer's Odysseus, besieger of Troy and wandering hero of *The Odyssey; ethnic* Pagan, i.e., non-Christian.
2   [Coryate's Note] I call her not thus in respect of any sovereignty that she has over other nations, in which sense Rome was in former times called queen of the world, but in regard of her incomparable situation, surpassing wealth and most magnificent buildings.
3   *litto maggior* Italian: great shore.

Istrian marble.[1] Their roofs do much differ from those of our English buildings. For they are all flat and built in that manner as men may walk upon them, as I have often observed. [...] Again, I noted another thing in these Venetian palaces that I have very seldom seen in England, and it is very little used in any other country that I could perceive in my travels, saving only in Venice and other Italian cities. Somewhat above the middle of the front of the building, or (as I have observed in many of their palaces) a little beneath the top of the front they have right opposite unto their windows a very pleasant little terrace, that juts or butts out from the main building: the edge whereof is decked with many pretty little turned pillars, either of marble or free-stone to lean over. These kind of terraces or little galleries of pleasure Suetonius calls *meniana*.[2] They give great grace to the whole edifice, and serve only for this purpose, that people may from that place as from a most delectable prospect contemplate and view the parts of the city round about them in the cool evening. [...] The foundations of their houses are made after a very strange manner. For whereas many of them are situate in the water, whensoever they lay the foundation of any house they remove the water by certain devices from the places where they lay the first fundamental matter. Most commonly they drive long stakes into the ground, without the which they do *aggerere molem*,[3] that is, raise certain heaps of sand, mud, clay, or some other such matter to repel the water. Then they ram in great piles of wood, which they lay very deep, upon the which they place their brick or stone, and so frame the other parts of the building. These foundations are made so exceeding deep, and contrived with so great labour, that I have heard they cost them very near the third part of the charge of the whole edifice.

[...]

There is only one bridge to go over the great channel, which is the same that leads from St. Mark's to the Rialto,[4] and joins together both

---

1   *Istrian marble* Stone from nearby Istria, used in many Venetian buildings.
2   *Suetonius* Roman historian (c. 70–130); *meniana* Latin: balconies.
3   *aggerere molem* Latin: to heap up a mass (of something).
4   *St. Mark's* St. Mark's Basilica, a Venetian cathedral named for Mark the Evangelist; *Rialto* Commercial district in Venice.

the banks of the channel. This bridge is commonly called *Ponte de Rialto*,[1] and is the fairest bridge by many degrees for one arch that ever I saw, read, or heard of. For it is reported that it cost about fourscore[2] thousand crowns, which do make four and twenty thousand pound sterling.

[…]

There are in Venice thirteen ferries or passages, which they commonly call *traghetti*, where passengers may be transported in a gondola to what place of the city they will. Of which thirteen one is under this Rialto bridge. But the boatmen that attend at this ferry are the most vicious and licentious varlets about all the city. For if a stranger enters into one of their gondolas, and does not presently tell them whither he will go, they will incontinently[3] carry him of their own accord to a religious house forsooth, where his plumes shall be well pulled before he comes forth again. Then he may afterward with Demosthenes buy too dear repentance for seeing Lais, except he does for that time either with Ulysses stop his ears, or with Democritus pull out his eyes.[4] Therefore I counsel all my countrymen whatsoever, gentlemen or others that determine hereafter to see Venice, to beware of the Circean cups, and the sirens' melody, I mean these seducing and tempting gondoliers of the Rialto bridge, least they afterward cry *peccavi*[5] when it is too late. For

————————————*facilis descensus Averni,*
Noctes atque dies patet atri janua Ditis.[6]

---

1 *Ponte de Rialto* Rialto Bridge.
2 *fourscore* Eighty; a score is twenty.
3 *incontinently* Immediately.
4 *Demosthenes … Lais* Lais was a famous ancient Greek prostitute who charged Demosthenes ten times her normal rate after noticing he was ugly; *Ulysses … ears* In Homer's *Odyssey*, Odysseus/Ulysses is tied to the ship's mast so he can withstand the call of the sirens, monstrous women whose songs lure sailors to shipwreck. It is his men rowing the ship, not Odysseus, who have their ears stopped (with wax); *Democritus … eyes* Democritus the philosopher (c. 460–370 BCE), who according to some sources blinded himself.
5 *Circean cups* In Homer's *Odyssey*, the witch Circe transforms Greeks who drink at her table into wild animals; *peccavi* Latin: I have sinned. An acknowledgment of guilt.
6 [Coryate's Note] *Virgil. Aenei.*6 [ll. 126–27. Latin: easy is the path to Avernus; the door to black Dis stands open day and night. Avernus is the entrance to Dis, the underworld].

Besides they shall find the iniquity of them to be such, that if the passenger commands them to carry him to any place where his serious and urgent business lies, which he cannot but follow without some prejudice unto him, these impious miscreants will either strive to carry him away maugre[1] his heart to some irreligious place whither he would not go, or at the least tempt him with their diabolical persuasions.

[...]

The channels (which are called in Latin *euripi or aestuaria,*[2] that is, pretty little arms of the sea, because they ebb and flow every six hours) are very singular ornaments to the city, through the which they run even as the veins do through the body of a man, and do disgorge into the *Canal il grande*, which is the common receptacle of them all. They impart two principal commodities to the city, the one that it carries away all the garbage and filthiness that falls into them from the city, which by means of the ebbing and flowing of the water, is the sooner conveyed out of the channels, though indeed not altogether so well, but that the people do eftsoons[3] add their own industry to cleanse and purge them; the other that they serve the Venetians instead of streets to pass with far more expedition on the same, than they can do on their land streets, and that by certain little boats, which they call gondolas the fairest that ever I saw in any place. For none of them are open above, but fairly covered, first with some fifteen or sixteen little round pieces of timber that reach from one end to the other, and make a pretty kind of arch or vault in the gondola; then with fair black cloth which is turned up at both ends of the boat, to the end that if the passenger means to be private, he may draw down the same, and after row so secretly that no man can see him. In the inside the benches are finely covered with black leather, and the bottoms of many of them together with the sides under the benches are very neatly garnished with fine linen cloth, the edge whereof is laced with bone-lace: the ends are beautified with two pretty and ingenuous devices. For each end has a crooked thing made in the

---

1   *maugre* Despite.
2   *euripi or aestuaria* Latin: channels or inlets.
3   *eftsoons* Occasionally.

form of a dolphin's tail, with the fins very artificially represented, and it seems to be tinned over.[1] The watermen that row these never sit as ours do in London, but always stand, and that at the farther end of the gondola, sometimes one, but most commonly two; and in my opinion they are altogether as swift as our rowers about London. Of these gondolas they say there are ten thousand about the city, whereof six thousand are private, serving for the gentlemen and others, and four thousand for mercenary men, which get their living by the trade of rowing.

The fairest place of all the city (which is indeed of that admirable and incomparable beauty, that I think no place whatsoever, either in Christendom or paganism may compare with it) is the piazza, that is, the marketplace of St. Mark or (as our English merchants commorant in Venice, do call it) the place of S. Mark, in Latin *Forum* or *Platea Di. Marci*. Truly such is the stupendious (to use a strange epitheton[2] for so strange and rare a place as this) glory of it, that at my first entrance thereof it did even amaze or rather ravish my senses. For here is the greatest magnificence of architecture to be seen, that any place under the sun does yield. Here you may both see all manner of fashions of attire, and hear all the languages of Christendom, besides those that are spoken by the barbarous ethnics; the frequency of people being so great twice a day, betwixt six of the clock in the morning and eleven, and again betwixt five in the afternoon and eight, that (as an elegant writer says of it) a man may very properly call it rather *orbis* then *urbis forum*, that is, a marketplace of the world, not of the city.

[...]

But I will descend to the particular description of this peerless place, wherein if I seem too tedious, I crave pardon of thee (gentle reader) seeing the variety of the curious objects which it exhibits to the spectator is such, that a man shall much wrong it to speak a little of it. The like tediousness thou art like to find also in my description of the duke's palace, and St. Mark's church, which are such glorious works, that I endeavoured to observe as much of them as I might,

---

1   *tinned over* Covered with tin.
2   *stupendious* Astounding; *epitheton* Epithet.

because I knew it was uncertain whether I should ever see them again, though I hoped for it. [...] This part of the piazza together with all the other is fairly paved with brick, which makes a show fair enough; but had it been paved either with diamond pavier[1] made of freestone, as the halls of some of our great gentlemen in England are, (amongst the rest that of my honourable and thrice-worthy Mecoenas Sir Edward Phillips in his magnificent house of Montague,[2] in the county of Somerset within a mile of Odcombe my sweet native soil) or with other pavier *ex quadrato lapide*, which we call ashlar[3] in Somersetshire, certainly it would have made the whole piazza much more glorious and resplendent than it is.

The second part which reaches from the clock at the entrance of St. Mark's from the merceria,[4] as I have before said, to the two huge marble pillars by the shore of the Adriatic gulf, is exceeding fair also, but is something inferior to the first. This is in length two hundred and thirty paces, and in breadth threescore and seven. This part of the piazza is worthy to be celebrated for that famous concourse and meeting of so many distinct and sundry nations twice a day, betwixt six and eleven of the clock in the morning, and betwixt five in the afternoon and eight, as I have before mentioned, where also the Venetian long-gowned gentlemen do meet together in great troupes. For you shall not see as much as one Venetian there of the patrician rank without his black gown and tippet.[5] There you may see many Polonians, Slavonians, Persians, Grecians, Turks, Jews, Christians of all the famousest regions of Christendom, and each nation distinguished from another by their proper and peculiar habits. A singular show, and by many degrees the worthiest of all the European countries. There are two very goodly and sumptuous rows of building in this part also, as in the other that I have already described, which do confront each other. One of these rows is the west front of the duke's

---

1 *diamond pavier* Diamond-shaped paving stones.
2 *Mecoenas* Gaius Maecenas (c. 70–8 BCE), whose name is traditionally invoked to describe a wealthy patron; *Sir Edward Phillips* Wealthy Somerset nobleman (c. 1555–1614) whose influence landed Coryate a position in Prince Henry Frederick's household; *Montague* Montacute House, Somersetshire.
3 *ex quadrato lapide* Latin: out of square stone; *ashlar* Square-shaped building stone.
4 *merceria* Chief market street of Venice.
5 *tippet* Long piece of hanging cloth worn as a scarf or attached to various articles of clothing, e.g., hoods and sleeves.

palace which is adorned with a fair walk about fourscore and sixteen paces long, and sixteen feet broad. [...] Above this walk is a fair long gallery contrived in the front of the palace, having seven and thirty pillars of white stone at the side thereof, or rather Istrian marble. But of those seven and thirty there are two made of red marble, betwixt which one of their dukes was beheaded for many years since,[1] as a gentleman told me in Venice. For a memorial whereof those pillars were erected as a monument to posterity. Also betwixt every couple of pillars in this high gallery there goes a pretty little terrace of white stone, containing three small marble pillars. Above the top of the arch of the gallery there are seven fair glass windows a pretty way distant asunder, whereof the middle is exceeding fair, having two goodly rows of red marble and alabaster pillars, that run up to the very top of the frontispiece. Which rows are garnished with the statues of women cunningly[2] wrought. A little without the window there is a fair terrace butting out made of white and red marble to lean over, serving for a fair prospect. These kind of windows were heretofore used in Rome amongst the ancient Romans, which they called *meniana*, as I have before written. Above the top of this window within a fair circle of alabaster is portrayed a mother with her three infants about her, and on both sides without that compass are presented the statues of two women more, above which the arms of Venice are displayed, that is, the winged lion with the duke in his ducal ornaments kneeling before it. All these things are expressed in alabaster. Again, above that three men are curiously carved with books in their hands, which fit within a hollow place made of red marble. At the top of all this the image of dame justice[3] is erected at large, according to the whole proportion of a body in alabaster as the rest, with a pair of scales in one hand, and a sword in the other. In this manner is the middle window of the south side of the duke's palace made.

[...]

---

1 *for many ... since* Many years ago.
2 *cunningly* Skilfully.
3 *dame justice* Justice was traditionally personified as female.

In this row of building are some of the *clarissimoes'* dwelling houses, whereof one belonging to one of the *procurators*[1] of St. Mark's, is exceeding beautifully built all with white stone, with a fair quadrangular court, about the walls whereof many worthy antiquities are to be seen, as ancient statues of Roman worthies made in alabaster and other stone. There I read this inscription written in a certain stone which is about three feet high, and a foot and half broad. *Marce Tulli Cicero have, & tu Terentia Antoniana.*[2] I have read that this stone was kept within these few years in Zacynthos now called Zante a famous island in the Ionian Sea, from whence it was afterward brought to Venice. There also I saw a statue of one of the Roman emperors, portrayed at length in alabaster with a garland of laurel about his temples, a cap upon his head, and a mantle wrapped about his body. About the top of the base whereon this statue stands there is a Greek inscription which I could not understand by reason of the antiquity of those exolete[3] letters.

[...]

It happened that when I was very diligently surveying these antiquities, and writing out inscriptions, there came a youth unto me, who because he thought I was a great admirer and curious observer of ancient monuments, very courteously brought me into a fair chamber, which was the next room to Cardinal Bessarion's library,[4] so famous for ancient manuscripts both Greek and Latin.

[...]

At the farther end of this second part of the piazza of S. Mark there stand two marvellous lofty pillars of marble, which I have before

---

1   *clarissimoes* Venetian noblemen; *procurators* Church financial managers.
2   *Marce ... Antoniana* Latin: Hail to Marcus Tullius Cicero, and to you Terentia Antoniana. Cicero (106–43 BCE) was a Roman statesman and orator; Terentia Antoniana (98 BCE–4 CE) was his first wife.
3   *exolete* Obsolete.
4   [Coryate's Note] This library did first belong to Francis Petrarcha, who by his last will and testament made the senate of Venice heir thereof. [Francesco Petrarca (1304–74) was an Italian humanist and influential poet]; *Cardinal Bessarion's library* Core of St. Mark's Library, the Biblioteca Nazionale Marciana, donated by Cardinal Bessarion (1403–72).

mentioned, of equal height and thickness very near to the shore of the Adriatic gulf, the fairest certainly for height and greatness that ever I saw till then. For the compass of them is so great, that I was not able to clasp them with both mine arms at thrice, their diameter in thickness containing very near four feet (as I conjecture). Besides they are of such an exceeding height, that I thought a good while there were scarce the like to be found in any place of Christendom, till at length I called to my remembrance that wondrous high pillar in a certain marketplace of Rome, on whose top the ashes of the emperor Trajan[1] were once kept. For that pillar was about one hundred and forty feet high, but this I think is scarce above thirty. They are said to be made of Phrygian marble,[2] being solid and all one piece. They were brought by sea from Constantinople for more than four hundred years since. Upon the top of one of them are advanced the arms of Venice, the winged lion made all of brass; on the other the statue of S. Theodorus[3] gilt, and standing upon a brazen crocodile, with a spear in one hand, and a shield in another. This S. Theodorus was a valiant warrior, and the general captain of the Venetian armies, whom by reason of his invincible courage, and fortunate success in martial affaires that he achieved for the good of this city, the Venetians caused to be canonized for a saint, and do with many ceremonious solemnities celebrate his feast every year. There was a third pillar also brought from Constantinople at the same time that these were: which through the exceeding force of the weight when they were drawing of it out of the ship into the land, fell down into the water, by reason that the tackling and instruments that those men used which were set a work about it, broke asunder. That same pillar is yet to be felt within some ten paces of the shore: those two that do now stand hard by the seashore were erected about some eighteen paces asunder, by one Nicolas Beratterius a Lombard, and a very cunning architect. It is reported that this man craved no other reward of the senate for his labour, than that it might be lawful for any man to play at dice at all times betwixt those pillars without any contradiction, which was granted, and is continually performed. In this distance betwixt the pillars condemned men and malefactors are put to death. For whensoever there

---

1   *Trajan* Roman Emperor (c. 53–117), commemorated by Trajan's Column in Rome.
2   *Phrygian marble* Marble from Asia Minor, modern-day Turkey.
3   *S. Theodorus* Theodore Stratelates (d. 319 CE), warrior saint.

is to be any execution, upon a sudden they erect a scaffold there, and after they have beheaded the offenders (for that is most commonly their death) they take it away again.

[...]

There are many notable things to be considered in this piazza of St. Mark, the principal whereof I will relate before I come to the description of St. Mark's church and the duke's palace: most memorable is the tower of St. Mark, which is a very fair building, made all of brick till towards the top, being distant from St. Mark's church about some eighty feet. It is from the bottom to the top about some two hundred and eighty feet, and has such an exceeding deep foundation, that some do think the very foundation cost almost as much as the rest of the building from the ground to the top. [...] The stairs are made after such a strange manner that not only a man, or woman, or child may with great ease ascend to the top of it, but also a horse, as it is commonly reported in the city. But I think this will seem such a paradox and incredible matter to many, that perhaps they will say I may lie by authority (according to the old proverb) because I am a traveller. Indeed I confess I saw no horse ascend the stairs, but I heard it much reported in Venice, both by many of my countrymen, and by the Venetians themselves; neither is it unlikely to be true. For these stairs are not made as other common stairs, by which a man can ascend by no more than a foot higher from stair to stair till he comes to the highest, but there are made flat, and ascend so easily by little and little in height, that a man can hardly be weary, and scarce perceive any pains or difficulty in the ascent. [...] When you have ascended almost as high as you can, you shall leave the stairs, and enter into a void loft, and from that you are conveyed by a short ladder into a little square gallery butting out from the tower, and made in the form of a terrace, being supported with fair round pillars of alabaster. From every side of which square gallery you have the fairest and goodliest prospect that is (I think) in all the world. For therehence may you see the whole model and form of the city *sub uno intuito*,[1] a sight that does in my opinion far surpass all the shows under the cope of

---

1   *sub uno intuito* Latin: under one view.

heaven.[1] There you may have a *synopsis*, that is, a general view of little Christendom (for so do many entitle this city of Venice) or rather of the Jerusalem of Christendom. For so methinks may a man not improperly call this glorious city of Venice: not in respect of the religion thereof, or the situation, but of the sumptuousness of their buildings, for which we read Jerusalem in former times was famoused above all the eastern cities of the world. There you may behold all their sumptuous palaces adorned with admirable variety of beautiful pillars: the church of S. Mark which is but a little way therehence distant, with the duke's stately palace adjoining unto it, being one of the principal wonders of the Christian world; the lofty Rialto, the piazza of Saint Stephen,[2] which is the most spacious and goodly place of the city except St. Mark's; all the six parts of the city. For into so many it is divided as I have before said: their streets, their churches, their monasteries, their marketplaces, and all their other public buildings of rare magnificence. Also many fair gardens replenished with diversity of delicate fruits, as oranges, citrons, lemons, apricots, musk-melons, *anguriaes*,[3] and what not together with their little islands bordering about the city wonderfully frequented and inhabited with people, being in number fifty or thereabout. Also the Alps that lead into Germany two ways, by the city of Trent, and the Grisons country,[4] and those that lead into France through Savoy, the Apennines, the pleasant Euganean hills, with a little world of other most delectable objects; therefore whatsoever thou art that means to see Venice, in any case forget not to go up to the top of Saint Mark's tower before thou come out of the city. For it will cost thee but a gazet,[5] which is not fully an English penny: on the top of the tower is erected a brazen angel[6] fairly gilt, which is made in that sort that he seems to bless the people with his hand.

[...]

---

1   *cope of heaven* Dome of the sky.
2   *Saint Stephen* First Christian martyr (d. 34 CE)
3   *anguriaes* Angurie (Italian: watermelons).
4   *Grisons country* Graubünden, the easternmost canton of Switzerland, bordering Italy.
5   *gazet* Small Venetian coin.
6   [Coryate's Note] This angel was erected Anno Domi[ni]. 1517.

The fairest street of all Venice saving Saint Mark's, which I have already described, is that adjoining to St. Mark's place which is called the *merceria*, which name it has because many mercers dwell there, as also many stationers,[1] and sundry other artificers. [...] There is a very fair gate at one end of this street even as you enter into St. Mark's place when you come from the Rialto bridge which is decked with a great deal of fair marble, in which gate are two pretty conceits[2] to be observed, the one at the very top, which is a clock with the images of two wild-men by it made in brass, a witty device and very exactly done. At which clock there fell out a very tragic and rueful accident on the twenty-fifth day of June being Monday about nine of the clock in the morning, which was this. A certain fellow that had the charge to look to the clock was very busy about the bell, according to his usual custom every day, to the end to amend something in it that was amiss. But in the meantime one of those wild-men that at the quarters of the hours do use to strike the bell, struck the man in the head with his brazen hammer, giving him such a violent blow, that therewith he fell down dead presently in the place, and never spoke more. Surely I will not justify this for an undoubted truth, because I saw it not. For I was at that time in the duke's palace observing of matters: but as soon as I came forth some of my countrymen that told me they saw the matter with their own eyes, reported it unto me, and advised me to mention it in my journal for a most lamentable chance. The other conceit that is to be observed in this gate is the picture of the Virgin Mary made in a certain door above a fair dial, near to whom on both sides of her are painted two angels on two little doors more. These doors upon any principal holiday do open of themselves, and immediately there come forth two kings to present themselves to our Lady, unto whom, after they have done their obeisance by uncovering of their heads, they return again into their places: in the front of this sumptuous gate are presented the twelve celestial signs, with the sun, moon, and stars, most excellently handled.

[...]

---

1   *mercers* Fabric merchants; *stationers* Booksellers.
2   *conceits* Devices.

At the south corner of St. Mark's church as you go into the duke's palace there is a very remarkable thing to be observed. A certain porphyry[1] stone of some yard and a half or almost two yards high, and of a pretty large compass, even as much as a man can clasp at twice with both arms. On this stone are laid for the space of three days and three nights, the heads of all such as being enemies or traitors to the state, or some notorious offenders, have been apprehended out of the city, and beheaded by those that have been bountifully hired by the senate for the same purpose. In that place do their heads remain so long, though the smell of them doth breed a very offensive and contagious annoyance. For it has been an ancient custom of the Venetians, whensoever any notorious malefactor has for any enormous crime escaped out of the city for his security, to propose a great reward to him that shall bring his head to that stone. Yea I have heard that there have been twenty-thousand ducats given to a man for bringing a traitor's head to that place.

Near to this stone is another memorable thing to be observed. A marvellous fair pair of gallows made of alabaster, the pillars being wrought with many curious borders and works, which serves for no other purpose but to hang the duke whensoever he shall happen to commit any treason against the state. And for that cause it is erected before the very gate of his palace to the end to put him in mind[2] to be faithful and true to his country, if not, he sees the place of punishment at hand. But this is not a perfect gallows, because there are only two pillars without a transverse beam, which beam (they say) is to be erected when there is any execution, not else. Betwixt this gallows malefactors and condemned men (that are to go to be executed upon a scaffold betwixt the two famous pillars before mentioned at the south end of St. Mark's street, near the Adriatic Sea) are wont to say their prayers to the image of the Virgin Mary, standing on a part of S. Mark's church right opposite unto them.

[...]

---

1   *porphyry* Highly valued reddish-purple rock.
2   *to the end ... in mind* For the purpose of reminding him.

The palace of the duke which was built by Angelus Participatius a duke of Venice[1] in the year 809 is absolutely the fairest building that ever I saw, exceeding all the king of France's palaces that I could see, yea his most delectable paradise at Fontainebleau.

Which indeed for delicate walks, springs, rivers, and gardens, excels this, but not for sumptuousness of building, wherein this surpasses the best of his three that I saw, namely the Louvre, the Tuileries, and Fontainebleau. [...] When you are once entered in at the gate you shall pass through a most magnificent porch before you can come into the court, which porch is vaulted over, and has six several partitions that are distinguished from each other by six fair marble pillars on each side: this porch is paved with brick, and is in length three and forty paces, and in breadth seven. On both sides of the inner gate of the porch within the court are erected two most exquisite statues in alabaster of Adam and Eve naked, covering their shame with fig leaves. That statue of Eve is done with that singularity of cunning, that it is reported the Duke of Mantua has offered to give the weight of it in gold for the image, yet he cannot have it. These are placed right opposite to the statues of Neptune and Pallas,[2] which are upon the top of the stairs on the other side. The architecture over this gate which is within the palace is exceeding glorious, being adorned with many marble pillars, some of white colour, some of red, some of changeable.[3]

[...]

The room wherein the duke does usually sit in his throne with his greatest councilors, which is commonly called the college or the senate house, is a very magnificent and beautiful place, having a fair roof sumptuously gilt, and beautified with many singular pictures that represent diverse notable histories. At the higher end of this room is the duke's throne, and the picture of Venice made in the form of a royal queen, wearing a crown upon her head, and crowning the duke: this is the place where the duke with his noble peers treats

---

1   *Angelus ... Venice* Agnello Participazio, Doge of Venice (811–27).
2   *Neptune and Pallas* Roman god of the sea and goddess of wisdom, respectively.
3   [Coryate's Note] I mean that which we call in Latin *versicolor*. [Latin: color-changing, but here used to mean "parti-colored."]

about affairs of state, and hears the ambassadors both of foreign nations, and of them that are sent from the cities subject to the signiory of Venice.

[...]

After that I went into a third room, which was the sumptuousest of all, exceeding spacious, and the fairest that ever I saw in my life, either in mine own country, or France, or any city of Italy, or afterward in Germany. Neither do I think that any room of all Christendom doth excel it in beauty. This lies at the south side of the palace, and looks towards the sea: it is called the great council hall. For there is assembled sometimes the whole body of the council, which consists of one thousand and six hundred persons: there do they give their suffrages and voices for the election of the magistrates of all degrees. [...] All this east wall where the duke's throne stands is most admirably painted. For there is presented paradise, with Christ and the Virgin Mary at the top thereof, and the souls of the righteous on both sides. This workmanship, which is most curious and very delectable to behold, was done by a rare painter called Tinctoretus.[1]

[...]

One thing more there is in this magnificent and beautiful palace, which (as I have heard many that have seen it report) is the fairest ornament of the whole palace, even the armoury, which it was not my fortune to see, for the which I have often since not a little repented, because the not seeing of it has deprived me of much worthy matter, that would have added great luster to this description of the duke's palace. For indeed it is a thing of that beauty and riches that very few have access unto it but great personages, neither can any man whatsoever be permitted to see it without a special mandate under the hand of one of the Council of Ten.[2] I would advise any English gentleman of special mark that determines to see Venice in his travels, to use all means for obtaining the sight of this room. For many gentlemen that

---

1 *Tinctoretus* Tintoretto (1518–94), whose *Paradise* in the Palazzo Ducale Coryate describes here.
2 *Council of Ten* Venetian administrative body responsible for state security.

have been very famous and great travellers in the principal countries of Christendom, have told me that they never saw so glorious an armoury for the quantity thereof, in the whole course of their travels. Here they say is marvellous abundance of armour of all sorts, and that most curiously gilt and enameled, as helmets, shields, belts, spears, swords, lances: the store being so great that it is thought it can well arm ten thousand men, and the beauty so incomparable that no armoury of Christendom does match it.

[…]

Next unto the duke's palace the beautiful church of Saint Mark does of its own accord as it were offer itself now to be spoken of. Which though it be but little, yet it is exceeding rich, and so sumptuous for the stateliness of the architecture, that I think very few in Christendom of the bigness do surpass it. It is recorded, that it had the first beginning of the foundation in the year 829 which was full twenty years after the building of the duke's palace adjoining unto it; many pillars, and other notable matter being brought thither from Athens, and diverse other places of Greece, for the better grace of the fabric.[1] And it is built in that manner that the model of it doth truly resemble our savior's cross. Truly, so many are the ornaments of this glorious church, that a perfect description of them will require a little volume. The principal whereof I will relate by way of an epitome, according to that slender and inelegant manner that I have hitherto continued this discourse of Venice. The pavement of this church is so passing curious, that I think no church in Christendom can show the like. For the pavement of the body of the church, the quire, and the walks round about before you come within the body, are made of sundry little pieces of Thasian, Ophitical, and Laconical marble in checker work,[2] and other most exquisite conveyances, and those, of many several colours, that it is very admirable and rare to behold, the rareness such that it does even amaze all strangers upon their first view thereof. The west front towards St. Mark's street is most beautiful, having five several partitions, unto which there belong as many

---

1 *fabric* Structure.
2 *Thasian … checker work* Marble made from ophite, as well as marbles from Thasos and Laconia, arranged in a mosaic pattern.

brazen doors, whereof the middle, through which they usually go into the church, is made of solid brass, the other four in the form of lattice windows. This front is very stately adorned with beautiful pillars of marble, whereof in one part of the front, I told[1] a hundred and two and fifty, in the higher two and forty. In all one hundred fourscore and fourteen. Some greater, some lesser. Some of one colour and some of another. At the sides of the great gate are eight rich pillars of porphyry, four in one side, and as many in another, whereof each would be worth twenty pound with us in England. Over the top of this middle gate is to be seen a very ancient and remarkable monument, four goodly brazen horses[2] made of Corinthian metal,[3] and fully as great as the life. Some say they were cast by Lysippus[4] that singular statuary of Alexander the Great above three hundred years before Christ; some say that the Romans made them at what time Hiero King of Syracuse triumphed of the Parthians,[5] and placed them in a certain arch that they dedicated to him. It is reported that Tyridates King of Armenia bestowed them on the Emperor Nero, when he was entertained by him in Rome with such pompous magnificence, as is mentioned by Tacitus and Suetonius.[6] And that Constantine the Great[7] brought them from Rome to Constantinople, and therehence they were lastly brought to Venice by the Venetians, when they possessed Constantinople. At what time they brought many other notable things from that city, for the better ornament both of their public and private buildings. These horses are advanced on certain curious and beautiful pillars, to the end they may be the more conspicuous and eminent to be seen of every person. Of their forefeet, there is but one set on a pillar, and that is of porphyry marble, the other foot he holds up very

---

1 *told* Counted.

2 [Coryate's Note] These horses were brought to Venice in the time of their duke Petrus Zanus, which was about the year of our lord 1206. [Pietro Ziani reigned from 1205 to 1229.]

3 *Corinthian metal* Bronze from Corinth.

4 *Lysippus* Greek sculptor (fl. fourth century BCE) who made several statues of Alexander the Great (356–323 BCE).

5 *Hiero King of Syracuse* Hieron II, tyrant of Syracuse (c. 308–216/215 BCE); *Parthians* People who lived in what is now north-eastern Iran.

6 *Tyridates ... Nero* Tiridates I (first century CE) was crowned King of Armenia by Nero (37–68 CE), Roman emperor; *Tacitus and Suetonius* Roman historians.

7 *Constantine the Great* Constantine I (c. 274–337), first Roman emperor to convert to Christianity.

bravely in his pride, which makes an excellent show. The two hinder feet are placed upon two pretty pillars of marble, but not porphyry. Two of these horses are set on one side of that beautiful alabaster border full of imagery and other singular devices, which is advanced over the middle great brass gate at the coming into the church, and the other two on the other side. Which yields a marvellous grace to this frontispiece of the church, and so greatly they are esteemed by the Venetians, that although they have been offered for them their weight in gold by the king of Spain, as I have heard reported in Venice, yet they will not sell them.

[…]

Over the gate as you pass into the body of the church, is to be seen the picture of St. Mark (if at the least a man may properly call such a piece of work a picture) made most curiously with pieces of marble (as I conceive it) exceeding little, all gilt over in a kind of work very common in this church, called mosaic work. He is made looking up to heaven with his hands likewise elevated, and that wearing of a marvellous rich cope.

[…]

The inner walls of the church are beautified with a great multitude of pictures gilt, and contrived in mosaic[1] work, which is nothing else but a pretty kind of picturing consisting altogether of little pieces and very small fragments of gilt marble, which are square, and half as broad as the nail of a man's finger; of which pieces there concurs[2] a very infinite company to the making of one of these pictures. I never saw any of this kind of picturing before I came to Venice, nor ever either read or heard of it, of which Saint Mark's church is full in every wall and roof. It is said that they imitate the Grecians in these mosaic works.

---

1   [Coryate's Note] This is the same that was called of the ancient writers *opus musiuum*. Adrian Turnebus *Adversa*. lib. I. cap. 17. [Adrien Turnèbe was a French scholar whose *Adversia* (1564–65) Coryate cites here.]
2   *concurs* Comes together.

[...]

There are three very notable and ancient monuments kept in this church, besides those that I have above mentioned, being worthy to be seen by an industrious traveller, if that be true which they report of it. The first is the body of S. Mark the Evangelist and patron of Venice, which was brought hither by certain merchants from Alexandria in Egypt (where he lived a long time, and died a glorious martyr of Jesus Christ) in the year 810. To whose honour they built this church about nineteen years after, and made him the patron of their city. The second, his gospel written in Greek with his own hand: the sight of these two worthy things to my great grief I omitted. The third is the picture of the Virgin Mary, which they say was made by S. Luke the Evangelist: but that is altogether uncertain whether Luke were a painter or no. That he was a physician we read in the holy scriptures,[1] but not that he was a painter. This picture is adorned with exceeding abundance of precious stones, and those of great worth; and the hue of it does witness that it is very ancient. It was my hap to see it twice: once when it was presented all the day upon the high altar of this church, upon the great feast day of our Lady's assumption,[2] at what time I saw that rich table also, whereof I have before spoken. Secondly when it was carried about St. Mark's place in a solemn procession, in the which the duke, the senators, the gentlemen of the city, the clergy, and many other both men and women walked. This was in the time of a great drought, when they prayed to God for rain. For they both say and believe that this picture has so great virtue, as also that of Padua, whereof I have before spoken, that whensoever it is carried abroad in a solemn procession in the time of a great drought it will cause rain to descend from heaven either before it is brought back into the church, or very shortly after. For mine own part I have had some little experience of it, and therefore I will censure the matter according as I find it. Surely that either pictures or images should have that virtue to draw drops from heaven, I never read either in God's word, or any other authentic author. So that I cannot be induced to attribute so much to the virtue of a picture, as the Venetians do, except I had seen

---

1 [Coryate's Note] *Col[ossians]* 4.14.
2 *feast day ... assumption* Feast day celebrating the Assumption of Mary, Mary's ascension into heaven.

some notable miracle wrought by the same. For it brought no drops at all with it: only about two days after it rained (I must needs confess) amain.[1] But I hope they are not so superstitious to ascribe that to the virtue of their picture. For it is very likely it would have rained at that time, though they had not at all carried their picture abroad. Therefore, except it doth at other times produce greater effects than it did when I was in Venice, in my opinion that religious relic of our Lady's picture, so devoutly worshipped and honoured of the Venetians, has no more virtue in working miracles than any other that is newly come forth of the painter's shop.

The last notable thing that is in the church with relation whereof I will shut up this discourse of S. Mark's church, is the treasure of Saint Mark kept in a certain chapel in the south side of the church near to the stately porch of the duke's palace. But here methinks I use the figure *hysteron proteron*,[2] in that I conclude my tract of St. Mark's church with that which was worthiest to be spoken of at the beginning. For this treasure is of that inestimable value, that it is thought no treasure whatsoever in any one place of Christendom may compare with it, neither that of St. Denis in France, which I have before described, nor St. Peter's in Rome, nor that of Madonna di Loreto in Italy, nor that of Toledo in Spain,[3] nor any other. Therefore I am sorry I must speak so little of it. For I saw it not though I much desired it, because it is very seldom shown to any strangers but only upon St. Mark's day; therefore that little which I report of it is by the tradition of other men, not of mine own certain knowledge. Here they say is kept marvellous abundance of rich stones of exceeding worth, as diamonds, carbuncles, emeralds, chrysolites, jacinths,[4] and great pearls of admirable value: also three unicorns' horns; an exceeding great carbuncle which was bestowed upon the senate by the Cardinal Grimannus, and a certain pitcher adorned with great variety of precious stones, which Usumcassanes[5] King of Persia bestowed upon the

---

1 *amain* Torrentially.

2 *hysteron proteron* Greek: latter prior, referring to a rhetorical device in which the expected temporal order is reversed.

3 *St. Peter's ... Spain* Coryate lists sumptuous Christian churches.

4 *carbuncles* Red gems, especially ones that have been polished smooth; *chrysolites* Green gems; *jacinths* Blue or yellow gems.

5 *Usumcassanes* Persian king referenced in several early modern sources.

signiory, with many other things of wonderful value, which I must needs omit, because I saw none of them.

[...]

I was at the arsenal which is so called, *quasi ars navalis*,[1] because there is exercised the art of making tackling, and all other necessary things for shipping. Certainly I take it to be the richest and best furnished storehouse for all manner of munition both by sea and land not only of all Christendom, but also of all the world, in so much that all strangers whatsoever are moved with great admiration when they contemplate the situation, the greatness, the strength, and incredible store of provision thereof. [...] It is situate at the east end of the city, in compass two miles, and fortified with a strong wall that goes round about it, in which are built many fair towers for the better ornament thereof. There are continually one thousand five hundred men working in it, unto whom there is paid every week two thousand crowns which do amount to six hundred pound sterling, in the whole year twenty-eight thousand and six hundred pound. Also those workmen that have wrought so long in the arsenal that they are become decrepit and unable to work any longer, are maintained in the same at the charge of the city during their lives. Here are always kept two hundred and fifty galleys, each having a several[2] room fairly roofed over to cover and defend it from the injury of the weather, and fifty more are always at sea. The fairest galley of all is the Bucentoro,[3] the upper parts whereof in the outside are richly gilt. It is a thing of marvellous worth, the richest galley of all the world: for it cost one hundred thousand crowns which is thirty thousand pound sterling. A work so exceeding glorious that I never heard or read of the like in any place of the world, these only excepted, *viz*: that of Cleopatra, which she so exceeding sumptuously adorned with cables of silk and other passing beautiful ornaments; and those that the Emperor Caligula built

---

1 *arsenal* Dockyard; *quasi ars navalis* Latin: as though *ars navalis* (that is, drawing attention to the phonetic similarity of "ars navalis" and "arsenal," which is a portmanteau word derived from "ars navalis," which means in Latin "the art of the navy").

2 *galleys* Mediterranean ships typically rowed by slaves; *several* Separate.

3 *Bucentoro* Bucentaur, the duke's barge.

with timber of cedar and poops and sterns of ivory.[1] And lastly that most incomparable and peerless ship of our gracious prince called the Prince Royal, which was launched at Wollige about Michaelmas last,[2] which indeed does by many degrees surpass this Bucentoro of Venice, and any ship else (I believe) in Christendom. In this galley the duke launches into the sea some few miles off upon the Ascension day,[3] being accompanied with the principal senators and patricians of the city, together with all the ambassadors and personages of greatest mark that happen to be in the city at that time. At the higher end there is a most sumptuous gilt chair for the duke to sit in, at the back whereof there is a loose board to be lifted up, to the end he may look into the sea through that open space, and throw a golden ring into it, in token that he does as it were betroth himself unto the sea, as the principal lord and commander thereof. A ceremony that was first instituted in Venice by Alexander the third pope of that name, when Sebastianus Zanus was duke, *Anno* 1174 unto whom he delivered a golden ring from his own finger, in token that the Venetians having made war upon the Emperor Frederick Barbarossa[4] in defence of his quarrel, discomfited his fleet at Istria, and he commanded him for his sake to throw the like golden ring into the sea every year upon Ascension day during his life, establishing this withal, that all his successors should do the like; which custom has been ever since observed to this day.

[...]

---

1   *viz* Abbreviation of the Latin *videlicet*, meaning "namely" or "that is to say"; *Cleopatra* Cleopatra VII (69–30 BCE), Queen of Egypt. Her opulent barge is described in William Shakespeare's *Antony and Cleopatra* (2.2.200–07); *Caligula ... ivory* Caligula (12–41), Roman emperor, built the elaborately decorated Nemi ships, named after Lake Nemi (near Rome), where they were built and eventually sank.

2   *that most ... Michaelmas last* The royal ship of Henry Frederick (1594–1612), Prince of Wales, was launched from Woolwich (in southeast London) on the feast of St. Michael (29 September, or 19 September old style).

3   *Ascension day* Feast of the Ascension, held forty days after Easter in commemoration of Christ's ascension into heaven.

4   *Alexander the third pope* Pope Alexander III (c. 1105–81); *Sebastianus Zanus* Sebastiano Ziani, Doge of Venice from 1172 to 1178; *Frederick Barbarossa* Frederick I (c. 1123–90), Holy Roman Emperor.

I saw but one horse in all Venice during the space of six weeks that I made my abode there, and that was a little bay nag feeding in this churchyard of St. John and Paul,[1] whereat I did not a little wonder, because I could not devise what they should do with a horse in such a city where they have no use for him. For you must consider that neither the Venetian gentlemen nor any others can ride horses in the streets of Venice as in other cities and towns, because their streets being both very narrow and slippery, in regard they are all paved with smooth brick, and joining to the water, the horse would quickly fall into the river, and so drown both himself and his rider. Therefore the Venetians do use gondolas in their streets instead of horses, I mean their liquid streets, that is, their pleasant channels. So that I now find by mine own experience that the speeches of a certain English gentleman (with whom I once discoursed before my travels) a man that much vaunted of his observations in Italy, are utterly false. For when I asked him what principal things he observed in Venice, he answered me that he noted but little of the city, because he rode through it in post. A fiction as gross and palpable as ever was coined.

[…]

That day I saw a marvellous solemn procession. For every order and fraternity of religious men in the whole city met together, and carried their crosses and candlesticks of silver in procession to the Redeemer's church,[2] and so back again to their several convents. Besides there was much good fellowship in many places of Venice upon that day. For there were many places, whereof each yielded allowance of variety of wine and cakes and some other pretty junkets[3] to a hundred good fellows to be merry that day, but to no more: this I know by experience. For a certain stationer of the city, with whom I had some acquaintance, one Joannes Guerilius met me by chance at the Redeemer's church, and after he had shown me the particular places of the Capuchins' monastery, brought me to a place where we had very

---

1   *St. John and Paul* Basilica di San Giovanni e Paolo, completed in the fifteenth century.
2   *Redeemer's church* Il Redentore, built in the sixteenth century.
3   *junkets* Delicacies.

good wine, cakes, and other delicates[1] *gratis*, where a priest served us all.

I visited the church of the Grecians called S. Georges,[2] which is in the Parish of S. Martin, a very fair little church. It was my hap to be there at their Greek liturgy[3] in the morning. [...] They use beads as the papists do, and cross themselves, but much more than the papists. For as soon as they come into the church, standing about the middle thereof right opposite to the chapel where the priest does his ceremonies, they cross themselves six or seven times together, and use a very strange form in their crossings. For after they have crossed their forehead and breast, they cast down one of their hands to their knees, and then begin again. Though their language be very corrupt, and degenerates very much from the pure elegancy that flourished in St. Chrysostom's and Gregory Nazianzen's time,[4] yet they say their liturgy in very good Greek. When they sing in the church to answer the priest, they have one kind of gesture, which seems to me both very unseemly and ridiculous. For they wag their hands up and down very often. The priest says not divine service in so open and public a place to be seen as the papistical priests do. For he says service in a little private chapel, before whom most commonly there is a taffeta[5] curtain drawn at the door, that the people may not see him, yet sometimes he removes it again.

[...]

It was my chance after the Greek liturgy was done, to enter into some Greek discourse in the church with the Greek bishop Gabriel, who is Archbishop of Philadelphia, where I scoured up some of my old Greek, which by reason of my long desuetude[6] was become almost rusty, and according to my slender skill had some parley with him in his own language. He spoke the purest and elegantest natural

---

1   *Joannes Guerilius* Giovanni Guerigli (fl. 1591–1628), Venetian printer; *Capuchins* Strict branch of the Franciscan order; *delicates* Delicacies.
2   *S. Georges* San Giorgio dei Greci, built in the sixteenth century.
3   *Greek liturgy* Public worship conducted according to the Greek orthodox tradition.
4   *St. Chrysostom's ... time* John Chrysostom (347–407) and Gregory of Nanzianus (329–89) were key figures in the history of the Greek church.
5   *taffeta* Silk.
6   *desuetude* Period of disuse.

Greek that ever I heard, insomuch that his phrase came something near to that of Isocrates,[1] and his pronunciation was so plausible, that any man which was skillful in the Greek tongue, might easily understand him. He told me that they differ from the Roman church in some points of doctrine, especially about purgatory. For that they utterly reject: neither do they attribute to the pope the title of ecumenical or universal bishop that the Romanists do. Also in his parley betwixt him and me, he made worthy mention of two Englishmen, which did even tickle my heart with joy. For it was a great comfort unto me to hear my countrymen well spoken of by a Greek bishop. He much praised Sir Henry Wotton our ambassador in Venice[2] for his rare learning, and that not without great desert, as all those do know that have tried his excellent parts: and he commended one Mr. Samuel Slade[3] unto me, a Dorsetshire man born, and one of the fellows of Merton College in Oxford, but now a famous traveller abroad in the world. For I met him in Venice. The Grecian commended him for his skill in the Greek tongue, and told me that he had communicated unto him some manuscript fragments of S. Chrysostom's Greek works, the fruits whereof I hope we shall one day see.

I was at a place where the whole fraternity of the Jews dwells together, which is called the ghetto,[4] being an island: for it is enclosed round about with water. It is thought there are of them in all betwixt five and six thousand. They are distinguished and discerned from the Christians by their habits on their heads; for some of them do wear hats and those red, only those Jews that are born in the western parts of the world, as in Italy, &c. but the eastern Jews being otherwise called the Levantine[5] Jews, which are born in Jerusalem, Alexandria, Constantinople, &c. wear turbans upon their heads as the Turks do. But the difference is this: the Turks wear white, the Jews yellow. By that word turban I understand a roll of fine linen wrapped together upon their heads, which serves them instead of hats, whereof many

---

1   *Isocrates* Famous orator and rhetorician of ancient Greece (436–338 BCE).
2   *Sir Henry Wotton … Venice* Sir Henry Wotton was English ambassador to Venice from 1604–12.
3   *Samuel Slade* English traveler and antiquary (1568–c. 1612).
4   *ghetto* Area where Venetian Jews were constrained to live from 1516.
5   [Coryate's Note] They are so called from the Latin word *levare*, which sometimes signifies as much as *elevare*, that is to elevate or lift up. Because the sun elevates and raises itself in height every morning in the East: herehence also comes the Levant sea, for the eastern sea.

have been often worn by the Turks in London. They have diverse synagogues in their ghetto, at the least seven, where all of them, both men, women and children do meet together upon their Sabbath, which is Saturday, to the end to do their devotion, and serve God in their kind, each company having a several synagogue. In the midst of the synagogue they have a round seat made of wainscot, having eight open spaces therein, at two whereof which are at the sides, they enter into the seat as by doors. The Levite[1] that reads the law to them has before him at the time of divine service an exceeding long piece of parchment, rolled up upon two wooden handles, in which is written the whole sum and contents of Moses' law in Hebrew: that does he (being discerned from the lay people only by wearing of a red cap, whereas the others do wear red hats) pronounce before the congregation not by a sober, distinct, and orderly reading, but by an exceeding loud yelling, indecent roaring, and as it were a beastly bellowing of it forth. And that after such a confused and huddling[2] manner, that I think the hearers can very hardly understand him: sometimes he cries out alone, and sometimes again some others serving as it were his clerks hard without his seat, and within, do roar with him, but so that his voice (which he strains so high as if he sung for a wager) drowns all the rest. Amongst others that are within the room with him, one is he that comes purposely thither from his seat, to the end to read the law, and pronounce some part of it with him, who when he is gone, another rises from his seat, and comes thither to supply his room. This order they keep from the beginning of service to the end. One custom I observed amongst them very irreverent and profane, that none of them, either when they enter the synagogue, or when they sit down in their places, or when they go forth again, do any reverence or obeisance answerable to such a place of the worship of God, either by uncovering their heads, kneeling, or any other external gesture, but boldly dash into the room with their Hebrew books in their hands, and presently sit in their places, without any more ado; every one of them whatsoever he be, man or child, wears a kind of light yellowish veil, made of linsey-woolsey (as I take it) over his shoulders, something worse than our coarser Holland,[3] which reaches

---

1   *Levite* Assistant to the temple priest.
2   *huddling* Jumbled.
3   *linsey-woolsey* Textile made from a blend of linen and wool; *Holland* Linen from Holland.

a little beneath the middle of their backs. They have a great company of candlesticks in each synagogue made partly of glass, and partly of brass and pewter, which hang square about their synagogue. For in that form is their synagogue built: of their candlesticks I told above sixty in the same synagogue.

I observed some few of those Jews especially some of the Levantines to be such goodly and proper men, that then I said to myself our English proverb: to look like a Jew (whereby is meant sometimes a weather beaten warp-faced fellow, sometimes a frenetic[1] and lunatic person, sometimes one discontented) is not true. For indeed I noted some of them to be most elegant and sweet-featured persons, which gave me occasion the more to lament their religion. For if they were Christians, then could I better apply unto them that excellent verse of the poet, than I can now.

Gratior est pulchro veniens è corpore virtus.[2]

In the room wherein they celebrate their divine service, no women sit, but have a loft or gallery proper to themselves only, where I saw many Jewish women, whereof some were as beautiful as ever I saw, and so gorgeous in their apparel, jewels, chains of gold, and rings adorned with precious stones, that some of our English countesses do scarce exceed them, having marvellous long trains like princesses that are born up by waiting women serving for the same purpose. An argument to prove that many of the Jews are very rich. One thing they observe in their service which is utterly condemned by our savior Christ, *battologia,*[3] that is a very tedious babbling, and an often repetition of one thing, which cloyed mine ears so much that I could not endure them any longer, having heard them at least an hour; for their service is almost three hours long. They are very religious in two things only, and no more, in that they worship no images, and that they keep their Sabbath so strictly, that upon that day they will neither buy nor sell, nor do any secular, profane, or irreligious exercise,

---

1   *warp-faced* Having distorted features; *frenetic* Insane.

2   *Gratior ... virtus* Latin: Even more graceful is virtue associated with corporeal beauty. Cf. Virgil, *Aeneid* 5.344. Coryate (or his source) misquotes the line, which should read "gratior et pulchro veniens in corpore virtus."

3   [Coryate's Note] Mat[thew] 6. ver. 7.; *battalogia* Greek: babbling.

(I would to God our Christians would imitate the Jews herein) no not so much as dress their victuals,[1] which is always done the day before, but dedicate and consecrate themselves wholly to the strict worship of God. Their circumcision they observe as duly as they did any time betwixt Abraham[2] (in whose time it was first instituted) and the incarnation of Christ. For they use to circumcise every male child when he is eight days old, with a stony knife. But I had not the opportunity to see it. Likewise they keep many of those ancient feasts that were instituted by Moses. Amongst the rest the feast of tabernacles[3] is very ceremoniously observed by them. From swine's flesh they abstain as their ancient forefathers were wont to do, in which the Turks do imitate them at this day. Truly it is a most lamentable case for a Christian to consider the damnable estate of these miserable Jews, in that they reject the true messiah and savior of their souls, hoping to be saved rather by the observation of those Mosaic ceremonies, (the date whereof was fully expired at Christ's incarnation) than by the merits of the savior of the world, without whom all mankind shall perish. And as pitiful it is to see that few of them living in Italy are converted to the Christian religion. For this I understand is the main impediment to their conversion: all their goods are confiscated as soon as they embrace Christianity. And this I heard is the reason, because whereas many of them do raise their fortunes by usury, in so much that they do sometimes not only shear, but also flay[4] many a poor Christian's estate by their griping extortion; it is therefore decreed by the pope, and other free princes in whose territories they live, that they shall make a restitution of all their ill gotten goods, and so disclog their souls and consciences, when they are admitted by holy baptism into the bosom of Christ's church. Seeing then when their goods are taken from them at their conversion, they are left even naked, and destitute of their means of maintenance, there are fewer Jews converted to Christianity in Italy, than in any country of Christendom. Whereas in Germany, Poland, and other places the Jews that

---

1   *dress their victuals* Prepare their food.
2   *Abraham* Hebrew patriarch whose life is recounted in Genesis.
3   *feast of tabernacles* Sukkot, a Jewish festival celebrating the sheltering of the Israelites during their forty years in the wilderness.
4   *flay* Strip of money or goods.

are converted (which does often happen, as Emanuel Tremellius[1] was converted in Germany) do enjoy their estates as they did before.

But now I will make relation of that which I promised in my treatise of Padua, I mean my discourse with the Jews about their religion. For when as walking in the court of the ghetto, I casually met with a certain learned Jewish rabbi that spoke good Latin, I insinuated myself after some few terms of compliment into conference with him, and asked him his opinion of Christ, and why he did not receive him for his messiah; he made me the same answer that the Turk did at Lyons, of whom I have before spoken, that Christ forsooth was a great prophet, and in that respect as highly to be esteemed as any prophet amongst the Jews that ever lived before him. But [he] derogated altogether from his divinity, and would not acknowledge him for the messiah and savior of the world, because he came so contemptibly, and not with that pomp and majesty that beseemed the redeemer of mankind. I replied that we Christians do, and will even to the effusion of our vital blood confess him to be the true and only messiah of the world, seeing he confirmed his doctrine while he was here on earth, with such an innumerable multitude of divine miracles, which did most infallibly testify his divinity; and that they themselves, who are Christ's irreconcilable enemies, could not produce any authority either out of Moses, the prophets, or any other authentic author to strengthen their opinion concerning the temporal kingdom of the messiah, seeing it was foretold to be spiritual. And [I] told him, that Christ did as a spiritual king reign over his subjects in conquering their spiritual enemies the flesh, the world, and the devil. Withal I added that the predictions and sacred oracles both of Moses, and all the holy prophets of God, aimed altogether at Christ as their only mark, in regard he was the full consummation of the law and the prophets, and I urged a place of Esay[2] unto him concerning the name Emanuel, and a virgin's conceiving and bearing of a son; and at last descended to the persuasion of him to abandon and

---

1   *Emanuel Tremellius* John Immanuel Tremmelius (1510–80), an Italian Jew who converted to Catholicism and, later, to Protestantism.
2   [Coryate's Note] Cap. 17. ver. 14. [Isaiah 7.14: "Therefore the Lord himself will give you a sign. Look, the young woman is with child and shall bear a son, and shall name him Immanuel." "Esay" refers to "Isaiah," but Coryate (or the printer) provides an incorrect chapter number.]

renounce his Jewish religion and to undertake the Christian faith, without the which he should be eternally damned. He again replied that we Christians do misinterpret the prophets, and very perversely wrest them to our own sense, and for his own part he had confidently resolved to live and die in his Jewish faith, hoping to be saved by the observations of Moses' law. In the end he seemed to be somewhat exasperated against me, because I sharply taxed their superstitious ceremonies. For many of them are such refractory[1] people that they cannot endure to hear any reconciliation to the church of Christ, in regard they esteem him but for a carpenter's son, and a silly poor wretch that once rode upon an ass, and most unworthy to be the messiah whom they expect to come with most pompous magnificence and imperial royalty, like a peerless monarch, guarded with many legions of the gallantest worthies,[2] and most eminent personages of the whole world, to conquer not only their old country Judaea and all those opulent and flourishing kingdoms, which heretofore belonged to the four ancient monarchies[3] (such is their insupportable pride) but also all the nations generally under the cope of heaven, and make the king of Guiana, and all other princes whatsoever dwelling in the remotest parts of the habitable world his tributary vassals. Thus has God justly infatuated their understandings, and given them the spirit of slumber (as Saint Paul speaks out of the prophet Esay) eyes that they should not see, and ears that they should not hear unto this day.[4] But to shut up this narration of my conflict with the Jewish rabbi, after there had passed many vehement speeches to and fro betwixt us, it happened that some forty or fifty Jews more flocked about me, and some of them began very insolently to swagger with me, because I dared reprehend their religion: whereupon fearing lest they would have offered me some violence, I withdrew myself by little and little towards the bridge at the entrance into the ghetto, with an intent to fly from them, but by good fortune our noble ambassador Sir Henry Wotton passing under the bridge in his gondola at that

---

1 *refractory* Stubborn.
2 *worthies* Eminent people.
3 *four ancient monarchies* Babylon, Media-Persia, Greece, and Rome.
4 *as Saint Paul ... this day* 1 Corinthians 2.9: "But, as it is written, 'What no eye has seen, nor ear heard, nor the human heart conceived, what God has prepared for those who love him.'" The passage cites Isaiah 64.4.

very time, espied me somewhat earnestly bickering with them, and so incontinently sent unto me out of his boat one of his principal gentlemen Master Belford his secretary, who conveyed me safely from these unchristian miscreants, which perhaps would have given me just occasion to forswear any more coming to the ghetto.

[…]

Here again I will once more speak of our most worthy ambassador Sir Henry Wotton, *honoris causa*,[1] because his house was in the same street (when I was in Venice) where the Jewish ghetto is, even in the street called St. Hieronimo, and but a little from it. Certainly he has greatly graced and honoured his country by that most honourable port that he has maintained in this noble city, by his generous carriage and most elegant and gracious behaviour amongst the greatest senators and *clarissimoes*, which like the true adamant,[2] had that attractive virtue to win him their love and grace in the highest measure. And the rather I am induced to make mention of him, because I received many great favours at his hands in Venice, for the which (I must confess) I am most deservedly engaged unto him in all due observance and obsequious respects while I live. Also those rare virtues of the mind wherewith God has abundantly enriched him, his singular learning and exquisite knowledge in the Greek and Latin, and the famousest languages of Christendom, which are excellently beautified with a plausible volubility of speech, have purchased him the inward friendship of all the Christian ambassadors resident in the city; and finally his zealous conversation, (which is the principal thing of all) piety, and integrity of life, and his true worship of God in the midst of popery, superstition, and idolatry (for he has service and sermons in his house after the Protestant manner, which I think was never before permitted in Venice, that solid divine and worthy scholar Mr. William Bedel[3] being his preacher at the time of my being in Venice) will be very forcible motives (I doubt not) to win many souls to Jesus Christ, and to draw diverse of the famous papists of the city to the true reformed religion, and profession of the gospel.

---

1 *honoris causa* Latin: for the sake of the honor.
2 *adamant* Lodestone, which attracts through magnetism.
3 *William Bedel* William Bedell (d. 1642), Wotton's chaplain in Venice.

[...]

I was at the monastery of the Benedictine monks called Saint George's,[1] which is situate in a very delectable island about half a mile southward from Saint Mark's place. [...] There is an exceeding rich altar a little without the quire, made of marble stones of different colours, at the top whereof are erected four brazen men, supporting an exceeding great brazen globe, and at the top thereof stands the image of Christ, made in brass also. [...] They have an exceeding delectable and large garden full of great variety of dainty fruits, which is the fairest not only of all Venice, but also of all the gardens I saw in Italy, surpassing even that notable garden of the Benedictines in Padua, which I have before mentioned. Insomuch that I have heard this conceit of this garden: that as Italy is the garden of the world, Lombardy the garden of Italy, Venice the garden of Lombardy, so this is κατ' ἐξοχὴν[2] the garden of Venice.

[...]

There are two very fair and spacious piazzas or marketplaces in the city, besides that of St. Mark before mentioned, whereof the fairest is St. Stephen's, being indeed of a notable length, even two hundred eighty-seven paces long, for I paced it; but of a mean breadth, only sixty-one. Here every Sunday and holy-day in the evening the young men of the city do exercise themselves at a certain play that they call balloon,[3] which is thus: six or seven young men or thereabout wear certain round things upon their arms, made of timber, which are full of sharp pointed knobs cut out of the same matter. In these exercises they put off their doublets, and having put this round instrument upon one of their arms, they toss up and down a great ball, as great as our football in England: sometimes they will toss the ball with this instrument, as high as a common church, and about one hundred paces at the least from them. About them sit the *clarissimoes* of Venice, with many strangers that repair thither to see their game. I have

---

1   *Saint George's* San Giorgio Monastery, founded in the tenth century on the island of San Giorgio Maggiore.
2   κατ' ἐξοχὴν Greek: kat exochen, preeminently.
3   *balloon* Game involving an inflated ball.

seen at the least a thousand or fifteen hundred people there: if you will have a stool it will cost you a gazet, which is almost a penny. The other piazza is a fair one also, that of St. Paul, being all green, whereas the other being paved with brick is bare and plain without any grass.

[...]

I was at one of their playhouses where I saw a comedy acted. The house is very beggarly and base in comparison of our stately playhouses in England: neither can their actors compare with us for apparel, shows and music. Here I observed certain things that I never saw before. For I saw women act, a thing that I never saw before, though I have heard that it has been sometimes used in London,[1] and they performed it with as good a grace, action, gesture, and whatsoever convenient for a player, as ever I saw any masculine actor. Also their noble & famous courtesans came to this comedy, but so disguised, that a man cannot perceive them. For they wore double masks upon their faces, to the end they might not be seen: one reaching from the top of their forehead to their chin and under their neck; another with twiskes[2] of downy or woolly stuff covering their noses. And as for their necks round about, they were so covered and wrapped with cobweb lawn[3] and other things, that no part of their skin could be discerned. Upon their heads they wore little black felt caps very like to those of the *clarissimoes* that I will hereafter speak of. Also each of them wore a black short taffeta cloak. They were so graced that they sat on high alone by themselves in the best room of all the playhouse. If any man should be so resolute to unmask one of them but in merriment only to see their faces, it is said that were he never so noble or worthy a personage, he should be cut in pieces before he should come forth of the room, especially if he were a stranger. I saw some men also in the playhouse, disguised in the same manner with double vizards,[4] those were said to be the favourites of the same courtesans: they sit not here in galleries as we do in London. For there is but one or two

---

1   *women act ... London* Female actors were unlawful in London until the reopening of theaters in 1660.
2   *twiskes* Tufts.
3   *cobweb lawn* Thin transparent linen.
4   *vizards* Masks.

little galleries in the house, wherein the courtesans only sit. But all the men do sit beneath in the yard or court, every man upon his several stool, for the which he pays a gazet.

I passed in a gondola to pleasant Murano, distant about a little mile from the city, where they make their delicate Venice glasses, so famous over all Christendom for the incomparable fineness thereof, and in one of their working houses made a glass myself. Most of their principal matter whereof they make their glasses is a kind of earth which is brought thither by sea from Drepanum a goodly haven town of Sicily, where Aeneas buried his aged father Anchises.[1] This Murano is a very delectable and populous place, having many fair buildings both public and private. [...] Here did I eat the best oysters that ever I did in all my life. They were indeed but little, something less then our Wainfleet oysters about London, but as green as a leek, and *gratissimi saporis & succi*.[2]

By the way betwixt Venice and Murano I observed a most notable thing, whereof I had often heard long before, a fair monastery of Augustinian monks built by a second Flora or Lais.[3] I mean a rich courtesan of Venice, whose name was Margarita Aemiliana. I have not heard of so religious a work done by so irreligious a founder in any place of Christendom: belike she hoped to make expiation unto God by this holy deed for the lascivious dalliances of her youth, but *tali spe freti sperando pereant*.[4]

[...]

I was at three very solemn feasts in Venice, I mean not comessa-tions or banquets, but holy and religious solemnities, whereof the first was in the church of certain nuns in St. Laurence parish,[5] which are dedicated to St. Laurence. This was celebrated the one and thirtieth. of July being Sunday, where I heard much singular music. The second

---

1   *Drepanum* Trepani; *Aeneas ... Anchises* Anchises' tomb in Drepanum is the setting for the funeral games held in his honor in Virgil's *Aeneid*, Book 5.

2   *Wainfleet oysters* Oysters from Wainfleet All Saints, a port town in Lincolnshire; *gratissimi saporis & succi* Latin: of most agreeable flavor and juice.

3   [Coryate's Note] These were rich courtesans the one in Rome, the other in Corinth.

4   *tali ... pereant* Latin: let them die trusting in such expected hope.

5   *comessations* Feasts; *St. Laurence parish* San Lorenzo, built in the tenth century. St. Laurence (d. 258) was a Roman martyr.

was on the day of our Lady's Assumption, which was the fifth of August being Friday;[1] that day in the morning I saw the duke in some
of his richest ornaments, accompanied with twenty-six couple of
senators, in their damask-long-sleeved gowns[2] come to Saint Mark's.
Also there were Venetian knights and ambassadors, that gave attendance upon him, and the first that went before him on the right hand,
carried a naked sword in his hand. He himself then wore two very
rich robes or long garments, whereof the uppermost was white, of
cloth of silver, with great massy buttons of gold, the other cloth of silver also, but adorned with many curious works made in colours with
needlework. His train was then held up by two gentlemen. At that
time I heard much good music in Saint Mark's church, but especially
that of a treble viol[3] which was so excellent, that I think no man could
surpass it. Also there were sackbuts and cornets[4] as at St. Laurence
feast which yielded passing good music. The third feast was upon
Saint Roch's day[5] being Saturday and the sixth day of August, where I
heard the best music that ever I did in all my life both in the morning
and the afternoon, so good that I would willingly go a hundred miles
afoot at any time to hear the like. [...] This feast consisted principally of music, which was both vocal and instrumental, so good, so
delectable, so rare, so admirable, so superexcellent, that it did even
ravish and stupefy[6] all those strangers that never heard the like. But
how others were affected with it I know not. For mine own part I can
say this: that I was for the time even rapt up with Saint Paul into the
third heaven.[7] Sometimes there sang sixteen or twenty men together,
having their master or moderator to keep them in order; and when
they sang, the instrumental musicians played also. Sometimes sixteen
played together upon their instruments, ten sackbuts, four cornets,
and two viol-de-gambaes[8] of an extraordinary greatness; sometimes
ten, six sackbuts and four cornets; sometimes two, a cornet and a

---

1   our Lady's ... Friday The feast day is now held on 15 August; Coryate refers to the old style
    date of the Assumption of 5 August, following the Julian calendar.
2   damask ... gowns Richly woven long-sleeved gowns of silk.
3   treble viol Stringed instrument common in early modern Europe, played with a bow.
4   sackbuts Trumpets with slides; cornets Horn-like wind instruments.
5   Saint Roch's day Feast day for St. Roch (c. 1295–1327), which is on 16 August. Coryate
    refers to the old style feast day of 6 August, following the Julian calendar.
6   stupefy Astound.
7   rapt up ... heaven Cf. 2 Corinthians 12.2–4.
8   viol-de-gambaes Viols held upright between the legs.

treble viol. Of those treble viols I heard three several there, whereof each was so good, especially one that I observed above the rest that I never heard the like before. Those that played upon the treble viols, sang and played together, and sometimes two singular fellows played together upon theorboes,[1] to which they sang also, who yielded admirable sweet music, but so still that they could scarce be heard but by those that were very near them. These two theorbists concluded that night's music, which continued three whole hours at the least. For they began about five of the clock, and ended not before eight. Also it continued as long in the morning: at every time that every several music played, the organs, whereof there are seven fair pair in that room, standing all in a row together, played with them. Of the singers there were three or four so excellent that I think few or none in Christendom do excel them, especially one, who had such a peerless and (as I may in a manner say) such a supernatural voice for sweetness, that I think there was never a better singer in all the world, insomuch that he did not only give the most pleasant contentment that could be imagined, to all the hearers, but also did as it were astonish and amaze them. I always thought that he was an eunuch, which if he had been, it had taken away some part of my admiration, because they do most commonly sing passing well; but he was not, therefore it was much the more admirable. Again it was the more worthy of admiration, because he was a middle-aged man, as about forty years old. For nature doth more commonly bestow such a singularity of voice upon boys and striplings, than upon men of such years. Besides it was far the more excellent, because it was nothing forced, strained, or affected, but came from him with the greatest facility that ever I heard. Truly I think that had a nightingale been in the same room, and contended with him for the superiority, something perhaps he might excel him, because God has granted that little bird such a privilege for the sweetness of his voice, as to none other: but I think he could not much. To conclude, I attribute so much to this rare fellow for his singing, that I think the country where he was born, may be as proud for breeding so singular a person as Smyrna was of her Homer, Verona of her Catullus,[2] or Mantua of Virgil. But exceeding happy may that city, or town, or person be that possesses this miracle of nature. These

---

1 *theorboes* Large lutes with double necks.
2 *Catullus* Roman poet (c. 84–54 BCE).

musicians had bestowed upon them by that company of Saint Roch a hundred ducats, which is twenty-three pound six shillings eight pence sterling.

[...]

There is one very memorable thing (besides all the rest that I have before named) to be seen in Venice, if it be true that I heard reported of it, even the head of a certain friar which is set upon the top of one of their steeples: he was beheaded for his monstrous and inordinate luxury, as some affirm. For I heard many say in Venice that he begat with child no less then ninety-nine nuns, and that if his courage had served him to have begotten one more with child, that he might have made up the full number of a hundred, his life should have been saved. I asked many Venetians whether this were true, who denied it unto me, but with such a kind of smiling and laughter, that that denying seemed a kind of confessing of the matter. Again some others extenuating the heinousness of the crime, told me that that was but a mere fable, and said the truth was, that he committed sacrilege by robbing one of the churches of the city, stealing away their chalices and other things of greatest worth, after the which he fled out of the Venetian signiory: but being afterward apprehended, he was executed for this fact, and not for the other.

On the fourth day of August being Thursday, I saw a very tragic and doleful spectacle in Saint Mark's place. Two men tormented with the strapado, which is done in this manner. The offender having his hands bound behind him, is conveyed into a rope that hangs in a pulley, and after hoisted up in the rope to a great height with two several swings, where he sustains so great torments that his joints are for the time loosed and pulled asunder; besides such abundance of blood is gathered into his hands and face, that for the time he is in the torture, his face and hands do look as red as fire.

The manuary[1] arts of the Venetians are so exquisite and curious, that I think no artificers in the world do excel them in some, especially painting. For I saw two things in a painter's shop in Saint Mark's, which I did not a little admire: the one was the picture of a hinder

---

1   *manuary* Performed by hand.

quarter of veal hanged up in his shop, which a stranger at the first sight would imagine to be a natural and true quarter of veal, but it was not; for it was only a counterfeit of a hinder quarter of veal, the rarest invention that ever I saw before. The other was the picture of a gentlewoman, whose eyes were contrived with that singularity of cunning, that they moved up and down of themselves, not after a seeming manner, but truly and indeed. For I did very exactly view it. But I believe it was done by a vice which the Grecians call ἀυτόματον.[1]

[...]

The burials are so strange both in Venice, and all other cities, towns, and parishes of Italy, that they differ not only from England, but from all other nations whatsoever in Christendom. For they carry the corpse to church with the face, hands, and feet all naked, and wearing the same apparel that the person wore lately before it died, or that which it craved to be buried in: which apparel is interred together with their bodies. Also I observed another thing in their burials that savours of intolerable superstition: many a man that has been a vicious and licentious liver, is buried in the habits of a Franciscan friar; the reason forsooth is, because they believe there is such virtue in the friar's cowl, that it will procure them remission of the third part of their sins—a most fond and impious opinion. We in England do hope, and so does every good Christian besides, to obtain remission of our sins, through the mere merits of Christ, and not by wearing of a friar's frock, to whom we attribute no more virtue than to a *bardocucullus*, that is, a shepherd's ragged and weather beaten cloak.

[...]

There happened at the time of my being in Venice a very prodigious thing upon the first day of July being Friday. For that day there fell a shower of hail, lasting for the space of half an hour, that yielded stones as great as pigeon's eggs; a thing that amazed all that beheld it. Also there was another strange thing that fell out when I was there: the ball or globe of a certain tower in the city, together with the cross

---

1 *vice* Device; ἀυτόματον Greek: automaton, self-moving machine.

that stood thereon, was so extremely scorched with lightning, that it was turned coal black. For indeed two or three nights one after another it lightened[1] as terribly in Venice as ever I saw in my life, and that most incessantly for many hours together.

Amongst many other things that moved great admiration in me in Venice, this was not the least, to consider the marvellous affluence and exuberancy of all things tending to the sustentation[2] of man's life. For albeit they have neither meadows, nor pastures, nor arable grounds near their city (which is a matter impossible, because it is seated in the sea, and distinguished with such a multitude of channels) to yield them corn and victuals; yet they have as great abundance (a thing very strange to be considered) of victuals, corn and fruits of all sorts whatsoever, as any city (I think) of all Italy. Their victuals and all other provision being very plenteously ministered unto them from Padua, Vicenza, and other bordering towns and places of Lombardy, which are in their own dominion. For I have seen their shambles[3] and marketplaces (whereof they have a great multitude) exceedingly well furnished with all manner of necessaries. As for their fruits I have observed wonderful plenty amongst them, as grapes, pears, apples, plums, apricots, all which are sold by weight, and not by tale:[4] figs most excellent of three or four sorts, as black, which are the daintiest, green, and yellow. Likewise they had another special commodity when I was there, which is one of the most delectable dishes for a summer fruit of all Christendom, namely muskmelons. I wondered at the plenty of them, for there was such store brought into the city every morning and evening for the space of a month together, that not only St. Mark's place, but also all the marketplaces of the city were super-abundantly furnished with them: insomuch that I think there were sold so many of them every day for that space, as yielded five hundred pound sterling. They are of three sorts, yellow, green, and red, but the red is most toothsome of all. [...] But I advise thee (gentle reader) if thou meanest to see Venice, and shall happen to be there in the summertime when they are ripe, to abstain from the immoderate eating of them. For the sweetness of them is such as has

---

1 *lightened* Flashed lightning.
2 *sustentation* Sustenance.
3 *shambles* Stalls where meat is sold.
4 *tale* Number.

allured many men to eat so immoderately of them, that they have therewith hastened their untimely death: the fruit being indeed γλυκὺ πικρον,[1] that is, sweet-sour. Sweet in the palate, but sour in the stomach, if it be not soberly eaten. For it doth often breed the *dysenteria*, that is, the bloody flux. [...] Moreover the abundance of fish, which is twice a day brought into the city, is so great, that they have not only exceeding plenty for themselves, but also do communicate that commodity to their neighbour towns. Amongst many other strange fishes that I have observed in their marketplaces, I have seen many tortoises, whereof I never saw but one in all England. [...] I have observed a thing amongst the Venetians, that I have not a little wondered at, that their gentlemen and greatest senators, a man worth perhaps two millions of ducats, will come into the market, and buy their flesh, fish, fruits, and such other things as are necessary for the maintenance of their family: a token indeed of frugality, which is commendable in all men; but methinks it is not an argument of true generosity, that a noble spirit should deject itself to these petty and base matters, that are fitter to be done by servants than men of a generous parentage. Therefore I commend mine own countryman, the English gentleman that scorns to go into the market to buy his victuals and other necessaries for housekeeping, but employs his cook or cater[2] about those inferior and sordid affairs.

It is said there are of all the gentlemen of Venice, which are there called *clarissimoes*, no less than three thousand, all which when they go abroad out of their houses, both they that bear office, and they that are private, do wear gowns: wherein they imitate

Romanes rerum Dominos, gentemque togatam.[3]

Most of their gowns are made of black cloth, and over their left shoulder they have a flap made of the same cloth, and edged with black taffeta: also most of their gowns are faced before with black taffeta. There are others also that wear other gowns according to their distinct offices and degrees; as they that are of the Council of Ten (which are

---

1 γλυκὺ πικρον Greek: glyky pikron, sweet-sour.
2 *cater* Member of the household who buys provisions.
3 *Romanes ... togatam* Virgil, *Aeneid* 1.282. Latin: Romans, lords of the world and a toga-wearing people.

as it were the main body of the whole estate) do most commonly wear black chamlet[1] gowns, with marvellous long sleeves, that reach almost down to the ground. Again they that wear red chamlet gowns with long sleeves, are those that are called *savi*, whereof some have authority only by land, as being the principal overseers of the *podestaes* and *praetors*[2] in their land cities, and some by sea. There are others also that wear blue cloth gowns with blue flaps over their shoulders, edged with taffeta. These are the secretaries of the Council of Ten. Upon every great festival day the senators, and greatest gentlemen that accompany the duke to church, or to any other place, do wear crimson damask gowns, with flaps of crimson velvet cast over their left shoulders. Likewise the Venetian knights wear black damask gowns with long sleeves: but hereby they are distinguished from the other gentlemen. For they wear red apparel under their gowns, red silk stockings, and red pantofles.[3] All these gowned men do wear marvellous little black flat caps of felt, without any brims at all, and very diminutive falling bands, no ruffs[4] at all, which are so shallow, that I have seen many of them not above a little inch deep. The colour that they most affect and use for their other apparel, I mean doublet, hose, and jerkin, is black: a colour of gravity and decency. Besides the form and fashion of their attire is both very ancient, even the same that has been used these thousand years amongst them, and also uniform. For all of them use but one and the same form of habit, even the slender doublet made close to the body, without much quilting or bombast, and long hose plain, without those new fangled curiosities, and ridiculous superfluities of panes, pleats,[5] and other light toys used with us Englishmen. Yet they make it of costly stuff, well beseeming gentlemen and eminent persons of their place, as of the best taffeta, and satin that Christendom doth yield, which are fairly garnished also with lace of the best sort. In both these things they much differ from us Englishmen. For whereas they have but one colour, we use many more than are in the rainbow, all the most light, garish, and unseemly colours that are in the world. Also for fashion we are much inferior to

---

1 *chamlet* Fine exotic fabric.
2 *podestaes and praetors* Civic administrators.
3 *pantofles* Loose shoes.
4 *ruffs* Starched linen frills worn about the neck.
5 *quilting* Quilted patterning; *bombast* Cotton down; *panes* Furs; *pleats* Cloth folds.

them. For we wear more fantastical fashions than any nation under the sun does, the French only excepted; which has given occasion both to the Venetian and other Italians to brand the Englishman with a notable mark of levity, by painting him stark naked with a pair of shears in his hand, making his fashion of attire according to the vain invention of his brain-sick head, not to comeliness and decorum.

But to return to these gowned gentlemen: I observed an extraordinary custom amongst them, that when two acquaintances meet and talk together at the walking times of the day, whereof I have before spoken, either in the duke's palace, or S. Mark's place, they give a mutual kiss when they depart from each other, by kissing one another's cheek: a custom that I never saw before, nor heard of, nor read of in any history. Likewise when they meet only and not talk, they give a low congee[1] to each other by very civil and courteous gestures, as by bending of their bodies, and clapping their right hand upon their breasts, without uncovering of their heads, which sometimes they use, but very seldom.

Most of the women when they walk abroad, especially to church, are veiled with long veils, whereof some do reach almost to the ground behind. These veils are either black, or white, or yellowish. The black either wives or widows do wear; the white maids, and so the yellowish also, but they wear more white than yellowish. It is the custom of these maids when they walk in the streets, to cover their faces with their veils, *verecundiae causa*,[2] the stuff being so thin and slight, that they may easily look through it. For it is made of a pretty slender silk, and very finely curled: so that because she thus hoodwinks herself, you can very seldom see her face at full when she walks abroad, though perhaps you earnestly desire it, but only a little glimpse thereof.

[...]

Almost all the wives, widows and maids do walk abroad with their breasts all naked, and many of them have their backs also naked even almost to the middle, which some do cover with a slight linen, as

---

1   *congee* Bow.
2   *verecundiae causa* Latin: for reason of modesty.

cobweb lawn, or such other thin stuff: a fashion methinks very uncivil and unseemly, especially if the beholder might plainly see them. For I believe unto many that have *prurientem libidinem*,[1] they would minister a great incentive & fomentation of luxurious desires. Howbeit it is much used both in Venice and Padua. For very few of them do wear bands[2] but only gentlewomen, and those do wear little lawn or cambric[3] ruffs. There is one thing used of the Venetian women, and some others dwelling in the cities and towns subject to the signiory of Venice, that is not to be observed (I think) amongst any other women in Christendom, which is so common in Venice, that no woman whatsoever goes without it, either in her house or abroad; a thing made of wood, and covered with leather of sundry colours, some with white, some red, some yellow. It is called a chapiney,[4] which they wear under their shoes. Many of them are curiously painted; some also I have seen fairly gilt: so uncomely a thing (in my opinion) that it is pity this foolish custom is not clean banished and exterminated out of the city. There are many of these chapineys of a great height, even half a yard high, which makes many of their women that are very short, seem much taller than the tallest women we have in England. Also I have heard that this is observed amongst them, that by how much the nobler a woman is, by so much the higher are her chapineys. All their gentlewomen, and most of their wives and widows that are of any wealth, are assisted and supported either by men or women when they walk abroad, to the end they may not fall. They are borne up most commonly by the left arm, otherwise they might quickly take a fall. For I saw a woman fall a very dangerous fall, as she was going down the stairs of one of the little stony bridges with her high chapineys alone by herself; but I did nothing pity her, because she wore such frivolous and (as I may truly term them) ridiculous instruments, which were the occasion of her fall. For both I myself, and many other strangers (as I have observed in Venice) have often laughed at them for their vain chapineys.

---

1   *prurientum libidinem* Latin: prurient desire.
2   *bands* Close-fitting collars.
3   *cambric* White linen originally from Cambray, Flanders.
4   *chapiney* Chopine, an overshoe with a platform sole.

All the women of Venice every Saturday in the afternoon do use to anoint their hair with oil, or some other drugs,[1] to the end to make it look fair, that is whitish. For that colour is most affected of the Venetian dames and lasses. And in this manner they do it: first they put on a reeden[2] hat, without any crown at all, but brims of exceeding breadth and largeness; then they sit in some sun-shining place in a chamber or some other secret room, where having a looking-glass before them they sophisticate[3] and dye their hair with the foresaid drugs, and after cast it back round upon the brims of the hat, till it be thoroughly dried with the heat of the sun, and last of all they curl it up in curious locks with a frizzling or crisping pin of iron, which we call in Latin *calamistrum*, the top whereof on both sides above their forehead is acuminated[4] in two peaks. That this is true, I know by mine own experience. For it was my chance one day when I was in Venice, to stand by an Englishman's wife, who was a Venetian woman born, while she was thus trimming of her hair: a favour not afforded to every stranger.

But since I have taken occasion to mention some notable particulars of their women, I will insist farther upon that matter, and make relation of their courtesans also, as being a thing incident and very proper to this discourse, especially because the name of a courtesan of Venice is famoused over all Christendom. And I have here inserted a picture[5] of one of their nobler courtesans, according to her Venetian habits, with my own near unto her, made in that form as we saluted each other. Surely by so much the more willing I am to treat something of them, because I perceive it is so rare a matter to find a description of the Venetian courtesans in any author, that all the writers that I could ever see, which have described the city, have altogether excluded them out of their writings. Therefore seeing the history of these famous gallants is omitted by all others that have written just commentaries of the Venetian state, as I know it is not impertinent

---

1   [Coryate's Note] These kind of ointments wherewith women were wont to anoint their hair, were heretofore called *capillaria unguenta*. Turnebus *Adversari*. lib. I. ca. 7. [Latin: hair unguent. The reference is to Adrien Turnèbe's *Adversaria* (1564–65).]
2   *reeden* Made of reeds or reed-like.
3   *sophisticate* Make artificial.
4   *acuminated* Sharpened.
5   *inserted a picture* See the image on the following page. This is one of five engraved plates included in Coryate's travelogue.

Venetian Courtesan, from *Coryats Crudities*.

to this present discourse to write of them; so I hope it will not be ungrateful to the reader to read that of these notable persons, which no author whatsoever doth impart unto him but myself. Only I fear lest I shall expose myself to the severe censure and scandalous imputations of many carping[1] critics, who I think will tax me for luxury and wantonness to insert so lascivious a matter into this treatise of Venice. Wherefore at the end of this discourse of the courtesans I will add some apology[2] for myself, which I hope will in some sort satisfy them, if they are not too captious.

The woman that professes this trade is called in the Italian tongue *cortezana*, which word is derived from the Italian word *cortesia* that signifies courtesy. Because these kind of women are said to receive courtesies of their favourites. Which word has some kind of affinity

---

1   *carping* Fault-finding.
2   *apology* Defense.

with the Greek word ἑταίρα[1] which signifies properly a sociable woman, and is by Demosthenes, Athenaeus,[2] and diverse other prose writers often taken for a woman of a dissolute conversation. As for the number of these Venetian courtesans it is very great. For it is thought there are of them in the whole city and other adjacent places, as Murano, Malomocco, &c. at the least twenty thousand, whereof many are esteemed so loose, that they are said to open their quivers to every arrow. A most ungodly thing without doubt that there should be a toleration of such licentious wantons in so glorious, so potent, so renowned a city. For methinks that the Venetians should be daily afraid lest their winking at such uncleanness should be an occasion to draw down upon them God's curses and vengeance from heaven, and to consume their city with fire and brimstone, as in times past he did Sodom and Gomorrah.[3] But they not fearing any such thing do grant large dispensation and indulgence unto them, and that for these two causes. First, *ad vitanda majora mala*.[4] For they think that the chastity of their wives would be the sooner assaulted, and so consequently they should be capricornified,[5] (which of all the indignities in the world the Venetian cannot patiently endure) were it not for these places of evacuation. But I marvel how that should be true though these courtesans were utterly rooted out of the city. For the gentlemen do even coop up their wives always within the walls of their houses for fear of these inconveniences, as much as if there were no courtesans at all in the city. So that you shall very seldom see a Venetian gentleman's wife but either at the solemnization of a great marriage, or at the christening of a Jew, or late in the evening rowing in a gondola. The second cause is for that the revenues which they pay unto the senate for their toleration, do maintain a dozen of their galleys, (as many reported unto me in Venice) and so save them a great charge. The consideration of these two things has moved them to tolerate for the space of these many hundred years these kind of Laides and Thaides,

---

1   ἑταίρα Greek: etaira, courtesan. – PROSTITUTES
2   *Demosthenes* Ancient Greek orator (384–322 BCE); *Athenaeus* Rhetorician (fl. c. 200 CE) of ancient Greece.
3   *Sodom and Gomorrah* Cities destroyed in Genesis 18 and 19.
4   *ad vitanda ... mala* Latin: to avoid a greater evil.
5   *capricornified* Literally, made horned. Cuckolds—men with unfaithful wives—are often described as wearing horns.

who may as fitly be termed the stales[1] of Christendom as those were heretofore of Greece. For so infinite are the allurements of these amorous Calypsos,[2] that the fame of them has drawn many to Venice from some of the remotest parts of Christendom, to contemplate their beauties, and enjoy their pleasing dalliances. And indeed such is the variety of the delicious objects they minister to their lovers, that they want nothing tending to delight. For when you come into one of their palaces (as indeed some few of the principalest of them live in very magnificent and portly buildings fit for the entertainment of a great prince) you seem to enter into the paradise of Venus. For their fairest rooms are most glorious and glittering to behold. The walls round about being adorned with most sumptuous tapestry and gilt leather, such as I have spoken of in my treatise of Padua. Besides you may see the picture of the noble courtesan most exquisitely drawn. As for herself she comes to thee decked like the queen and goddess of love, in so much that thou wilt think she made a late transmigration from Paphos, Cnidos, or Cythera,[3] the ancient habitations of Dame Venus. For her face is adorned with the quintessence of beauty. In her cheeks thou shalt see the lily and the rose strive for the supremacy, and the silver trammels[4] of her hair displayed in that curious manner besides her two frizzled peaks standing up like pretty pyramids, that they give thee the true *cos amoris*.[5] But if thou hast an exact judgment, thou may easily discern the effects of those famous apothecary drugs heretofore used amongst the noble ladies of Rome, even *stibium*, *cerussa*, and *purpurissum*.[6] For few of the courtesans are so much beholding to nature, but that they adulterate their faces, and supply her defect with one of these three. A thing so common amongst them, that many of them which have an elegant natural beauty, do varnish their faces (the observation whereof made me not a little pity their vanities) with these kind of sordid trumperies.[7] Wherein methinks they seem *ebur atramento candefacere*, according to that excellent

---

1 *Laides and Thaides* Prostitutes of ancient Greece; *stales* Low-class prostitutes.
2 *Calypsos* Reference to Calypso of Ogygia, who kept Odysseus on her island for seven years in Homer's *Odyssey*.
3 *Paphos ... Cythera* Three Greek islands where Aphrodite/Venus lived.
4 *trammels* Braids.
5 *cos amoris* Latin: Whetstone of love, i.e., object for sharpening sexual desire.
6 *stibium ... purpurissum* Antimony, white lead, and cosmetic paste, respectively.
7 *trumperies* Trifles, tricks.

proverb[1] of Plautus; that is, to make ivory white with ink. Also the ornaments of her body are so rich, that except thou dost even geld thy affections (a thing hardly to be done) or carry with thee Ulysses' herb called moly which is mentioned by Homer, that is, some antidote against those venereous titillations, she will very near benumb and captivate thy senses, and make reason vale bonnet to affection.[2] For thou shall see her decked with many chains of gold and orient pearl like a second Cleopatra, (but they are very little) diverse gold rings beautified with diamonds and other costly stones, jewels in both her ears of great worth. A gown of damask (I speak this of the nobler courtesans) either decked with a deep gold fringe (according as I have expressed it in the picture of the courtesan that I have placed about the beginning of this discourse) or laced with five or six gold laces each two inches broad. Her petticoat of red chamlet edged with rich gold fringe, stockings of carnation silk, her breath and her whole body, the more to enamour thee, most fragrantly perfumed. Though these things will at the first sight seem unto thee most delectable allurements, yet if thou shall rightly weigh them in the scales of a mature judgment, thou will say with the wise man, and that very truly, that they are like a golden ring in a swine's snout. Moreover she will endeavour to enchant thee partly with her melodious notes that she warbles out upon her lute, which she fingers with as laudable a stroke as many men that are excellent professors in the noble science of music; and partly with that heart-tempting harmony of her voice. Also thou will find the Venetian courtesan (if she be a selected[3] woman indeed) a good rhetorician, and a most elegant discourser, so that if she cannot move thee with all these foresaid delights, she will assay thy constancy with her rhetorical tongue. And to the end she may minister unto thee the stronger temptations to come to her lure, she will show thee her chamber of recreation, where thou shall see all manner of pleasing objects, as many fair painted coffers wherewith it is garnished round about, a curious milk-white canopy of needlework, a silk quilt embroidered with gold, and generally all

---

1 [Coryate's Note] Eras. ada. Chil. I. Cent. 3. adag. 70. [Desiderius Erasmus, *Adagia* (1500).]
2 *Ulysses' herb ... Homer* In Homer's *Odyssey*, Odysseus must deploy the herb moly to break the goddess Circe's enchantments; *venereous* Libidinous, literally "related to Venus"; *make reason ... affection* Make reason give way to affection.
3 *selected* Choice.

her bedding sweetly perfumed. And amongst other amiable ornaments she will show thee one thing only in her chamber tending to
mortification, a matter strange amongst so many *irritamenta
malorum*;[1] even the picture of our Lady by her bedside, with Christ in
her arms, placed within a crystal glass. But beware notwithstanding
all these *illecebrae & lenocinia amoris*,[2] that thou enter not into terms
of private conversation with her. For then thou shall find her such a
one as Lipsius[3] truly calls her, *callidam & calidam Solis filiam*, that is,
the crafty and hot daughter of the sun. Moreover I will tell thee this
news which is most true, that if thou should wantonly converse with
her, and not give her that *salarium iniquitatis*, which thou hast promised her, but perhaps cunningly escape from her company, she will
either cause thy throat to be cut by her ruffiano,[4] if he can after catch
thee in the city, or procure thee to be arrested (if thou art to be found)
and clapped up in the prison, where thou shall remain till thou has
paid her all thou did promise her. Therefore for avoiding of those inconveniences, I will give thee the same counsel that Lipsius did to a
friend of his that was to travel into Italy, even to furnish thyself with
a double armour, the one for thine eyes, the other for thine ears. As
for thine eyes, shut them and turn them aside from these venereous
Venetian objects. For they are the double windows that convey them
to thy heart. Also thou must fortify thine ears against the attractive
enchantments of their plausible speeches. Therefore even as wrestlers
were wont heretofore to fence their ears against all exterior annoy-
ances, by putting to them certain instruments called ἀμφωτιδες:[5] so
do thou take unto thyself this firm foundation against the amorous
wounds of the Venetian courtesans, to hear none of their wanton
toys. Or if thou will need both see and hear them, do thou only cast
thy breath upon them in that manner as we do upon steel, which is
no sooner on but incontinent it falls off again: so do thou only breathe
a few words upon them, and presently be gone from them, for if thou
dost linger with them thou will find their poison to be more perni-
cious than that of the scorpion, asp, or cockatrice.[6] Amongst other

---

1 *irritamenta malorum* Latin: stimuli of evils.
2 *illecebrae ... amoris* Latin: allurements and enticements of love.
3 *Lipsius* Justus Lipsius (1547–1606), humanist scholar.
4 *salarium iniquitatis* Latin: payment for iniquity; *ruffiano* Italian: pimp.
5 *ἀμφωτιδες* Greek: amphotides, ear-guards worn by wrestlers.
6 *cockatrice* Mythical beast with a killing glance.

things that I heard of these kind of women in Venice, one is this, that when their *cos amoris* begins to decay, when their youthful vigor is spent, then they consecrate the dregs of their old age to God by going into a nunnery, having before dedicated the flower of their youth to the devil. Some of them also having scraped together so much pelf by their sordid faculty as doth maintain them well in their old age: for many of them are as rich as ever was Rhodope in Egypt, Flora in Rome, or Lais in Corinth.[1] One example whereof I have before mentioned in Margarita Aemiliana that built a fair monastery of Augustinian monks. There is one most notable thing more to be mentioned concerning these Venetian courtesans, with the relation whereof I will end this discourse of them. If any of them happen to have any children (as indeed they have but few, for according to the old proverb the best carpenters make the fewest chips) they are brought up either at their own charge, or in a certain house of the city appointed for no other use but only for the bringing up of the courtesans' bastards, which I saw eastward above Saint Mark's street near to the sea side. In the south wall of which building that looks towards the sea, I observed a certain iron grate inserted into a hollow piece of the wall, betwixt which grate and a plain stone beneath it, there is a convenient little space to put in an infant. Hither doth the mother or somebody for her bring the child shortly after it is born into the world; and if the body of it be no greater, but that it may conveniently without any hurt to the infant be conveyed in at the foresaid space, they put it in there without speaking at all to anybody that is in the house to take charge thereof. And from thenceforth the mother is absolutely discharged of her child. But if the child be grown to that bigness that they cannot convey it through that space, it is carried back again to the mother, who takes charge of it herself, and brings it up as well as she can. Those that are brought up in this foresaid house are removed therehence when they come to years of discretion, and many of the male children are employed in the wars, or to serve in the arsenal, or galleys at sea, or some other public service for the commonweal. And many of the females if they be fair do *matrizare*, that is, imitate their mothers in their gainful faculty, and get their living by prostituting their bodies to their favourites. Thus have I described unto thee the

---

1   *Rhodope ... Corinth* Famous ancient prostitutes.

Venetian courtesans; but because I have related so many particulars of them, as few Englishmen that have lived many years in Venice can do the like, or at the least if they can, they will not upon their return into England, I believe thou will cast an aspersion of wantonness upon me, and say that I could not know all these matters without mine own experience. I answer thee, that although I might have known them without my experience, yet for my better satisfaction, I went to one of their noble houses (I will confess) to see the manner of their life, and observe their behaviour, but not with such an intent as we read Demosthenes went to Lais, to the end to pay something for repentance; but rather as Panutius did to Thais,[1] of whom we read that when he came to her, and craved a secret room for his pastime, she should answer him that the same room where they were together, was secret enough, because nobody could see them but only God; upon which speech the godly man took occasion to persuade her to the fear of God and religion, and to the reformation of her licentious life, since God was able to pry into the secretest corners of the world. And so at last [he] converted her by this means from a wanton courtesan to a holy and religious woman. In like manner I both wished the conversion of the courtesan that I saw, and did my endeavour by persuasive terms to convert her, though my speeches could not take the like effect that those of Panutius did. Withal I went thither partly to the end to see whether those things were true that I often heard before both in England, France, Savoy, Italy, and also in Venice itself concerning these famous women, for

Segnius irritant animos demissa per aures
quam quae sunt oculis subjecta fidelibus, & quae
ipse sibi tradit spectator———[2]

Neither can I be persuaded that it ought to be esteemed for a stain or blemish to the reputation of an honest and ingenuous man to see a courtesan in her house, and note her manners and conversation, because according to the old maxim, *cognitio mali non est mala*, the

---

1   *Demosthenes ... Lais* Demosthenes intended to sleep with Lais; *Panutius ... Thais* Panutius intended to reform Thais.
2   *Segnius ... spectator* Latin: What we hear more slowly moves the mind than what we see. Horace, *Ars poetica* ll. 180–82.

knowledge of evil is not evil but the practice and execution thereof. For I think that a virtuous man will be the more confirmed and settled in virtue by the observation of some vices, than if he did not at all know what they were. For which cause we may read that the ancient Lacedaemonians were wont sometimes to make their slaves drunk, which were called *helotae*,[1] and so present them to their children in the midst of their drunken pangs, to the end that by seeing the ugliness of that vice in others, they might the more loathe and detest it in themselves all the days of their life afterward. As for mine own part I would have thee consider that even as the river Rhone (to use that most excellent comparison, that eloquent *Kirchnerus* doth in his oration that I have prefixed before this book) doth pass through the lake Losanna, and yet mingles not his waters therewith; and as the fountain Arethusa[2] runs through the sea, and confounds not her fresh water with the salt liquor of the sea; and as the beams of the sun do penetrate into many unclean places, and yet are nothing polluted with the impurity thereof. So did I visit the palace of a noble courtesan, view her own amorous person, hear her talk, observe her fashion of life, and yet was nothing contaminated therewith, nor corrupted in manners. Therefore I instantly request thee (most candid reader) to be as charitably conceited of me, though I have at large deciphered and as it were anatomized[3] a Venetian courtesan unto thee, as thou would have me of thyself upon the like request.

I hope it will not be esteemed for an impertinency to my discourse, if I next speak of the mountebanks[4] of Venice, seeing amongst many other things that do much famous this city, these two sorts of people, namely the courtesans and the mountebanks, are not the least: for although there are mountebanks also in other cities of Italy, yet because there is a greater concourse of them in Venice than elsewhere,

---

1   *Lacedaemonians* Spartans; *helotae* Spartan slaves, named after their hometown Helos.
2   *Kirchnerus* Hermann Kirchner (1562–1620), German author who wrote an essay on travel that Coryate translated and appended to the beginning of Crudities as "a most elegant oration ... in praise of travel in general"; *lake Losanna* Lake Leman, bordering both Zurich and Lausanne, Switzerland; *Arethusa* Mythological spring on the Greek island of Ortygia, named after a nereid (sea-nymph) who was transformed into the spring while being pursued by the river god Alpheus.
3   *anatomized* Analyzed.
4   *mountebanks* Roving peddlers who endorsed quack salves and medicines in elaborate public performances.

and that of the better sort and the most eloquent fellows, and also for that there is a larger toleration of them here than in other cities (for in Rome, &c. they are restrained from certain matters as I have heard which are here allowed them) therefore they use to name a Venetian mountebank κατ᾽ ἐξοχὴν for the coryphaeus[1] and principal mountebank of all Italy; neither do I much doubt but that this treatise of them will be acceptable to some readers, as being a mere novelty never before heard of (I think) by thousands of our English gallants. Surely the principal reason that has induced me to make mention of them is because when I was in Venice, they oftentimes ministered infinite pleasure unto me. I will first begin with the etymology of their name: the word mountebank (being in the Italian tongue *monta'inbanco*) is compounded of two Italian words: *montare* which signifies to ascend or go up to a place, and *banco* a bench, because these fellows do act their part upon a stage, which is compacted of benches or forms, though I have seen some few of them also stand upon the ground when they tell their tales, which are such as are commonly called *ciaratanoes* or *charlatans*, in Latin they are called *circulatores* and *agyrtae*, which is derived from the Greek word ἀγείρειν which signifies to gather or draw a company of people together, in Greek Θαυματόποιοι.[2] The principal place where they act is the first part of Saint Mark's street that reaches betwixt the west front of S. Mark's church, and the opposite front of Saint Geminian's church. In which, twice a day, that is, in the morning and in the afternoon, you may see five or six several stages erected for them: those that act upon the ground, even the foresaid charlatans being of the poorer sort of them, stand most commonly in the second part of S. Mark's, not far from the gate of the duke's palace. These mountebanks at one end of their stage place their trunk, which is replenished with a world of new-fangled trumperies. After the whole rabble of them is gotten up to the stage, whereof some wear vizards being disguised like fools in a play, some that are women (for there are diverse women also amongst them) are attired with habits according to that person that they sustain; after (I say) they are all upon the stage, the music begins—sometimes vocal,

---

1 κατ᾽ ἐξοχὴν Greek: kat exochen, preeminent; *coryphaeus* Leader of the chorus in ancient Greek drama.
2 *circulatores and agyrtae* Latin: itinerant peddlers and roving beggars; ἀγείρειν Greek: ageirein, to bring together; Θαυματόποιοι Greek: Thaumatopoioi, jugglers.

sometimes instrumental, and sometimes both together. This music is a preamble and introduction to the ensuing matter: in the meantime while the music plays, the principal mountebank which is the captain and ring-leader of all the rest, opens his trunk, and sets abroach[1] his wares; after the music has ceased, he makes an oration to the audience of half an hour long, or almost an hour. Wherein he does most hyperbolically extol the virtue of his drugs and confections:

Laudat venales qui vult extrudere merces.[2]

Though many of them are very counterfeit and false. Truly I often wondered at many of these natural orators. For they would tell their tales with such admirable volubility and plausible grace, even extempore, and seasoned with that singular variety of elegant jests and witty conceits, that they did often strike great admiration into strangers that never heard them before: and by how much the more eloquent these naturalists[3] are, by so much the greater audience they draw unto them, and the more ware they sell. After the chiefest mountebank's first speech is ended, he delivers out his commodities by little and little, the jester still playing his part, and the musicians singing and playing upon their instruments. The principal things that they sell are oils, sovereign waters,[4] amorous songs printed, apothecary drugs, and a commonweal of other trifles. The head mountebank at every time that he delivers out any thing, makes an extemporal speech, which he does eftsoons intermingle with such savoury jests (but spiced now and then with singular scurrility) that they minister passing mirth and laughter to the whole company, which perhaps may consist of a thousand people that flock together about one of their stages. For so many according to my estimation I have seen giving attention to some notable eloquent mountebank. I have observed marvellous strange matters done by some of these mountebanks. For I saw one of them hold a viper in his hand, and play with his sting a quarter of an hour together, and yet receive no hurt; though another man should have

---

1   *sets abroach* Sets out in public.

2   *Laudat ... merces* Latin: [Seller] who's willing to push out saleable merchandise praises [them]. Horace, *Epistle to Julius Florus* 2.2.11.

3   *naturalists* People whose behavior is natural to their being, i.e., not acquired through study.

4   *sovereign waters* Medicinal tinctures containing water.

been presently stung to death with it. He made us all believe that the same viper was lineally descended from the generation of that viper that leapt out of the fire upon S. Paul's[1] hand, in the Island of Melita now called Malta, and did him no hurt; and told us moreover that it would sting some, and not others. Also I have seen a mountebank hackle[2] and gash his naked arm with a knife most pitifully to behold, so that the blood has streamed out in great abundance, and by and by after he has applied a certain oil unto it, wherewith he has incontinent both stanched the blood, and so thoroughly healed the wounds and gashes, that when he has afterward shown us his arm again, we could not possibly perceive the least token of a gash. Besides there was another black-gowned mountebank that gave most excellent contentment to the company that frequented his stage. This fellow was born blind, and so continued to that day: he never missed Saint Mark's place twice a day for six weeks together. He was noted to be a singular fellow for singing extemporal songs, and for a pretty kind of music that he made with two bones betwixt his fingers. Moreover I have seen some of them do such strange juggling tricks as would be almost incredible to be reported. Also I have observed this in them, that after they have extolled their wares to the skies, having set the price of ten crowns upon some one of their commodities, they have at last descended so low, that they have taken for it four gazets, which is something less than a groat. These merry fellows do most commonly continue two good hours upon the stage, and at last when they have fed the audience with such passing variety of sport, that they are even cloyed with the superfluity of their conceits, and have sold as much ware as they can, they remove their trinkets and stage till the next meeting.

[...]

The heat of Venice about the hottest time of summer is oftentimes very extreme, especially betwixt eleven of the clock in the morning, and two in the afternoon, insomuch that about noon you shall see very few in the whole city walking abroad, but asleep either in their

---

1 [Coryate's Note] *Act*[s]. 28.5.
2 *hackle* Hack.

own houses, or in the public walks or other open places abroad in the city. For mine own part I can speak by experience, that for the whole time almost that I was in Venice the heat was so intolerable, that I was constrained to lie stark naked most commonly every night, and could not endure any clothes at all upon me.

There are certain desperate and resolute villains in Venice, called braves,[1] who at some unlawful times do commit great villainy. They wander abroad very late in the night to and fro for their prey, like hungry lions, being armed with a privy[2] coat of mail, a gauntlet upon their right hand, and a little sharp dagger called a stiletto. They lurk commonly by the water side, and if at their time of the night, which is betwixt eleven of the clock and two, they happen to meet any man that is worth the rifling,[3] they will presently stab him, take away all about him that is of any worth, and when they have thoroughly pulled his plumes, they will throw him into one of the channels: but they buy this booty very dear if they are after apprehended. For they are presently executed.

I observed one thing in Venice that I utterly condemned, that if two men should fight together at sharp openly in the streets, whereas a great company will suddenly flock together about them, all of them will give them leave to fight till their hearts ache, or till they welter in their own blood, but not one of them has the honesty to part them, and keep them asunder from spilling each other's blood. Also if one of the two should be slain they will not offer to apprehend him that slew the other (except the person slain be a gentleman of the city) but suffer him to go at random whither he list,[4] without inflicting any punishment upon him. A very barbarous and unchristian thing to wink at[5] such effusion of Christian blood, in which they differ (in my opinion) from all Christians. The like I understand is to be observed in Milan and other cities of Italy.

[...]

---

1   *braves* Mercenary assassins.
2   *privy* Hidden.
3   *rifling* Robbing.
4   *whither he list* Wherever he wants.
5   *wink at* Ignore.

There have been some authors that have distinguished the orders or ranks of the Venetians into three degrees, as the patricians, the merchants, and the plebeians: but for the most part they are divided into two, the patricians, which are otherwise called the *clarissimoes* or the gentlemen, & the plebeians. By the patricians are meant those that have the absolute sway and government of the state or signiory both by sea and land, and administer justice at home and abroad. By the plebeians those of the vulgar sort that use mechanical and manuary trades, and are excluded from all manner of authority in the commonweal.

[...]

It is a matter very worthy the consideration, to think how this noble city has like a pure virgin and uncontaminated maid (in which sense I called her a maiden city in the front of my description of her, as also we read in the scripture, 2 King. 19.21.[1] Jerusalem was called a virgin, because from the first foundation thereof to the time that God honoured her with that title, when she was like to be assaulted by Sennacherib[2] King of the Assyrians, she was never taken by the force of any foreign enemy) kept her virginity untouched these thousand two hundred and twelve years (for so long it is since the foundation thereof) though emperors, kings, princes and mighty potentates, being allured with her glorious beauty, have attempted to deflower her, every one receiving the repulse: a thing most wonderful and strange. In which respect she has been ever privileged above all other cities.

[...]

Seeing I have related unto thee so many notable things of this renowned city, as of her first foundation, situation, name, the division thereof, her goodly temples, palaces, streets, monasteries, towers, armouries, monuments, and memorable antiquities, &c. I think thou

---

1 *2 King. 19.21* "This is the word that the Lord has spoken concerning him: 'She despises you, she scorns you—virgin daughter Zion; she tosses her head—behind your back, daughter Jerusalem.'"

2 *Sennacherib* Assyrian king (d. 681 BCE) who invaded Palestine.

will expect this also from me, that I should discover[1] unto thee her form of government, and the means wherewith she both maintains herself in that glorious majesty, and also rules those goodly cities, towns, and citadels that are subject to her dominion. If thou doth require this at my hands (as I believe thou will) I would have thee consider that I am neither politician, nor statist,[2] but a private man, and therefore I often thought to myself when I was in Venice, that it would be a matter something impertinent to me to pry into their government, observe their laws, their matters of state, their customs, their courts of justice, their judicious proceedings, their distributions of offices, &c. seeing I should make but little use thereof upon my return into my country. Or were it so that I had had a great desire to have informed myself with the knowledge of the principal particularities of their government (which I must need say had been a most laudable and excellent thing, especially in such a city as has the fame to be as well governed as any city upon the face of the whole earth ever was, or at this day is) yet to attain to an exact knowledge thereof in so short a space as I spent there, over and above these my poor observations which I have communicated unto thee, truly I confess I was not able. Therefore for as much as thou may gather even by these my notes of Venice (which are more I am sure than every English man can show thee out of six weeks abode there) that I was not altogether idle when I lay in the city, I hope thou wilt deign to pardon me, though I cannot answer thy expectation about the government thereof, especially because I will promise thee (if God shall graciously prolong my life that I may once more see it, which I earnestly wish and hope for) that I will endeavour to observe as much of their government as may be lawful for a stranger, and so *tandem aliquando*[3] to impart the same unto thee with other observations of my future travels, which perhaps will not be altogether unworthy the reading. But because thou shall not think that I am utterly ignorant of all matters touching their government, I will give thee only a superficial touch, and no more. [...] I could tell thee some notable ceremonies concerning the election of their duke, but those I will defer till my next observations of this city. Only I will impart one unto thee, which is this. As soon as the duke

---

1 *discover* Reveal.
2 *statist* One knowledgeable about political affairs.
3 *tandem aliquando* At last.

is proclaimed, he is carried about St. Mark's place in a chair upon certain men's shoulders that are appointed for the same purpose, and all the while he flings money about the street for the poor to gather up. The duke is not a sovereign prince, to say *sic volo, sic jubeo*;[1] but his authority is so curbed & restrained, that without the consent of the councils he can neither establish nor abrogate a law, nor do any other matter whatsoever that belongs to a prince. So that the government of this city is a compounded form of state, containing in it an idea of the three principal governments of the ancient Athenians and Romans, namely the monarchical, the oligarchical, and democratical. The duke sits at the stern of the commonweal with glorious ornaments beseeming his place and dignity, adorned with a diadem and other ensigns of principality, so that he seems to be a kind of monarch; yet there is that limitation of his power that without the approbation of the senate he cannot do anything that carries a mark of sovereignty. Next is the Council of Ten commonly called *Consilio di dieci*, which were first instituted by way of imitation of the ancient Roman *Decemviri*.[2] These are as it were the main sinews and strength of the whole Venetian empire. For they are the principal lords of the state that manage the whole government thereof, both by sea and land. This Council presents unto thee a singular form of an oligarchy or aristocracy. The last is the great Council which consists of a thousand and six hundred gentlemen, who are likewise other subordinate members of the state, and are a notable pattern of a democracy.

[...]

That day that I came forth of Venice I observed a thing which did even tickle my senses with great joy and comfort; for on the right hand of the second walk of Saint Mark's place, as you go betwixt the clock and the two great pillars by the sea side, even in the outward wall of the duke's palace, and within that fair walk that is supported with pillars, I saw the pictures of certain famous kings, and other great personages, and our King James his picture in the very midst of them, as being the worthiest person of them all. The pictures were

---

1   *sic volo, sic jubeo* Latin: thus I wish, thus I command.
2   *Decemviri* Latin: Ten men. The Decemviri were Roman administrative groups with different functions.

these: one of the present king of Spain, Philip the second; one of the king of France, Henry the fourth; One of the last duke of Venice, Marino Grimanno;[1] and one of a certain noble woman whose name nobody could tell me. And in the very middle our king's picture, which I think was placed there not without great consideration; for I believe they remembered the old speech when they hanged up his picture: *in medio consistit virtus*.[2] Again the same day I saw his picture very gallantly advanced in another place of the city, even at the Rialto bridge, with Queen Anne[3] and Prince Henry on one side of him, and the king of France on the other; a thing that ministered singular contentment unto me.

Having now so amply declared unto thee most of the principal things of this thrice-renowned and illustrious city, I will briefly by way of an epitome mention most of the other particulars thereof, and so finally shut up this narration: there are reported to be in Venice and the circumjacent islands[4] two hundred churches in which are one hundred forty-three pair of organs, fifty-four monasteries, twenty-six nunneries, fifty-six tribunals or places of judgment, seventeen hospitals, six companies or fraternities, whereof I have before spoken; one hundred sixty-five marble statues of worthy personages, partly equestrial, partly pedestrial,[5] which are erected in sundry places of the city, to the honour of those that either at home have prudently administered the commonweal, or abroad valiantly fought for the same. Likewise of brass there are twenty-three, whereof one is that of Bartholomew Coleon[6] before mentioned. Also there are twenty-seven public clocks, ten brazen gates, a hundred and fourteen towers for bells to hang in, ten brazen horses, one hundred fifty-five wells for the common use of the citizens, one hundred eighty-five most delectable gardens, ten thousand gondolas, four hundred and fifty bridges partly stony, partly timber, one hundred and twenty palaces, whereof one hundred are very worthy of that name, one hundred seventy-four

---

1   *Philip the second* King Philip II of Spain (1527–98); *Henry the fourth* King Henri IV of France (1553–1610); *Marino Grimmano* Marino Grimani (1532–1605).

2   *in medio ... virtus* Latin: in the middle stands virtue.

3   *Queen Anne* Anne of Denmark (1574–1619), wife of King James I of England.

4   [Coryate's Note] Which are in number twenty-five.

5   *partly equestrial ... pedestrial* Some equestrian, some on foot.

6   *Bartholomew Coleon* Bartolomeo Colleoni (1400–75), famous condottiero (leader of mercenary soldiers).

courts: and the total number of souls living in the city and about the same is thought to be about five hundred thousand, something more or less. For sometimes there is a catalogue made of all the persons in the city of what sex or age soever they be, as we may read there was heretofore in Rome in the time of Augustus Caesar:[1] and at the last view there were found in the whole city as many as I have before spoken.

Thus have I related unto thee as many notable matters of this noble city, as either I could see with mine eyes, or hear from the report of credible and worthy persons, or derive from the monuments of learned and authentic writers that I found in the city; hoping that diverse large circumstances which I have inserted into this history, will not be unpleasant unto thee, because many of them do tend to the better illustration of some things, whose glory would have been even eclipsed if I had not enlarged the same with these amplifications; and so at length I finish the treatise of this incomparable city, this most beautiful queen, this untainted virgin, this paradise, this Tempe, this rich diadem and most flourishing garland of Christendom: of which the inhabitants may as proudly vaunt, as I have read the Persians have done of their Ormus,[2] who say that if the world were a ring, then should Ormus be the gem thereof: the same (I say) may the Venetians speak of their city, and much more truly. The sight whereof has yielded unto me such infinite and unspeakable contentment (I must needs confess) that even as Albertus Marquess of Guasto said (as I have before spoken) were he put to his choice to be Lord of four of the fairest cities of Italy, or the arsenal of Venice, he would prefer the arsenal. In like manner I say, that had there been an offer made unto me before I took my journey to Venice, either that four of the richest manors of Somersetshire (wherein I was born) should be *gratis* bestowed upon me if I never saw Venice, or neither of them if I should see it, although certainly those manors would do me much more good in respect of a state of livelihood to live in the world, than the sight of Venice: yet notwithstanding I will ever say while I live, that the sight of Venice and her resplendent beauty, antiquities,

---

1   *Augustus Caesar* First Roman Emperor (63 BCE–19 CE).
2   *Ormus* Former Persian kingdom whose capital city was Hormuz, Iran.

and monuments, has by many degrees more contented my mind, and satisfied my desires, than those four manors could possibly have done.

Thus much of the glorious city of Venice.

I departed from Venice in a bark to Padua about eight of the clock in the evening the eighth day of August being Monday, after I had made my abode there six weeks and two days, and came to Padua about nine of the clock the next morning[....] I departed from Padua about two of the clock in the afternoon the same day, being conducted in my way by my kind friend Mr. George Rook, of whom I have made mention before in my discourse of Padua, and came to a solitary house thirteen miles beyond, about seven of the clock in the evening, where I lay that night.

[...]

I departed from the solitary house about six of the clock the next morning being Wednesday, and came to Vicenza about eight of the clock. The distance betwixt that house and Vicenza is five miles.

My observations of Vicenza [...]

There are four very memorable things to be seen in this city: the monastery of the Dominican[1] friars, the palace of the count or earl Leonardus Walmarana, his garden near to the west gate that leads to Verona, and a famous theatre, built *anno* M.D.LXXXIIII. In the monastery of the Dominican friars is to be seen the thorny crown of our savior Jesus Christ (as they say) which St. Louis King of France,[2] *anno* 1259 bestowed upon his brother at Paris, who happened afterward to be Bishop of Vicenza, and a Dominican friar. They report that he was the man that bestowed this crown upon the monastery. In my notes of Paris I have written something of this crown. For in Paris they say that they have the thorny crown: and here in Vicenza the Dominicans most constantly affirm, that none has it or can have

---

1   *Dominican* The Dominican order of preachers, founded by St. Dominic (c. 1174–1221), is notable for its focus on study.

2   *St. Louis ... France* Louis IX (1214–70).

it but themselves: either they must prove that Christ had two several crowns of thorns put upon his head (which is contrary to the history of the evangelists) or else it must needs follow that one of these crowns is false. Nevertheless I went thither to see it for my mind's sake, but I could not possibly obtain the favour, though the friars otherwise used me very courteously, affirming that it was never shown to any man whatsoever but upon *Corpus Christi* day, and that it was kept under three locks. One of the monks showed me a very memorable thing in this monastery. For he brought me into their kitchen, and told me, that where the chimney is, even where their meat is wont to be roasted and sodde, certain Arians[1] heretofore lived, their principal master reading from a chair that stood in the same place the Arian doctrine to his disciples and followers: but at last the holy Bishop Bartholomew[2] (of whom I have already spoken) chased them out of the city, and in their room placed the Dominicans.

The palace of the earl Leonardus Walmarana seems to be a very magnificent building, if the inside be correspondent to the front next to the street. For that front is very beautiful, having much pointed diamond work about the bottom, and about the top many pretty histories curiously cut in stone. [...] The third is the garden of the foresaid earl Leonardus, which is so delectable and pleasant that it seems a second paradise. [...] In both sides of this walk I saw cedar trees, orange, lemon, and pome-citron[3] trees, and fruits of all these kinds ripe. Amongst the rest I observed passing fair citrons, which made my mouth even water upon them, and caused me almost to transgress his law. One side of the walk is environed with a goodly wall, by the which the fruits do grow. About the middle of the walk there is built a pretty convenient house, wherein tame conies and diverse sorts of fine birds are kept, as turtles, &c. In the middle of the garden is built a fair round roof, supported with eight stately pillars of white stone; it is said that it shall be all covered with lead, but it was not when I was there. Also I saw a fine labyrinth made of box, but the door was locked that I could not get in. And many lofty pine trees, but some of them were so nipped with the cold frost and

---

1   *sodde* Boiled; *Arians* Believers in the Arian heresy, which asserts that Christ is a separate being from God the Father, contradicting conventional doctrine regarding the Trinity.
2   *Bishop Bartholomew* Bartholomew di Braganca (c. 1200–71).
3   *pome-citron* Citron, a citrus fruit resembling a large lemon.

snow that fell the winter before, as those were in the king of France's garden at the Tuileries, that they were even starved. Also for the more addition of pleasure to the place, there is a sweet river full of fine fish running by that fruitful walk, wherehence is ministered store of water to moisten the garden in time of drought. Finally to conclude, such is the affluence of all delights and pleasures in this garden, that it is the most peerless and incomparable plot for the quantity that ever I saw.

The fourth and last memorable thing of this city is a stately fair theatre, which was built by certain scholars in the year 1584 that were called *Academici Olympici*, but why so called I know not. It has an orchestra made in it according to the imitation of the Roman orchestras,[1] which is at the lower end of the degrees, or (as I may more properly term them) benches or seats, whereof there are fourteen, each above another, compassing something more than half the theatre, and contrived in the fashion of a half-moon. In that orchestra none sit but noble and eminent persons. He that showed me this theatre told me that the orchestra and fourteen benches would contain about some three thousand persons. The scene also is a very fair and beautiful place to behold. In this theatre was acted a play for many years since with diverse goodly shows before William Gonzaga Duke of Mantua, father to the present Duke Vincentius Gonzaga.[2] Again, afterward certain Moscovite[3] ambassadors that came from Rome, were very honourably entertained in this theatre with music and a banquet. And after them certain young noblemen of that far remote region in the East called Japan or Japona, being descended of the blood royal of the country, were received here with great state, at what time Livius Pajellus a singular orator pronounced an eloquent oration in praise of them. But one of the latest great shows that was made here was presented before the forenamed that famous earl Leonardus Walmarana, in the year 1585. For at that time the tragedy of Sophocles, which is entitled *Oedipus*,[4] was most excellently acted in this theatre. The history of the acting whereof is finely painted in the court wall at the very entrance to the theatre.

---

1 *Roman orchestras* Semicircular spaces in front of Roman stages.
2 *William ... Mantua* Guglielmo Gonzaga (1538–87); *Duke Vincentius Gonzaga* Vincenzo Gonzaga (1562–1612).
3 *Moscovite* Of Moscow, i.e., Russian.
4 *which ... Oedipus* Sophocles, *Oedipus Rex* (fifth century BCE).

[...]

For the sight of most of these notable things that I enjoyed in this fair city, I do acknowledge my self exceedingly beholding to two Italian young gentlemen that were Vicentines born, whose names were Thomas de Spanivellis, and Joannes Nicoletis; especially to one of them, who kept me company almost all that day that I spent there, and conducted me from place to place till he had showed me all the principal things of the city. For surely many Italians are passing courteous and kind towards strangers, of whose humanity I made trial in diverse other cities in Italy, as Padua, Venice, Verona, Brescia, Bergamo, &c. Therefore I will ever magnify and extol the Italian for as courteous a man to a stranger as any man whatsoever in Christendom. For I have had a little experience in my travels of some of every principal nation of Christendom.

[...]

That day that I came forth of Vicenza, being Thursday and the eleventh day of August, I saw a frantic and lunatic fellow run up and down the city with a gown about him, who kept a very furious stir, and drew many people about him.

[...]

I will now conclude my observations of Vicenza with two memorable Italian sayings, the one of the counts and knights of Vicenza, which is this:

Quanti ha Venetia ponti e Gondolieri,
Tanti ha Vicenza Conti e Cavallieri.

That is, look how many bridges and gondoliers Venice does yield, so many counts and knights does Vicenza.

The other, of the wine of Vicenza, which is in a manner proverbially spoken of, as other commodities are of other Italian cities, *viz.*

Vin Vicentin,
Pan Paduan.
Tripe Trevizan.
Putana Venetian

That is, *The Wine of Vicenza,*
The Bread of Padua.
The Tripes of Treviza.
The Courtesans of Venice

Thus much of Vicenza.

I departed from Vicenza about ten a clock in the morning, the eleventh day of August being Thursday, and came to Verona the next day about nine of the clock in the morning: the things that I observed betwixt Vicenza and Verona are these. Most of the horsemen that I met were furnished with muskets ready charged, and touch-boxes[1] hanging by their sides full of gunpowder, together with little pouches full of bullets; which is a thing so commonly used in most places of Italy, that a man shall scarce find a horseman in any place riding without them. I heard that this is the reason of it: because the people of the country are so given to villainies, that they will rob, rifle, and murder passengers, if they are not sufficiently provided to defend themselves against them.

[...]

My observations of Verona [...]

Surely it is a very delectable, large, and populous city, and most sweetly seated: for the noble river Athesis runs by it which Virgil calls *amoenus*, as

————*Athesin ceu propter amoenum.*[2]

---

1 *touch-boxes* Boxes filled with priming or "touch" powder. Once ignited by a spark, priming powder would ignite a larger explosive charge (also consisting of gunpowder).
2 *Athesis* Adige River; *amoenus* Latin: pleasant; *Athesin ... amoenum* Latin: Or near the pleasant Adige. Virgil, *Aeneid*, IX. 680.

It issues out of the Alps not far from the city of Trent.[1] This river yields a special commodity to the city. For although it be not able to bear vessels of a great burden, yet it carries pretty barges of convenient quantity, wherein great store of merchandise is brought unto the city, both out of Germany and from Venice itself. In one side of this river, I told nineteen water-mills, which were like to those that I saw upon the river Rhone at the city of Lyons. There are four bridges which join together both the banks of the river, whereof one is very fair and beautiful above the rest. [...] A certain Italian young gentleman, unto whom I was much beholding for the sight of many noble antiquities of this city, told me that this river Athesis does sometimes so extremely swell, that it has utterly overwhelmed all the bridges, and much annoyed the city.

[...]

So many notable antiquities and memorable monuments are to be seen in this noble city of Verona, as no Italian city whatsoever (Rome excepted) can show the like. But the worthiest and most remarkable of all is the amphitheatre commonly called the *Arena*, seated at the southwest end of the city where cattle are sold; whereof I have expressed a picture in this place,[2] according to the form of it, as it flourished in the time of the Roman monarchy. This word amphitheatre is derived from these two Greek words ἀμφὶ which signifies about, and Θεῶμαι[3] to behold, because which way soever a man does view it, he finds it of a circular and round form. So that herein an amphitheatre differs from a theatre, because an amphitheatre is everywhere round, but a theatre (according to the form of the ancient Roman building) is but half round, being made in the fashion of an half circle or half-moon. The model of these kind of amphitheatres which the ancient Romans built in Rome, and other places of Italy, was derived from the Athenians, who were the first that erected an amphitheatre. Certainly this present building, whereof I now speak, is a most stupendious mass of work. [...] For indeed it is such an admirable fabric that it

---

1   *Trent* Trento.
2   *a picture ... place* One of five engraved plates included in Coryate's travelogue; see the
    image on the following page.
3   *ἀμφὶ* Greek: amphi, around; *Θεῶμαι* Greek: Theomai, behold.

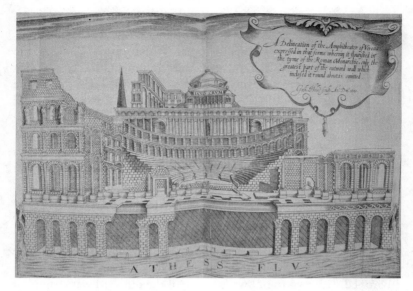

Theatre of Verona, from *Coryats Crudities*.

draws all strangers into admiration thereof: and I am persuaded that
the beauty thereof after it was first built and thoroughly consum-
mated, was so glorious, that it no less drew spectators from most of
the principal places of the world to contemplate the excellency thereof, than that famous Temple of Vespasian in Rome, dedicated to Pallas, which is so highly commended by Josephus the Jew.[1] It was
reported unto me by gentlemen of good note in this city of Verona,
that the like amphitheatre is not to be seen at this day in all Italy, no
not in Rome itself. Neither do I think that antiquity could ever show
a fairer piece of work for an amphitheatre; but it is very ruinous at this
time. For the principal ornaments thereof are demolished and de-
faced. So that it has lost more than half of its pristine glory: it is uncertain who was the first founder thereof. That it was built by one of

---

1   *Temple … Pallas* Temple of Vespasian and Titus, built in honor of Titus Flavius Vespasianus
    (9–79 CE), Roman Emperor. Pallas Athena is the Greek goddess of wisdom; *Josephus the Jew*
    Flavius Josephus (c. 37–c. 100 CE), Jewish historian. The reference is to Josephus' *Jewish War*
    (75–79 CE), which Coryate may have read as *The famous and memorable workes of Josephus*
    (1602): Josephus writes that "*Vespasian* built a Temple and dedicated it unto peace … [and]
    beautified it with diverse pictures and carved works" (7.24).

the Roman emperors every man believes, but by whom no chronicle, annals, or ancient history does certainly record. But Torellas Saraina,[1] a learned man born in Verona, who has written certain books of the antiquities of this city, is drawn by certain arguments and conjectures to affirm, that it was built by the Emperor Augustus, and that in the two and fortieth year of his empire, which was that very year that our blessed savior was born into the world. Were such a building to be made in England, I think it would cost at the least two millions of our pounds, that is, twenty hundred thousand pound, even as much as ten of our fairest cathedral churches. For it is all built with red marble: which although it were a very chargeable piece of workmanship, yet they could build it as cheap there as in any part of all Italy. For in the territory of Verona they have diverse marble quarries, and that of sundry colours, as white, black, red, &c. It was dedicated to Janus,[2] and has as yet many notable things to be seen, which do argue the singular beauty thereof when it flourished in his prime. For it was environed with two round walls, whereof the outward was a thing of rare magnificence. Which by the invasion of many barbarous people, as the Goths, Huns, (who under the conduct of their King Attila sacked this city) and Lombards under their King Alboinus,[3] has been so ruinated, that there is but a little part thereof standing, the marble stones being pulled down, and removed therehence, partly for the garnishing of the private houses of the city, and partly for other uses. This, together with all the other parts of the machine,[4] was built with red marble, all the pieces being cut square, which do very excellently garnish the work. That which remains at this day of the outward wall, though it be but little, does testify that it was a wondrous architecture. [...] But the inner wall itself does stand pretty well, and yields a most stately show, though some parts of the top be something blemished. [...] The lower arches are now converted to very base and sordid uses. For they serve partly for stables to put horses and hay in, and partly for tippling-houses[5] for poor folks to sell wine in, and other

---

1 *Torellas Saraina* Torella Saraina, historian of Verona whose *Le historie, e fatti de Veronesi* (1586) is referenced here.
2 *Janus* Two-faced Roman god of doorways.
3 *Alboinus* Alboin (d. 572), King of the Lombards.
4 *machine* Material structure.
5 *tippling-houses* Taverns.

necessaries. After I had exactly viewed all the outward parts, I was admitted into the inside by a fellow that gets his living altogether by showing the same to strangers, and as soon as I came in, I was driven into great admiration. For I saw so many things as will make a stranger not a little wonder. There I observed the seats, or benches, made of red marble, encompassing the *cavea*,[1] or plain within it round about, and ascending by degrees one above another to the very top, which are in number forty two: but the greatest part of the marble of these benches has been (to the great blemish of the work) carried away for many years since by those barbarous people that have much eclipsed the glorious beauty of this building. Yet the gentlemen of Verona have within these few years something repaired it again. For they have bestowed so great charges in mending them on both sides with new marble benches correspondent to the former, that those on the right hand cost them threescore thousand crowns, and those on the left six thousand, as a gentleman of Verona told me that showed me the particulars of the amphitheatre. These threescore and six thousand crowns being not the fiftieth part of the charge (as I think) that the whole building would cost, were it now to be built from the foundation, may give a man some conjecture what an infinite and excessive mass of money it cost in those days when it was first founded, though I believe their building was then much cheaper than now. Also these gentlemen of Verona do daily beautify it with new addition of marble benches, because they have oftentimes great shows exhibited here to the people upon festival days, as running at tilt, and other noble exercises, especially upon their carnival day, which is observed amongst them in the same manner as our Shrove-Tuesday[2] with us in England, being called carnival from the two Latin words, *caro* and *vale*, that is, farewell flesh, because after that day they eat no more flesh till Easter. These foresaid two and forty benches have in former times contained three and twenty thousand people that were the spectators of the games played therein, a foot and a half and no more being limited to every particular person. [...] All that open and void space at the top was wont to be covered over wholly with curtains at the time of their public games, to the end to keep off the

---

1   *cavea* Latin: hollow or cavity, here referring to the auditorium.
2   *Shrove-Tuesday* Celebration held on the Tuesday before Ash Wednesday, the first day of Lent.

scorching heat of the sun, which otherwise would very much annoy the people. The galleries in the inside are contrived after a very strange manner, not unlike unto labyrinths. For there are three degrees of them vaulted one above another, through the which both those that were above upon the benches did descend to go forth of the room, and they beneath ascended to their seats. Also I observed certain rooms where the beasts were kept, with whom the *gladiatores* were to fight. These rooms have at one end certain little open places to let in the air for the refreshing of the beasts, such as we call in Latin *spiracula*.[1] The *cavea* or green plain in the middle is made in the form of an egg, sharp at the ends, and broad at the sides, very like to a pond that I have seen in one of Sir Francis Carew's gardens in Middlesex: and it is in length nine & thirty perches,[2] in breadth two and twenty and a half. For I did exactly observe the length and breadth of it. Now it is divided in the very midst by a certain kind of pale, like to that of our tilt-yard at Whitehall,[3] where the Venetian gentlemen and noblemen of Verona do sometimes encounter at jousts and tournaments. In the midst of this plain diverse spectacles and games were wont to be shown in former times to the people, whereof some consisted especially of a most bloody kind of fight betwixt men and beasts, which was performed by their *gladiatores*. For according to the ancient custom of the Romans certain enormous malefactors that had committed some capital crimes, being condemned to fight for their lives with wild beasts, were in this place and such other (whereof Rome had many, as the *Circus maximus*, &c.) exposed with their swords and targets,[4] and such other weapons to the fury of savage beasts, as lions, bears, tigers, &c. If fortune favoured them so well that they slew those beasts, then both their lives were saved, and also they had some reward bestowed upon them, which was commonly called *brabium*,[5] in

---

1   *spiracula* Latin: vents.
2   *Sir Francis ... Middlesex* Sir Francis Carew (c. 1530–1611) kept famous gardens at Beddington, Surrey. Coryate incorrectly places these gardens in Middlesex, as an early modern reader has pointed out in the copy of *Crudities* held at Columbia University Rare Book and Manuscript Library; *nine & thirty perches* About 635 feet; a perch is a unit of measurement equal to 16.5 feet.
3   *pale* Fence; *tilt-yard at Whitehall* Tournament space at the Palace of Whitehall, London.
4   *Circus maximus* Roman arena used for races, ceremonies, athletic contests, and gladiatorial combat; *targets* Small shields.
5   *brabium* Latin: prize in the games.

token of their victory. But if they were slain by the beasts, it was esteemed as a just recompense for their wicked deserts. But to conclude this description of the amphitheatre of Verona, it is a work of such admirable magnificence that as I never saw the like before, so I think in all my future travels (which I determine God willing to undertake hereafter both in Christendom and paganism) I shall never see a fairer.

[...]

The principal marketplace of the city is very fair, which I take occasion to mention by reason of a notable thing that I observed there tending to idolatry. For on the front of a fair house adjoining to this marketplace, there stands the image of the Virgin Mary, made in white marble with Christ in one arm, and a book in one of her hands.

[...]

Also I saw about the middle of the same market place a marvellous pleasant fountain, adorned with a very ancient marble image, wearing a crown upon her head; that is said to be a representation of Verona. From diverse spouts of this statue, *jugis aquae fons*[1] does incessantly flow. Besides, at the higher end of this marketplace there is erected a very stately marble pillar with the winged lion advanced upon it. And in a gentleman's house of the city but a little way from that, I saw a very beautiful pair of winding stairs, made by that singular architect Andreas Palladius,[2] which by reason of the curious workmanship thereof are much shown to strangers.

[...]

The buildings of this city, especially those that belong to the gentlemen, are very fair, being for the most part built with brick: though I have seen some of the gentlemen's houses built with passing fair stone, and richly adorned with many goodly marble pillars; the

---

1 *jugis aquae fons* Latin: ever-flowing fountain of water.
2 *Andreas Palladius* Andrea Palladio (1508–80), Italian architect.

pentices or eaves of their houses being much broader than I have observed in other cities. Also many of their outward walls and their chimneys are very fairly painted, which gives great ornament to their houses.

[...]

I was admitted into the most magnificent palace of Count Augustinus Justus, but not without some favour. There I saw stones with very ancient inscriptions, which I could not read by reason of the antiquity of them. Also I was shown a certain higher room in the palace which was a place of that singular glory, that I saw not the like in any private house of Italy, the beauty thereof consisting especially of pictures which hanged round about the room, being in number one hundred fifty nine, and such as represented some of the worthiest and most eminent persons of the world in diverse ages. There I saw many of the Roman emperors most exquisitely painted, and some of the German emperors, and kings of Spain; also kings of France, many dukes of Venice, and diverse popes; of our English kings but one, and that was King Henry the eighth. But the Italian painter erred, for the picture more truly represented Henry the seventh, than H. the eighth.[1] [...] Therefore I counsel thee whatsoever thou art that means in thy travels to see Verona, to make means to be admitted into the palace of Count Augustinus Justus, and to see this noble and glorious room before thou does come forth of it: for many English gentlemen have seen it, as the Italian told me that showed it to me.

Also the Italian showed me his garden, which is a second paradise, and a passing delectable place of solace, beautified with many curious knots, fruits of diverse sorts and two rows of lofty cypress trees, three and thirty in a rank. Besides his walks at the top of the garden a little under St. Peter's castle,[2] are as pleasant as the heart of man can wish; being decked with excellent fruits, as figs, oranges, apricots, and with cypress trees. In one of these walks is a delicate little refectory: at one side whereof there is a curious artificial rock, adorned with many fine devices, as scallop shells, and great variety of other pretty

---

1   *Henry the seventh* Henry VII of England (1457–1509);   *H. the eighth* Henry VIII of England (1491–1547).
2   *St. Peter's castle* Castel San Pietro, built in the late-fourteenth century.

shells of fishes brought from Cyprus: and moss grows upon the same as if it were a natural rock. This place certainly is contrived with as admirable curiosity as ever I saw, and moistened with delicate springs and fountains conveyed into the same by leaden pipes. I have seen in England one place something like to this, even in one of the gardens of that noble knight Sir Francis Carew of Middlesex, who has one most excellent rock there framed all by art, and beautified with many elegant conceits, notwithstanding it is somewhat inferior unto this. Again in another walk I saw his fine chapel, wherein his chaplain does often say mass to him.

I observed a very mournful show performed by monks in Verona. For I saw eighteen couples of them accompany a corpse of one of their fraternity to church, being attired with black buckram[1] veils, and marked with the sign of the star on the left side of their breasts, girt with a black girdle, their heads covered with a black hood that came over all their shoulders, and hid all their face. Before their eyes were made two holes to look out: each of them carried a burning candle in his hand of virgin wax,[2] and some of them three candles, and there was put into every candle two pieces of their little tin money called gazets.

[...]

Besides those famous learned men born in Verona, that I have above mentioned, with many other most excellent wits, that it has ever bred from time to time, I have often read of two most worthy women born in this city, whereof each was esteemed the phoenix of her time for learning, with mention of whom I will end this description of Verona; the one was called Isotta Nogarola[3] a virgin,[4] who attained to so great knowledge, that she was very eloquent in the Greek and Latin tongues, and wrote many excellent Latin epistles to Nicolas, the fifth pope[5] of that name. Also she composed

---

1   *buckram* Fabric made from linen or cotton.
2   *virgin wax* Fresh beeswax.
3   *Isotta Nogarola* Italian humanist writer (1418–66).
4   [Coryate's Note] Fulgosus lib. 8. cap. 3. *Memorabilium.* [Battista Fregoso, *Factorum dictorumque memorabilium* (1578).]
5   *Nicolas ... pope* Pope Nicholas V (1397–1455).

an elegant dialogue, wherein she disputed the matter, who committed the greatest sin Adam or Eve. The other was Genebria,[1] who in the time of Pius the second[2] of that name pope, wrote sundry Latin epistles with a most elegant style; which two women have no less ennobled this famous city, with their learning than Aspasia and Diotima did Athens, Cornelia Rome, Cassandra Venice, or Hildegardis[3] the city of Bing in Germany.

Thus much of Verona.

[...]

My observations of Brescia [...]

It happened that the same Monday that I was in Brescia was Bartholomew day.[4] At what time there was a most solemn and ceremonious dedication of a new image to the Virgin Mary with Christ in her arms, which I saw performed in a certain little chapel with many superstitious rites. For they attired the image with a great many several robes, as of satin, taffeta, lawn, &c. and there was a great multitude of little waxen idols brought to the chapel, whereof some were only arms, some thighs, some presented all the parts of a man's body: although these toys were no novelties unto me. For I saw many of them before that time in diverse Italian cities. Yet I had a marvellous itching desire to finger one of them, only to this end, to bring it home into England, to show it to my friends as a token of their idolatry: but I saw there was some difficulty in the matter. Howbeit I gave the venture upon it in this manner. I stood at one corner of the chapel while

---

1   [Coryate's Note] Gesnerus *Biblioth.* [Conrad Gessner, *Bibliotheca universalis* (1545).]
2   *Pius the second* Pope Pius II (1405–64).
3   *Aspasia* Noted intellectual (late 470s–c. 400 BCE) who hosted gatherings attended by Athenian thinkers, including Socrates. She was also the mistress of the important rhetorician Pericles (c. 495–429 BCE); *Diotima* Socrates' tutor in Plato's *Symposium*, where she articulates the concept of Platonic love; *Cornelia* Cornelia (second century BCE), daughter of Scipio Africanus and mother of the Gracchi, whom she educated; *Cassandra* Cassandra Fedele (1465–1558), Italian scholar and orator, *Hildegardis* St. Hildegard of Bingen (1098–1179), German writer and mystic.
4   *Bartholomew day* St. Bartholomew the Apostle's feast day, which is 24 August. Coryate refers to the old style date of 14 August, following the Julian calendar.

many women were at their divine orisons prostrate before the image, and very secretly conveyed my fingers into a little basket (nobody taking notice thereof) where the images were laid; and so purloined one of them out, and brought him home into England. Which had it been at that time perceived, perhaps it might have cost me the lying in the Inquisition[1] longer than I would willingly have endured it.

[…]

I departed from Brescia about eight of the clock in the morning the sixteenth day of August being Tuesday, and came to Bergomum commonly called Bergamo the last city of the Venetian signiory about seven of the clock in the evening.

[…]

My observations of Bergamo […]

It was my chance to be here at the time of their fair the next day after Bartholomew day, which lasts a whole week; being kept in a large plain a little way distant from the lower part of the city. This was the greatest fair that ever I saw in my life, except that of Frankfurt in Germany, whereof I will hereafter speak. For there was a great concourse of people not only from the cities of Lombardy, but also from many other principal cities of Italy: besides many Germans both out of the Grisons country and Switzerland repair hither at this time, exceeding plenty of all manner of commodities being there sold.

[…]

This city yielded me the worst lodging for one night that I found in all my travels out of England. For all the inns were so extreme full of people by reason of the fair, that I could not get a convenient lodging though I would have given two or three ducats for it. So that I was fain to lie upon straw in one of their stables at the horses' feet,

---

1   *Inquisition* Ecclesiastical court of justice that presided over cases of heresy in Catholic countries from the sixteenth through the eighteenth centuries (mid-nineteenth in Spain).

according to a picture that I have made of it in the frontispiece of my book.[1] Where (notwithstanding my repose upon so uncouth a pallet) I slept in *utramque aurem*,[2] even as securely as upon a bed of down, because of my long journey the day before. And it was long before I could obtain this favour, which was at last granted me by the means of an honest Italian priest who had been a traveller. Unto whom I was not a little beholding for some courtesies that I received at his hands in Bergamo. He promised to revisit me the next morning, to the end to show me the antiquities of the city. But he was prevented to my great grief by the villainy of a certain blood-thirsty Italian, who for an old grudge he bare to him, shot him through the body in his lodging with a pewternell.[3]

Also a certain Dominican friar of this city called Vincentius de Petrengo [...] did so greatly gratify me in this city, that I cannot conveniently let him pass in this treatise of Bergamo, without some kind of mention of his name. For I received a special favour at his hands, which was this. When I was to go forth of the city towards the Grisons country, and so into Germany, being ignorant of the way, I repaired to the Augustinian friars to crave some directions of them for my journey. But none of them could direct me themselves, though very kindly they brought me acquainted with this foresaid Dominican, to the end he should satisfy me about the matter, because he had lived within these few years in the territory of the Grisons, as a chaplain to a certain *clarissimo* of Venice that was sent ambassador unto them, at what time he preached against the Calvinists of their country, as he himself told me. Truly he gave me as friendly counsel as any Protestant could have done. For he told me what dangers there were betwixt that and Germany, and the means how I might avoid them: that I was a Calvinist, he said he was fully persuaded, because I was an Englishman. Notwithstanding he would willingly give me the best counsel he could, in regard I was a stranger in those parts. Therefore he signified unto me that it would be very dangerous for me to pass in one place of the Grisons country within a few miles after the entrance thereof, if I were not very circumspect. For he said there was a certain castle seated by the lake of Como which was possessed and

---

1   *frontispiece ... book* See the engraved title page (page 212, illustration "M").
2   *utramque aurem* Latin: soundly.
3   *pewternell* Petronel, a large pistol.

guarded by a garrison of Spaniards, by which if I should happen to take my journey, they would lay their Inquisition upon me, as soon as they should perceive that I was an Englishman, and so consequently torture me with extreme cruelty, if they saw me constant in the profession of my religion, till they might compel me to abjure it, which if I would not do by the violence of their punishments, then at last they would put me to death, and excarnificate me after a very bitter and terrible manner. For the avoiding of which dangers he counseled me to leave the castle on the left hand of my way, and so to pass on the right hand towards a town called Chiavenna. Thus by the kind advice of this honest friar I took such a way in the Grisons country, that I shunned the Spanish Inquisition, which otherwise would not (I believe) have given me leave to bring thus much news out of Italy into England, except I would have renounced my religion, which God forbid I should ever do, notwithstanding any torments of Spaniards or any other enemies of the gospel of Christ. I am sure all kind of friars will not give Protestants the like counsel to eschew the bloody Spanish *carnificina*, (which is almost as cruel a punishment as Phalaris his brazen bull, or the exquisitest[1] torments that the Sicilian tyrants were wont to inflict upon offenders) but on the contrary side endeavour rather to entrap them therein. [...]

The end of my observations of Italy.

The beginning of my observations of Helvetia, otherwise called Switzerland [...]

This country of Switzerland is situate betwixt the mountain Jura,[2] the lake Lemanus (which is otherwise called the Lake Losanna), Italy, and the river Rhine.

[...]

---

1   *carnificina* Latin: torture; *Phalaris* Sixth-century Sicilian tyrant who placed his enemies inside a hollow brass bull statue heated by a fire beneath; *exquisitest* Most exquisite, i.e., excruciating.
2   *mountain Jura* Jura Mountains.

I [...] came to Zurich [...] about four of the clock the next morning being Friday, where I solaced myself all that day, and the better part of the next day with the learned Protestants of the city. I passed thirty-five English miles upon the Helvetian lake betwixt Walastat[1] and Zurich.

My observations of Zurich, in Latin Tigurum, the Metropolitan city of Switzerland

Such is the antiquity of this city, that it is thought it was built in the time of Abraham (which was about two thousand years before the incarnation of Christ, and thirteen hundred years before the foundation of Rome) as Rodolphus Hospinianus[2] that glittering lamp of learning, a most eloquent and famous preacher of this city told me; together with two more, Solodurum another fair city of Switzerland, & Trevirs[3] in the Netherlands, which by reason that they were built about one time are called the three sister cities of Germany.[4]

[...]

I was in their armoury unto the which I had access by the means of a worthy learned man of the city, a great professor of eloquence, a singular linguist. [...] Truly I have seen far greater armouries than this, as that of Milan, but especially those of the arsenal of Venice. Also our own in the Tower of London[5] yields more store of munition than this: but never in my life did I see so well a furnished place for the quantity. Amongst the rest of those things that this armoury does present, it yields more notable antiquities than ever I saw in any armoury before. For here I saw those arrows which the ancient

---

1 *Helvetian lake* Lake Zurich; *Walastat* Waldenstadt.
2 *Rodolphus Hospinianus* Swiss historian and theologian (1547–1626).
3 *Solodurum* Solothurn; *Trevirs* Trier, Germany, which borders Luxembourg and was once included in the historical region known as the Low Countries (i.e., not in the modern Netherlands).
4 *sister cities of Germany* These cities, located in Switzerland and "the Netherlands," are said to be "of Germany" because all three are located in the historic region of the Holy Roman Empire.
5 *Tower of London* London castle on the north bank of the Thames. Once a royal residence, the Tower was used as an arsenal and prison in the sixteenth and seventeenth centuries.

Helvetians[1] used in the time of Julius Caesar, when they fought with the Romans. They are very short, but exceeding big, being above two inches in compass, and headed with great three-forked heads. Of these arrows I saw a great quantity. Likewise the banners & ancients that the Helvetians displayed in the field against the Romans, which are almost eaten out with antiquity; and many of the Romans' ensigns with their arms in them, even the eagle, which the Helvetians won from them in fight. These banners are something less than those that are used in this age. Also I observed many shields which they used in their skirmishes with the Romans, being made of sinews, one whereof I saw exceedingly mangled, and hackled with strokes of swords, &c. All these things are shown in one of the higher rooms of the armoury. For it consists of many fair rooms most curiously kept. Also there is shown another most worthy monument in the same room, even the sword of William Tell[2][....] But to return once more to this higher room of the armoury; besides these foresaid antiquities, here I observed a marvellous multitude of costlets,[3] and head pieces, and a great deal of complete armour of proof,[4] for the whole body, which is so finely disposed in order, and so elegantly kept, that it yields a wondrous fair show.

At the upper end of this room I saw two artificial men standing a pretty distance from each other, even at the corners of the room, armed with their complete armour of proof, and crested helmets upon their heads, which a stranger at the first entrance of the room would conjecture to be living, and very natural men standing in their armour; this also gives no small grace to the room.

[...]

The habits of the citizens do in some things differ from the attire of any nation that ever I saw before. For all the men do wear round breeches[5] with codpieces. So that you shall not find one man in all

---

1   *Helvetians* Swiss, from Helvetica, the Latin name for Switzerland.
2   *William Tell* Legendary fourteenth-century Swiss freedom-fighter, coerced to fire an arrow at an apple placed atop his son's head.
3   *costlets* Corslets, or pieces of body armor.
4   *armour of proof* Proofed, or tested, armor.
5   *round breeches* Roomy (round) garment covering the legs down to the knees.

Zurich from a boy of ten years old to an old man of the age of a hundred years, but he wears a codpiece. Also all their men do wear flat caps and ruff bands.[1] For I could not see one man or boy in the whole city wear a falling band.[2] Many of their women, especially maids do use a very strange and fantastical fashion with their hair that I never saw before, but the like I observed afterward in many other places of Switzerland, especially in Basel. For they plait[3] it in two very long locks that hang down over their shoulders half a yard long. And many of them do twist it together with pretty silk ribbons or fillets of sundry colours.

[...]

About an English mile directly beyond the city westward, I saw a place where malefactors are punished, which is a certain green place, made in the form of a pit, near unto the which there stands a little chapel, wherein some clergyman does minister ghostly counsel unto the offender before he goes to execution. In that chapel I saw wheels.[4] If they should happen to tremble so much that they cannot stand upright (as sometimes offenders do) they are punished in the chapel. As about some fourteen years before I was at Zurich, three noble Tigurines[5] were beheaded in that chapel because they were so inclined to trembling that they could not stand upright. The punishments that are inflicted upon offenders are diverse, in number five, whereof the first is beheading, which punishment they only do sustain that are incestuous men or highway robbers. The second is the gallows, upon the which those are executed that commit burglary or burn houses. The third is the water, which incestuous women do suffer, being drowned therein. The fourth is the fire wherewith witches, sorcerers, and heretics are punished; and after their bodies are burnt, their ashes are cast into the River Sylla[6] aforesaid. The fifth and last punishment is wheeling, which is only for murderers.

---

1   *ruff bands* Stiff collars holding ruffs, or lacy frills, about the neck.
2   *falling band* Unstiffened collar draped over the back, chest, and shoulders.
3   *plait* Braid.
4   *wheels* Instruments of torture.
5   *Tigurines* Residents of Zurich.
6   *River Sylla* Sihl river.

[…]

To conclude this narration of Zurich: I attribute so much to this noble city, that for sweetness of situation, and that wonderful exuberancy of all things whatsoever tending both to profit and pleasure, I compare it at the least even with Mantua herself, in Italy, whom before I have so highly extolled, if not prefer it before the same: though indeed that be greater in compass than this. For that is four Italian miles about, but the circuit of this comprehends no more then half a Helvetian mile, which is but two English miles and a half.

Thus much of Zurich

[…]

I departed from Zurich upon a Saturday being the seven and twentieth of August, about two of the clock in the afternoon (being conducted about two miles in my way by my friends Mr. Thomannus and Marcus Buelerus, who at our final departing bedewed his cheeks with tears) and came to a place nine English miles beyond it called Maristella, which is hard by the river Limacus,[1] about eight of the clock in the evening. I passed the river in a boat, and lay that night in a solitary house by the riverside. Betwixt Zurich and Maristella I observed a passing fair and spacious country full of excellent fair cornfields. About eight miles beyond Zurich I passed by a certain chapel standing by the highway side wherein was an exceeding massy multitude of dead men's bones and skulls heaped together. These are said to be the skulls of the soldiers of Charles the Great Duke of Burgundy, (whom I have before mentioned in my notes of Zurich) and the Switzers, who not far from this place fought a great battle, in which there was great slaughter on both sides.

I departed from Maristella the next morning being Sunday and the eight and twentieth of August about seven of the clock, and came to

---

1   *Mr. Thomannus* "Prefect of the corn market" in Zurich, as Coryate mentions in a passage omitted from this edition; *Marcus Buelerus* As mentioned in a passage omitted from this edition, Buelerus was "a certain learned young man of the city … unto whom [Coryate] was exceedingly beholding for the sight of most of the principal things of Zurich"; *Maristella* Wettingen; *river Limacus* Limmat river.

the city of Baden commonly called ober Baden,[1] two English miles beyond it, about eight of the clock.

[...]

One thing I observed in the German cities that I could not perceive in any place of France, Savoy, Italy, or Rhetia,[2] namely, the heads of boars nailed upon the doors of dwelling houses of cities and towns. The first that I saw in Germany were in this city of Baden. For here I saw many of them hanged upon the doors both at the entrance into the city, and in the fairest street. These heads are of certain wild boars that the people do kill in hunting in the forests and woods of the country, which hunting of wild boars is more exercised by the Germans than by any other Christian nation. And it is the custom of the country whensoever they have killed any great boar to cut off his head, and erect it in that manner as I have already spoken. The like I observed afterward in many other German cities.

[...]

I departed from this city about ten of the clock the same Sunday, and took my journey directly towards the baths which are within half an English mile of the city. For Master Hospinian[3] of Zurich did earnestly counsel me to see them, as being a place very worthy my observation. But there happened such a sinister accident unto me upon the way, that it was very difficult for me to find them out; whereby I verified the old speech, though indeed the same be properly spoken in another sense, *difficilia quae pulchra*.[4] For by reason that I was ignorant of the Dutch[5] language, those that met me by the way could not understand my speeches, and so gave me no certain directions to find out the place. Whereupon I went five English miles beyond it before I could learn any news of it, even to the famous

---

1 *ober Baden* German: upper Baden, to distinguish Baden, Switzerland, from Baden-Baden, Germany.
2 *Rhetia* Historical region in Switzerland.
3 *Master Hospinian* Rodolphus Hospinianus, mentioned above.
4 *difficilia quae pulchra* Latin: Beautiful things are difficult.
5 *Dutch* German.

monastery of Kiningsfelden near the city of Brooke.[1] Which accident ministered occasion unto me to see certain memorable monuments in this foresaid monastery, which I had not seen, if this occurrence had not driven me thither. Here I happened to insinuate myself into the acquaintance of an honest sociable scholar, who very courteously walked with me five miles back to the baths. For I was struck with such an ardent desire to see them, that I could not be satisfied before I had been there, though it were forth and back ten miles out of my way. Therefore I will first describe them, and after return to the discourse of the monastery again.

My observations of the baths of Baden

Certainly this is the sweetest place for baths that ever I saw, by many degrees excelling our English baths both in quantity and quality. The antiquity of them is such, that (as a certain learned man told me in the same place) it is thought they were found out before the incarnation of Christ. The place is called Hinderhove, being seated in a low bottom about a bowshot from the highway, and about half an English mile westward from the highway, and about half an English mile westward from the city of Baden. They are much the more commodiously and pleasantly situate by reason of the sweet river Limacus running by them, which divides them into two parts, the greater and the lesser. For those on this side the river are called the greater, and those beyond it the lesser. The baths are distinguished asunder by several houses that are nothing else than inns serving for the entertainment of strangers. And whereas every inn has his proper sign, the baths have their names from the same signs. As in one inn which has the sign of the bear, the baths in the same place being in number six are called the bear baths, and so the rest of the baths have their denomination from their peculiar signs. In another inn called the sun are eight, in a place called the Statehove eleven, at the sign of the crown seven, at the flower three, at the ox six, in a place called by the same name that is the general appellation of all the baths, *viz*. Hinderhove, seventeen, in an open court *sub dio* two public baths, whereof one is the greatest of them all; in which I told seven and thirty poor people bathing of

---

1   *monastery of Kiningsfelden* Königsfelden Monastery; *Brooke* Brugg.

themselves. For these two serve only for the plebeian and poorer sort. So that the total number of them amounts to threescore. None are admitted to these baths in the inns but the richer sort, and such as do sojourn in the same. For many of the strangers are tabled there for a certain stinted[1] price by the week. And some of the thriftier sort only pay for their lodging, and procure them provision from the city. For it is a place of great charge to them that pay for their weekly diet. Although the number of the baths be so great as I have already spoken, yet the original fountains that feed them all are but few, no more than two, which are so hot at the first spring thereof, that a man can hardly endure to touch them with his bare hands, the like whereof I will report hereafter of the baths of the lower Baden in the Marquisate.[2] Howbeit the water of these baths themselves is of a very moderate temperature. Here was a great concourse of people at the time of my being there, which was at the autumn, even the eight and twentieth day of August; as at the same time every year many resort thither from Zurich, Basel, Bern, and most of the Helvetical cities, and from the city of Konstanz, &c. the strangers that are to be seen in Hinderhove, amounting sometimes to the number of a thousand persons, besides some few that lie abroad in the country for the bath's sake. Many of those people that lay at Hinderhove when I was there were gentlemen of great worth that repaired thither from the foresaid cities partly for infirmity's sake, and partly for mere pleasure and recreation. Most of the private baths are but little, but very delicate and pleasant places, being divided asunder by certain convenient partitions wherein are contrived diverse windows, to the end that those in the baths may have recourse to each other, and mutually drink together. For they reach out their drinking glasses one to another through the windows. The rooms overhead are lodgings for the strangers. Here I have observed the people in the baths feed together upon a table that has swum upon the superficies[3] of the water. Also I have noted another strange thing amongst them that I have not a little wondered at. Men and women bathing themselves together naked from the middle upward in one bath: whereof some of the women were wives (as I was told) and the men partly bachelors, and partly married men, but not

---

1   *tabled* Provided with hospitality; *stinted* Fixed.
2   *lower ... Marquisate* Baden-Baden, Germany, in the Margraviate of Baden.
3   *superficies* Surface.

the husbands of the same women. Yet their husbands have been at that time at Hinderhove, and some of them in the very place standing hard by the bath in their clothes, and beholding their wives not only talking and familiarly discoursing with other men, but also sporting after a very pleasant and merry manner. Yea sometimes they sing merrily together but especially that sweet & most amorous song of *solus cum sola*;[1] I mean another man's wife, & another man naked upward (as I have aforesaid) in one bath. Yet all this while the husband may not be jealous though he be at the baths, and sees too much occasion of jealousy ministered unto him. For the very name of jealousy is odious in this place. But let these Germans and Helvetians do as they list, and observe these kind of wanton customs as long as they will; for mine own part were I a married man, and meant to spend some little time here with my wife for solace and recreation sake, truly I should hardly be persuaded to suffer her to bathe herself naked in one and the selfsame bath with one only bachelor or married man with her, because if she was fair, and had an attractive countenance, she might perhaps cornify[2] me. For I might have just cause to fear lest if she went into the water with the effigies of a male lamb characterized upon her belly, the same might within a few hours grow to be an horned ram[3] (according to a merry tale that I have sometimes heard) before she should return again to my company. Here also I saw many passing fair young ladies and gentlewomen naked in the baths with their wooers and favourites in the same. For at this time of the year many wooers come thither to solace themselves with their beautiful mistresses. Many of these young ladies had the hair of their head very curiously plaited in locks, & they wore certain pretty garlands upon their heads made of fragrant and odoriferous flowers—a spectacle exceeding amorous. A certain learned man that I found bathing himself in one of the baths, told me that Henry Pantaleon[4] that famous philosopher and physician of Basel, (who made his abode two or three

---

1   *solus cum sola* Latin: a man and woman alone together. The English composer John Dowland wrote a piece of music of the same name for the lute.

2   *cornify* Literally, to fit with horns, here meaning to cuckold.

3   *effigies* Image; *characterized* Imprinted; *grow to be an horned ram* The lamb image would transform as her belly grew (through pregnancy), with the horns on the ram suggestive of the figurative horns worn by the cuckolded husband.

4   *Henry Pantaleon* Heinrich Pantaleon (1522–95), Swiss physician.

years in this place) has written a peculiar book of the virtue and effect of these baths. Moreover he affirmed that they are of very sovereign virtue for the curing of these infirmities, *viz.* the tertian and quartan ague, the itch, the colic and the stone;[1] and it has one most rare virtue that I never heard of any baths in all the world. For he told me that they are of admirable efficacy to cure the sterility of women, and make those that are barren, very fruitful bearers of children. A matter verified and certainly confirmed by the experience of many women. The water of the baths is mingled with great store of brimstone and a small quantity of alum, (as Munster affirms, from whom I derive these few lines following concerning the virtue of the baths) by means whereof it heats and dries up all noisome and cold humours.[2] Also it is good for those infirmities which proceed from the cold of the head, as the lethargy, the apoplexy,[3] the diseases of the ears and eyes. It consumes the fleame, heats and dries up the stomach, helps the digestive faculty, opens the obstructions of the liver and spleen, assuages the biting and fretting[4] of the guts, appeases the pain of the members that proceeds from cold, and to conclude, it cleanses the skin from spots and freckles. But it hurts those that have a hot and dry[5] complexion, and such as are weakened with the consumption. But old-folks, of what sex soever they are, reap no benefit by these baths. A place that imparts his virtue after a partial manner rather to the feminine than masculine kind. And so finally I end this discourse of the Helvetical baths of Hinderhove with that elegant elogium of Poggius the Florentine in praise of the same, even

---

1   *tertian and quartan ague* Fever occurring every third or fourth day, respectively; *the itch* Skin disease; *the colic* Severe stomach pain; *the stone* Disease marked by the formation of gall- or kidney-stones.

2   *Munster* Sebastian Münster (1448–1552), German scholar and author of *Cosmographia universalis* (1544), a text Coryate cites throughout the German sections of *Crudities*; *cold humours* According to ancient humoral theory, four substances influenced the human body (phlegm, blood, yellow bile, and black bile), each being associated with a state of mind (phlegmatic, sanguine, choleric, and melancholy, respectively). Between each of these humors lay the complexions of wet, hot, dry, and cold. Cold humors would involve phlegm and/or black bile, causing phlegmatic (apathetic) and/or melancholic behavior.

3   *apoplexy* Sudden illness affecting sense and movement.

4   *fleame* Phlegm, here meaning mucus; *biting and fretting* Pain.

5   *hot and dry* Someone having both hot and dry complexions would be choleric (irritable).

that it is a second paradise, the seat of the Graces,[1] the bosom of love, and the theatre of pleasure.

Thus much of the Helvetical baths of Hinderhove commonly called the baths of Baden.

[...]

My observations of Basel, in Latin Basilea [...]

Surely it is exceeding sweetly situate, having on one side of the Rhine a pleasant plain that yields great abundance of wine and corn, but especially corn; on the other side hills, in number three, whereon one part of the city stands. Also the air of this city is esteemed as sweet and comfortable as in any city of the whole world, as a certain English gentleman told me that sojourned in the university for learning sake at the time of my being there, who affirmed that it was the most delectable place for air that ever he lived in. Again, it is as finely watered as ever I saw a city, partly with goodly rivers, and partly with pleasant springs or fountains that do incessantly flow out of delicate conduits.

[...]

The cathedral church is dedicated to our Lady, and stands in the greater city. A building of singular magnificence and beauty, the sight whereof and that passing variety of worthy monuments in the same gave me such true content, that I must needs say I prefer it before the fairest church I saw in Germany, though the cathedral churches of Strasbourg, Spier, Worms, Mainz, and Cologne be greater. [...] But to return to this glorious and most elegant church of Basel the very queen of all the German churches that I saw, according as I have before entitled our Lady church at Amiens of the French churches; truly I extol it so highly that I esteem it the most beautiful Protestant

---

1   *elogium* Explanatory inscription; *Poggius the Florentine* Poggio Bracciolini (1380–1459), Italian humanist, manuscript hunter, and author of facetiae. Coryate refers to Bracciolini's letter to Nicholaus de Niccolis, dated 1416, in which he describes the baths at Baden; *Graces* Minor Greco-Roman goddesses representing splendor, cheerfulness, and mirth.

church that ever I saw, saving our two in London of Paul's and West-minster,[1] which do very little excel this in beauty (though something in greatness) if anything at all. [...] Truly I observed every thing in the body of this church disposed in such a comely order, and so trimly kept, that it did even tickle my soul with spiritual joy to behold the same, and so I think it will every zealous and godly Protestant, in so much that I did even congratulate and applaud the religious indus-try of the Baselians. And I am persuaded that one godly prayer pro-nounced in this church by a penitent and contrite-hearted Christian in the holy congregation of the citizens, to the omnipotent Jehovah through the only mediation of his son Jesus Christ, is of more efficacy, and does sooner penetrate into the ears of the lord, than a century yea a whole myriad of Ave Maries[2] mumbled out upon beads in that superstitious manner as I have often seen at the glittering altars of the popish churches. The quire is very decently graced with many fair pillars, and the frontispiece thereof marvellously adorned with gilt escutcheons and arms of diverse royal and princely potentates. On the left hand of the body of the church as you enter into the quire, I saw the sepulcher of that thrice-famous Erasmus Roterodamus[3] that phoenix of Christendom, and well deserving man of the common-weal of learning, who was so delighted with the noble city of Basel, that he studied here many years together, being a great benefactor to the city as I will hereafter mention, and at last finished his life in the same. His body lies interred under a flat stone, near to the which is erected a beautiful pillar of red marble about three yards high (ac-cording to my estimation) two foot thick, and an ell broad, at the top whereof the effigies of his face is expressed, with this word *Terminus* (by which impress[4] I think is meant that death is the end of all things) written under it in golden letters.

[...]

---

1   *Paul's and Westminster*   St. Paul's Cathedral and Westminster Abbey, London.

2   *century*   One hundred;   *Ave Maries*   Ave Marias (Hail Marys), common Catholic prayers devoted to the Virgin Mary.

3   *Erasmus Roterodamus*   Desiderius Erasmus (c. 1466–1536) of Rotterdam, Dutch humanist writer, editor, and theologian.

4   *ell*   The length of the historical English ell is forty-five inches;   *Terminus*   Latin: The end; *impress*   Motto.

Many other notable epitaphs I saw there, which the shortness of my abode in Basel and the urgent occasions of calling me away therehence would not permit me to write out, as of Hierom Frobenius, and Michael Isingrius,[1] two famous printers of the city, &c. But what is now wanting, I hope shall be hereafter supplied; for by God's grace I will one day see Basel again.

[...]

The men of this city wear great codpieces and ruff bands as the Tigurines do. Also they wear a strange kind of hat, wherein they differ from all other Switzers that I saw in Helvetia. It is made in the form of a cap, very long crowned, whereof some are made of felt, and some of a kind of stuff not unlike to shag in outward view. It has no brims at all, but a high flap turned up behind, which reaches almost to the top of the hat, being lesser and lesser towards the top. This fashion is so common in the city, that not only all the men generally do wear it both citizens and academics (in so much that Amandus Pollanus[2] wore the same in the divinity school) but also the women whatsoever, both young and old. Moreover their women, especially maids do wear two such plaited rolls of hair over their shoulders wherein are twisted ribbons of diverse colours at the ends, as the women of Zurich. I observed many women of this city to be as beautiful and fair as any I saw in all my travels: but I will not attribute so much to them as to compare them with our English women, whom I justly prefer, and that without any partiality of affection, before any women that I saw in my travels, for an elegant and most attractive natural beauty.

The diet in their principal inns is passing good, especially at their ordinaries.[3] For the variety of meat and that of the better sort, it is so great that I have not observed the like in any place in my whole journey saving at Zurich. But indeed it is something dear, no less than eight battes[4] a meal, which are twenty pence of our money. They use to sit long at supper, even an hour and a half at the least, or almost

---

1   *Hierom ... Isingrius* Hieronymus Froben (1501–63) and Michael Isengrin (1500–57), printers of Basel.
2   *Amandus Pollanus* Amandus Polanus von Polansdorf (1561–1610), Swiss theologian.
3   *ordinaries* Taverns.
4   *battes* Batz, small coin used in Switzerland and Southern Germany.

two hours. The first noble carousing that I saw in Germany was at mine inn in Basel. Where I saw the Germans drink helter-skelter very sociably, exempting myself from their liquid impositions as well as I could. It is their custom whensoever they drink to another, to see their glass filled up incontinent,[1] (for therein they most commonly drink) and then they deliver it into the hand of him to whom they drink, esteeming him a very courteous man that does pledge the whole, according to the old verse:

Germanus mihi frater eris si pocula siccas.[2]

But on the contrary side, they deem that man for a very rustic and unsociable peasant, utterly unworthy of their company, that will not with reciprocal turns mutually retaliate a health. And they verify the old speech ἢ πίθι ἢ ἄπιθι,[3] that is, either drink or be gone. For though they will not offer any villainy or injury unto him that refuses to pledge him the whole, (which I have often seen in England to my great grief) yet they will so little regard him, that they will scarce vouchsafe[4] to converse with him. Truly I have heard Germany much dispraised for drunkenness before I saw it; but that vice reigns no more there (that I could perceive) than in other countries. For I saw no man drunk in any place of Germany, though I was in many goodly cities, and in much notable company. I would to God the imputation of that vice could not be almost as truly cast upon mine own nation as upon Germany. Besides I observed that they impose not such an inevitable necessity of drinking a whole health, especially those of the greater size, as many of our English gallants do, a custom (in my opinion) most barbarous, and fitter to be used amongst the rude Scythians and Goths[5] than civil Christians: yet so frequently practised in England, that I have often most heartily wished it were clean

---

1 *incontinent* Without restraint.
2 *Germanus ... siccas* Latin: German, you will be my brother if you drain the cup.
3 ἢ πίθι ἢ ἄπιθι Greek: e pithi e apithi.
4 *vouchsafe* Permit.
5 *Scythians and Goths* Bywords for barbarian. Scythians came from Scythia, a historical region comprising parts of Europe and Asia, while Goths were warring Germanic tribes that invaded the Roman Empire.

abolished out of our land, as being no small blemish to so renowned and well governed a kingdom as England is.

[...]

I made my abode in Basel all Tuesday after nine of the clock in the morning, all Wednesday being the one and thirtieth and last of August, and departed therehence in a bark *secundo cursu*[1] upon the river Rhine betwixt five and six of the clock in the morning the first day of September being Thursday, and came to the city of Strasbourg, which is fourscore English miles beyond it, about eleven of the clock the next morning being Friday, and the second day of September.

[...]

My observations of some parts of high Germany [...]

My observations of Argentina or Argentoratum, commonly called Strasbourg the Metropolitan city of Alsatia [...]

Strasbourg stands in the lower Alsatia,[2] and is situate in a very pleasant and delectable plain about a quarter of an English mile distant from the Rhine, yet well watered with three other rivers, as the Kintzgus, the Ilia, and the Bruschus,[3] whereof the last runs through a part of the city; a place of such passing fatness and fertility (as a certain English merchant told me called Robert Kingman a Herefordshire man born, but then commorant in Strasbourg with his whole family when I was there) that for amenity of situation and exceeding plenty of all things that the heart of man can wish for, it does far excel all the other cities of the same territory, though some of them are very fair.

[...]

---

1   *secundo cursu* Latin: in a favorable course.
2   *lower Alsatia* Northern region of Alsace, a historically German region conquered by France in 1639.
3   *Kintzgus, the Illia, and the Bruschus* Ill river and two tributaries of the Rhine.

There are many goodly things in this renowned city that do much beautify the same. As the loftiness of the building, the multitude of their houses, the beauty and spaciousness of their streets and the clean keeping thereof, the great frequency of people, their strong walls made of hard stone, and adorned with stately battlements, diverse towers, strong bulwarks, fair gates, mighty and deep trenches that are moated round about. [...] But the principal things of all which do especially illustrate and garnish Strasbourg are but two, which because they are the most matchless and incomparable fabrics of all Christendom, no city whatsoever in all Europe yielding the like, I will something particularly discourse thereof. These are the tower of the cathedral church and a clock within the church.

[...]

Surely the same is by many degrees the exquisitest piece of work for a tower that ever I saw, as well for the height, as for the rare curiosity of the architecture; so that neither France, Italy, nor any city in Switzerland or vast Germany, nor of any province or island whatsoever within the precincts of the Christian world can show the like. It was begun in the year 1277 at what time Rodolph Earl of Habsburg[1] was emperor of Germany, and was continually building for the space of eight and twenty years together, till it was brought to full perfection. The principal architect was one Ervinus of Steinbach (as the author of those excellent hexameter verses[2] which I have prefixed before this description of Strasbourg does testify) who contrived the whole model of the work himself, and was the chief mason in the performing of this peerless machine, which he raised from the very foundation to the top with square stones most artificially and rarely cut. The stairs that lead up to the tower, are made windingly, being distinguished with four several degrees, and where the thickness does begin to be acuminated in a slender top, there are eight degrees more of those winding stairs that rise above the first four. The ball which stands

---

1 *Rodolph Earl of Habsburg* Rudolf I (1218–91), King of Germany and founder of the Habsburg dynasty.
2 *Ervinus of Steinbach* Erwin Von Steinbach (d. 1318), German architect; *excellent hexameter verses* Referring to Latin verses "in a certain elegant book" by George Sidenham; Coryate begins the section on Strasbourg with these verses (in a section omitted from this edition).

upon the highest top of all, seems to those that are beneath upon the ground, no greater than a bushel, yet the circumference thereof is so large that it will well contain five or six sufficient and stout men upon the same. The manifold images, pinnacles, & most curious devices carved in stone that are erected round about the compass of the tower, are things of such singular beauty, that they are very admirable to behold, and such as will by reason of the rare novelty of the work, drive a stranger that is but a novice into a very ecstasy of admiration. Also the altitude of it is so strange that from the bottom to the top it is said to contain five hundred seventy four geometrical feet, which much exceeds the famous Italian towers, as that of Cremona, which is esteemed the loftiest of all Italy, Saint Mark's of Venice, which although it be but two hundred eighty feet high, yet the Venetians do account it a tower of notable height, as indeed it seems to all those that come to Venice by sea. Likewise the slender tower of Vicenza is very high: but they all are much inferior to this unmatchable tower of Strasbourg. Wherefore to conclude this discourse of this tower, I attribute so much unto it, that I account it one of the principal wonders of Christendom.

The second notable thing is a clock (as I have already spoken) which stands at the south side of the church near to the door. A true figure or representation whereof, made according to the form itself as it stands at this day in the church I have expressed in this place.[1] Truly it is a fabric so extraordinarily rare and artificial that I am confidently persuaded it is the most exquisite piece of work of that kind in all Europe. I think I should not commit any great error if I should say in all the world: the bolder I am to affirm it, because I have heard very famous travellers (such as have seen this clock and most of the principal things of Christendom) report the same. It was begun to be built in the year 1571 in the month of June by a most excellent architect & mathematician of the city of Strasbourg, who was then alive when I was there. His name is Conradus Dasypodius,[2] once the ordinary professor of the mathematics in the university of this city: a man that for his excellent art may very fitly be called the

---

1 *true figure … this place* See the image on the next page, one of five engraved plates included in Coryate's travelogue.
2 *Conradus Dasypodius* Konrad Dasypodius (1532–1600), Strasbourg mathematician.

Strasbourg Cathedral Clock, from *Coryats Crudities*.

Archimedes[1] of Strasbourg. It was ended about three years after, even in the year 1574 in the same month of June about the feast of Saint John Baptist.[2] This work contains by my estimation about fifty feet in height betwixt the bottom and the top; it is compassed in with three several rails, to the end to exclude all persons that none may approach near it to disfigure any part of it, whereof the two outmost are made of timber, the third of iron about three yards high. On the left hand of it there is a very ingenious and methodical observation for the knowing of the eclipses of the sun and moon for thirty-two years. At the top whereof is written in fair Roman letters

Typi Eclipsium
Solis et Lunae
ad annos xxxii.[3]

On the same hand ascends a very fair architectonic[4] machine made of wainscot with great curiosity, the sides being adorned with pretty little pillars of marble of diverse colours, in which are three degrees, whereof each contains a fair statue carved in wainscot: the first the statue of Urania[5] one of the nine muses, above which her name is written in golden letters, and by the sides these two words in the like golden letters, *Arithmetica & Geometria*. The second the picture of a certain king with a regal scepter in his hand. But what king it is I know not. Above him is written Daniel 2. Cap.[6] The last is the picture of Nicolaus Copernicus that rare astronomer, under whom this is written in fair Roman letters: *Nicolai Copernici vera effigies ex ipsius autographo depicta.*[7] At the very top of this row or series of work is erected a most excellent effigies of a cock which does passing curiously represent the living shape of that vocal creature, and it crows

---

1   *Archimedes* Greek inventor and mathematician (287–212 BCE).
2   *feast of Saint John Baptist* 24 June. St. John the Baptist was a preacher who, according to the Gospels, foretold the coming of Christ.
3   *Typi … xxxii* Latin: Models of eclipses of the sun and moon for thirty-two years.
4   *architectonic* Relating to architecture.
5   *Urania* Classical muse of astronomy.
6   *Daniel 2. Cap.* Second chapter of the Book of Daniel.
7   *Nicolaus Copernicus* Nicolas Koppernik or Copernicus (1473–1543), Polish astronomer who devised the heliocentric model of the universe; *Nicolai … depicta* Latin: The true painted image of Nicolaus Copernicus himself, from the autograph.

at certain hours, yielding as shrill and loud a voice as a natural cock, yea and such a kind of sound (which makes it the more admirable) as counterfeits very near the true voice of that bird. The hours are eleven of the clock in the morning, and three in the afternoon. It was my chance to hear him at the third hour in the afternoon, whereat I wondered as much as I should have done if I had seen that famous wooden pigeon of Architus Tarentinus[1] the philosopher (so much celebrated by the ancient historians) fly in the air. On the right hand also of this goodly architecture there is another row of building correspondent to the foresaid in height, but differing from it in form. For the principal part thereof consists of a pair of winding stairs made of free-stone, and most delicately composed. I could not perceive for what use they serve, so that I conjecture they are made especially for ornament. Again in the middle work betwixt these two notable rows that I have now described, is erected that incomparable fabric wherein the clock stands. At the lower end whereof, just about the middle, I observed the greatest astronomical globe[2] that ever I saw, which is supported with an artificial pelican wounding his breast with his beak, wherewith they typically represent Christ, who was wounded for the salvation and redemption of the world: and about the midst goes a compass of brass which is sustained with very elegant little turned pillars. Opposite unto which is a very large sphere beautified with many cunning conveyances and witty inventions. Directly above that stands another orb which with a needle (this is a mathematical term signifying a certain instrument about a clock) points at four hours only that are figured at the four corners thus: 1, 2, 3, 4, each figure at a several corner. At the sides of the orb two angels are represented, whereof the one holds a mace in his hand, with which he strikes a brazen serpent every hour, and hard by the same stands a death's head[3] finely resembled; the other an hourglass, which he moves likewise hourly. Notable objects tending to mortification.[4] Both the lower ends of this middle engine are very excellently graced with the

---

1 *famous ... Tarentinus* Archytas (fl. c. 400–350 BCE), from Tarentum (southern Italy), was a Greek mathematician who built a self-propelling flying device, the "wooden pigeon" mentioned here.

2 *astronomical globe* Globe depicting the constellations.

3 *death's head* Skull.

4 *Notable ... mortification* I.e., the objects are memento mori, or reminders of death.

portraiture of two huge lions carved in marble. This part of the third fabric wherein stands the clock, is illustrated with many notable sentences of the holy scripture written in Latin. As, *In principio creavit Deus coelum et terram.*[1] Gene, i cap. *Omnis caro foenum,*[2] Pet. i. cap. i. *Peccati stipendium mors est.*[3] Rom. 6. *Dei donum vita aeterna per Christum.*[4] Rom. 6. *Ascendisti in altum, cepisti captivitatem.*[5] Psal. 68. Again under the same are written these sentences in a lower degree: *Ecce ego creo coelos novos et terram novam.*[6] Esaiae 65. *Expergiscimini et laetamini qui habitatis in pulvere.*[7] Esa. 26. *Venite benedicti patris mei, possidete regnum vobis paratum. Discedite a me maledicti in ignem aeternum.*[8] Math. 25. Above these sentences diverse goodly arms are advanced and beautified with fair escutcheons. Under the same many curious pictures are drawn which present only histories of the Bible. Again above that orb which I have already mentioned, there is erected another orb or sphere wherein are figured the hours distinguishing time, and a great company of mathematic conceits which do decipher some of the most abstruse & secret mysteries of the noble science of astronomy. Likewise another orb stands above this that I last spoke of, within the which is expressed the figure of a half moon and many glittering stars set forth most gloriously in gold, and again without are formed four half moons and two full moons. Above the higher part of this orb this empresa is written: *Quae est haec tam illustris, similis aurorae, pulchra ut Luna, pura ut Sol?*[9] At the sides of it beneath, this poesy is written, which is thus distributed: *Dominus lux mea*, on the left hand; & this on the right hand, *Quem timebo?*[10] Also above the same orb I observed another very exquisite device, even seven little pretty bells of brass (as I conceived it) standing together in one rank, and another little bell severally by itself above the rest. Within the

---

1   *In principio ... terram* Latin: In the beginning God created the heaven and the earth.
2   *Omnis caro foenum* Latin: All flesh is grass.
3   *Peccati ... est* Latin: The reward of sin is death.
4   *Dei ... Christum* Latin: The gift of God is eternal life through Christ.
5   *Ascendisti ... captivitatem* Latin: You ascended on high, leading captives.
6   *Ecce ... novam* Latin: Behold, I will create new heavens and a new earth.
7   *Expergiscimini ... pulvere* Latin: Awake and be joyful, you who dwell in dust.
8   *Venite ... aeternum* Latin: Come, you who are blessed of my father, possess the kingdom prepared for you. Depart from me, accursed ones, into the eternal fire.
9   *empresa* Motto; *Quae ... Sol?* Latin: Who is this so bright, like the dawn, beautiful as the moon, pure as the sun?
10 *Dominus lux mea* Latin: Lord, my light; *Quem timebo?* Latin: Whom shall I fear?

same is contrived a certain vacant or hollow place wherein stand certain artificial men so ingeniously made that I have not seen the like. These do come forth at every quarter of an hour with a very delightful and pleasant grace, holding small banners in their hands wherewith they strike these foresaid bells, every one in order *alternis vicibus*,[1] and supply each other with a pretty diligence and decorum in this quarterly function. Under the place where these two men do strike those foresaid bells, these two sacred emblems are written: *Ecclesia Christi exulans*: And, *Serpens antiquus Antichristus*.[2] The highest top of this fabric is framed with such surpassing curiosity that it yields a wonderful ornament to the whole engine, having many excellent little portraitures and fine devices contrived therein of free-stone, and garnished with borders and works of singular art. Moreover the corners of this middle work are decked with very beautiful little pillars of ash-coloured marble, whereof there stand two in a place, those above square, those beneath round. Thus have I something superficially described unto thee this famous clock of Strasbourg, being the phoenix of all the clocks of Christendom. For it does as far excel all other clocks that ever I saw before, as that of the piazza of St. Mark's in Venice, which I have already mentioned, that of Middelborough in Zeeland[3] which I afterward saw, and all others generally, as far (I say) as a fair young lady of the age of eighteen years that has been very elegantly brought up in the trimming of her beauty, does a homely and coarse trull[4] of the country, or a rich orient pearl a mean piece of amber.

But I am sorry I have not made that particular relation thereof as that excellent fabric does deserve. For these few observations which I have written of it I gathered in little more than half an hour, where I had no man's assistance to instruct me in the principal things that I doubted of, determining then to make a full description of those particulars that I have expressed in the effigies thereof, had I not been

---

1 *alternis vicibus* Latin: by alternate turns.
2 *Ecclesia Christi exulans* Latin: The church of Christ in exile; *Serpens antiquus Antichristus* Latin: The old serpent, antichrist.
3 *Middelborough in Zeeland* City of Middleburg in the southwestern region of the Netherlands.
4 *trull* Lass.

barred of opportunity by the sexton[1] that at that time that I was in the midst of my curious survey of the same, was to shut up the church doors. Howbeit I wish that that little which I have written of it (if it should happen to be read by any of the wealthy citizens of London) may be an encouragement to some wealthy fraternity to erect the like in Paul's church, or some other notable church of London for the better ornament of the metropolitan city of our famous island of Great Britain. A thing that I heartily wish I may one day see come to pass. Having therefore now ended this discourse of the clock (whereof I wish all English gentlemen that determine hereafter to see Strasbourg, to take an exact view, as a matter most worthy of their curious observation) I will return to the relation of some other memorable things of this city.

[...]

I observed that some of the women of this city do use that fashion of plaiting their hair in two long locks hanging down over their shoulders, as before in Zurich and Basel. But it is not a quarter so much used here as in Basel. As for those strange kind of caps that the women promiscuously[2] with the men do wear in Basel (as I have before said) none of them are used here, but most of the women, especially their matrons do wear very broad caps made of cloth, and furred, and many of them black velvet caps of as great a breadth.

[...]

I remained in Strasbourg all Friday after eleven of the clock in the morning, and departed therehence the Saturday following being the third day of September, about eleven of the clock in the morning. A little beyond the town's end of Strasbourg I passed a wooden bridge made over the Rhine that was a thousand fourscore and six paces long. For I paced it.

[...]

---

1 *sexton* Officer responsible for church maintenance.
2 *promiscuously* Indiscriminately.

About six of the clock in the afternoon I came to a Protestant town called Litenawe,[1] where I lay that night. This town is about sixteen English miles distant from Strasbourg.

[...]

I departed from the foresaid Litenawe a little after seven of the clock in the morning the next day being Sunday, and came to the city of Baden[2] the metropolis of the Marquisate of Baden, about four of the clock in the afternoon.

[...]

About a mile and half on this side Baden I observed a solitary monastery situate in a wood: being desirous to see it I went to the place, and craved to enter into it, but I could not by any means obtain access into the house: but one of the friars (for here dwell five Franciscans of the mendicant family)[3] to the end to give me some kind of recompense and amends for my repulse, like a very good fellow bestowed upon me a profound draught of good Rhenish wine, which gave great refection[4] to my barking stomach—a courtesy that I neither craved nor expected. Also he told me that their fraternity was much infested by the Lutheran faction of the country. As I departed therehence towards Baden I met one of the foresaid five riding homeward, who immediately returned again, and having overtaken me he discovered his grief unto me after a very pensive and disconsolate manner. For he told me that he had lost his breviary,[5] and asked me whether I had found any such book. This breviary is a certain kind of popish book containing prayers to their saints and other holy meditations, which priests and friars do as frequently use as we Protestants do the Bible. The first of them that I saw was in Venice. At last the friar after very diligent seeking having found his precious jewel, returned home once

---

1   *Litenawe* Lichtenau, Baden-Württemberg.
2   *Baden* Baden-Baden, Germany.
3   *Franciscans ... family* Franciscan friars living on alms alone.
4   *refection* Nourishment.
5   *breviary* Catholic liturgical book containing a daily "Divine Office," consisting of psalms, prayers, and readings.

more, and when he met me, told me with a cheerful countenance and merry heart that he had found that for the which he had before so much dejected his spirits.

One notable accident happened unto me in my way a little before I came to this monastery and the city of Baden, of which I will here make mention before I write any thing of Baden. It was my chance to meet two clowns commonly called boors,[1] who because they went in ragged clothes, struck no small terror into me; and by so much the more I was afraid of them, by how much the more I found them armed with weapons, myself being altogether unarmed, having no weapon at all about me but only a knife. Whereupon fearing lest they would either have cut my throat, or have robbed me of my gold that was quilted in my jerkin,[2] or have stripped me of my clothes, which they would have found but a poor booty. For my clothes being but a threadbare fustian case[3] were so mean (my cloak only except-ed) that the boors could not have made an ordinary supper with the money for which they should have sold them; fearing (I say) some ensuing danger, I undertook such a politic[4] and subtle action as I never did before in all my life. For a little before I met them, I put off my hat very courteously unto them, holding it a pretty while in my hand, and very humbly (like a mendicant friar) begged some money of them (as I have something declared in the front of my book)[5] in a language that they did but poorly understand, even the Latin, expressing my mind unto them by such gestures and signs, that they well knew what I craved of them: and so by this begging insinuation I both preserved myself secure & free from the violence of the clowns, and withal obtained that of them which I neither wanted or expected. For they gave me so much of their tin money called fennies[6] (as poor as they were) as paid for half my supper that night at Baden, even four pence half-penny.

---

1 *two clowns ... boors* Peasants.
2 *quilted in my jerkin* Covered with quilted material in a tight-fitting jacket for men.
3 *fustian case* Garment made of coarse cloth.
4 *politic* Crafty.
5 *declared ... book* Illustrated on the engraved title page (page 212, illustration "N").
6 *fennies* Pfennig, a German coin.

But having thus far digressed from my discourse of Baden, upon the occasion of mentioning the first institution of the Marquisate & the religion of the present prince, I will now return to the description of the city. There is one thing that makes this city very famous, namely the baths, which are of great antiquity. For authors do write that they were found out in the time of Marcus Antoninus surnamed *Philosophus*[1] the seventeenth emperor of Rome, about the year of our lord 160, who was so delighted with the baths of this place that he built the city for their sakes. Truly they are very admirable for two respects: first for the heat, secondly for the multitude. As for the heat it is so extreme that I believe they are the hottest of all Christendom, especially at their fountains, whereof I myself had some experience. For I did put my hand to one of the springs, which was so hot that I could hardly endure to handle the water, being of that force that it would scald my fingers very grievously if I had suffered it to run upon them till I had but told twenty. Yea the heat is so vehement, that it is reported it will seethe[2] eggs, and make them as ready to be eaten as if they were boiled in water over the fire. Also if one should cast any kind of bird or pig into the water at the original spring, where it is much hotter than in the baths themselves that are derived from the same, it will scald off the feathers from the one, and the hair from the other. Likewise the multitude of them is marvellous, which I will report, though many incredulous persons will (I believe) apply the old proverb unto me, that travellers may lie by authority. The number of them I heard does amount to three hundred several baths at the least. Which I did much the more wonder at because when I was at the baths of Hinderhove by the Helvetical Baden, I saw so great a company there, even sixty (which I esteemed a marvellous number in comparison of the fewness of our English baths at the city of Bath in my country of Somersetshire,[3] where we have no more than five) that I thought there were not so many particular baths so near together in any one town of Europe. But in this lower Baden the number of

---

1 *Marcus ... Philosophus* Marcus Aurelius Antoninus (121–180), author of the *Meditations* (second century CE).
2 *seethe* Boil.
3 *Bath ... Somersetshire* Bath Spa, renowned for its Roman baths.

them is so exceedingly multiplied, that it will seem almost incredible to many men that have ever contained themselves within at the limits of their own native soil, and never saw the wonders of foreign regions. For whereas the baths of the lower Baden are distinguished by several inns, in number thirteen, but after an unequal manner, so that some inns have more and some less: that inn wherein I lay, which was at the sign of the golden lion, contained more baths than all these fore-said threescore of Hinderhove. For in the same inn were no less than threescore & five several baths, as a learned man told me that lay in a house adjoining to my inn. All these baths are divided asunder by a great many rooms of the house, and covered overhead; the space that is limited for each bath being square and very narrow, so that in one and the selfsame room I observed four or five distinct baths. All these baths are of an equal heat, none hotter or colder than another. Also I heard that they are most frequented in the summer time, contrary to our English baths & those at Hinderhove, which are used only at the spring and autumn. The water of the baths is mingled with matter of three several kinds, brimstone, salt, and alum,[1] as Munster writes: unto whom I am beholding for this short ensuing discourse of the virtue of these baths, as I was before in the description of the baths of Hinderhove. Those that have tried them have found the virtue of them to be very sovereign for the curing of diverse diseases, as the asthma, which is an infirmity that proceeds from the difficulty of the breath, the moistness of the eyes, the cramp, the coldness of the stomach, the pain of the liver and the spleen proceeding from cold; also it helps the dropsy,[2] the griping of the bowels, the stone, the sterility of women; it appeases the pain of a woman's womb, keeps off the white menstrual matter, assuages the swelling of the thighs, cures the itch and blisters or whelks[3] rising in any part of the body; and to be short, it is said to be of greater efficacy for curing of the gout than any other baths whatsoever either of Germany or any other country of Christendom.

[...]

---

1   *alum* Mineral salt.
2   *dropsy* Condition marked by watery fluid build-up in membranes and connective tissue.
3   *whelks* Pustules.

My observations of Heidelberg [...]

The city is strongly walled, and has four fair gates in the walls, and one very goodly street above the rest both for breadth and length. For it is at the least an English mile long: and garnished with many beautiful houses, whereof some have their fronts fairly painted, which do yield an excellent show. [...] But the church of the holy ghost which adjoins to their great marketplace, is the fairest of all, being beautified with two singular ornaments above the other churches that do greatly grace the same: the one the Palatine library,[1] the other the monuments of their prince's. The Palatine library is kept by that most excellent and general scholar Mr. Janus Gruterus the prince's bibliothecary,[2] of whom I have reason to make a kind and thankful mention, because I received great favours of him in Heidelberg. For he entertained me very courteously in his house, showed me the library, and made means for my admission into the prince's court. [...] It is built over the roof of the body of the church—a place most beautiful, and divided into two very large and stately rooms that are singular well furnished with store of books of all faculties. Here are so many ancient manuscripts, especially of the Greek manuscripts and Latin fathers of the church,[3] as no library of all Christendom, no not the Vatican of Rome nor Cardinal Bessarion's of Venice can compare with it. Besides there is a great multitude of manuscripts of many other sorts, in so much that Mr. Gruterus told he could show in this library at the least a hundred more manuscripts than Mr. James[4] the public bibliothecary of Oxford could in his famous university library. For what books that library has or has not he knows by Mr. James his index or catalog that was printed in Oxford.[5] Amongst other books that he showed me one was a fair large parchment book written by the great grandfather of

---

1 *Palatine library* Bibliotheca Palatina, renowned German library founded by a Count Palatine, a nobleman who ruled a historical territory in the Holy Roman Empire.

2 *Janus Gruterus* Jan Gruter (1560–1627), German philologist; *bibliothecary* Librarian.

3 *Latin fathers of the church* Foundational theologians of the Catholic Church: Ambrose, Jerome, Augustine, St. Gregory the Great.

4 *Mr. James* Thomas James (1572/73–1629), who served as librarian at the Bodleian Library (Oxford University) from 1602–20.

5 *index ... Oxford* First published catalog of the Bodleian library, *Catalogus librorum bibliothecae publicae quam vir ornatissimus Thomas Bodleius* (1605).

Frederick the fourth[1] that was the count palatine when I was there. Truly the beauty of this library is such both for the notable magnificence of the building, and the admirable variety of books of all sciences and languages, that I believe none of those notable libraries in ancient times so celebrated by many worthy historians, neither that of the royal Ptolemies of Alexandria, burnt by Julius Caesar, not that of King Eumenes at Pergamum in Greece, nor Augustus his Palatine in Rome, nor Trajan's Ulpian, nor that of Serenus Sammonicus, which he left to the emperor Gordianus the younger,[2] nor any other whatsoever in the whole world before the time of the invention of printing, could compare with this Palatine. Also I attribute so much unto it that I give it the precedence above all the noble libraries I saw in my travels, which were especially amongst the Jesuits in Lyons, Speyer, and Mainz. Howbeit Mr. Gruterus will pardon me I hope if I prefer one library of my own nation before the Palatine, even that of our renowned University of Oxford, whereof the foresaid Mr. James is a keeper. For indeed I believe it contains a few more books (though not many) than this of Heidelberg. There happened one disaster unto me when I was in this library. For shortly after I came within it, and had surveyed but a few of the principal books, it chanced that two young princes of Anhalt[3] which are descended from the most ancient princely family of all Germany, came suddenly into the room upon me, being ushered by their golden-chained gentlemen. Whereupon I was constrained to withdraw myself speedily out of the library, all the attendance being given unto the princes: by which sinister accident I lost the opportunity of seeing those memorable antiquities and

---

1 *Frederick the fourth* Frederick IV, Elector Palatine (1574–1610). His great grandfather was Johann II, Count Palatine (1492–1557).
2 *that of the royal ... Caesar* Library of Alexandria, founded by the Ptolemies (Greek dynastic family) of Egypt in the third century BCE. The source of its destruction is a matter of debate: the fire Julius Caesar set there in 48 BCE is one of many contributing factors to its eventual destruction; *King Eumenes ... Greece* Pergamum was an ancient Greek city in Asia Minor famous for its library, built by Eumenes II (d. 158 BCE). The word parchment derives from the name Pergamum, where the use of parchment as a writing material is believed to have started; *Augustus ... Rome* The library adjoining the Temple of Palatine Apollo was founded by Augustus, first emperor of Rome; *Trajan's Ulpian* Bibliotheca Ulpia, part of Trajan's forum, commissioned by the Roman emperor Trajan (c. 53–117); *Serenus Sammonicus* Roman writer (d. 211); *Gordianus the younger* Gordian II (d. 238), briefly emperor of Rome.
3 *Anhalt* Anhalt-Dessau, historical principality in Germany.

rarities which Mr. Gruterus intended to have communicated unto me, and so consequently I myself the same to my country. Let this therefore suffice for the Palatine library.

[...]

Besides this foresaid church, there are two things more which do very notably adorn and beautify this stately city, the first the most gorgeous palace of the prince.[1] [...] The principal ornament that graces it [i.e., the palace], is the multitude of fair statues (which the outward front wants) very loftily advanced towards the fairest part of the court, whereof there are four distinct degrees or series made one above another. The same statues are carved in a singular fair milk-white stone, which seems as beautiful as the fairest alabaster, and formed in a very large proportion, expressing all the parts of a man's body, and done with that artificial curiosity, that I believe were those famous statuaries Polycletus and Praxiteles[2] alive again, they would praise the same, and confess they were not able to amend them. For they imitate the true natural countenance and living shape of those heroic and princely peers, whom they represent. Most of them are the statues of the famous palatine princes to the last of them Frederick the fourth. Also emperors, kings, and queens are there portrayed. This front is raised to a very great height, and decked with marvellous curious devices at the top, all which ornaments concurring together do exhibit to the eyes of the spectator a show most incomparable.

[...]

There is a notable thing to be seen in this palace, the sight whereof it was not my hap to enjoy, because I heard nothing of it before I went out of the palace: a matter of great antiquity. Namely certain ancient stony pillars, in number five, which the emperor Carolus Magnus above eight hundred and fifty years since brought from the city of Ravenna in Italy, and placed them afterward in his palace of

---

1 *two things more ... prince* The "second thing" is the University of Heidelberg, which Coryate treats briefly at the end of his relation of the city (in a passage omitted from this edition).
2 *statuaries* Sculptors; *Polycletus and Praxiteles* Polyclitus (fifth century BCE) and Praxiteles
   (fourth century BCE), Greek sculptors.

Ingelheim, a place of high Germany within a few miles of the city of Mainz, where he was born, and oftentimes kept his court. The same pillars were of late years removed from the said Ingelheim to Heidelberg by the prince Philip[1] of whom I have before made mention in my discourse of the church of the holy ghost, who erected them in this palace whereof I now speak, and are there showed for a principal ancient monument to this day.

But some of the gentlemen of the prince's family did sufficiently recompense my loss of the sight of these ancient pillars by showing me a certain piece of work that did much more please my eyes than the sight of those pillars could have done. For it is the most remarkable and famous thing of that kind that I saw in my whole journey, yea so memorable a matter, that I think there was never the like fabric (for that which they showed me was nothing else than a strange kind of fabric) in all the world, and I doubt whether posterity will ever frame so monstrously strange a thing: it was nothing but a vessel full of wine. Which the gentlemen of the court showed me after they had first conveyed me into diverse wine cellars, where I saw a wondrous company of extraordinary great vessels, the greatest part whereof was replenished with Rhenish wine, the total number containing one hundred and thirty particulars. But the main vessel above all the rest, that superlative moles[2] unto which I now bend my speech, was shown me last of all standing alone by itself in a wonderful vast room. I must needs say I was suddenly struck with no small admiration upon the first sight thereof. For it is such a stupendious mass (to give it the same epitheton that I have done before to the beauty of St. Mark's street in Venice) that I am persuaded it will affect the gravest and constantest man in the world with wonder. Had this fabric been extant in those ancient times when the Colossus of Rhodes, the Labyrinths of Egypt and Crete, the Temple of Diana at Ephesus, the hanging gardens of Semiramis, the tomb of Mausolus, and the rest of those decantated miracles did flourish in their principal glory, I think Herodotus and Diodorus Siculus[3] would have celebrated this rare work with their learned style as well as the rest, and have consecrated the memory

---

1   *prince Philip* Philip the Contentious (1503–48), Count Palatine.

2   *moles* Mass.

3   *Colossus of Rhodes … Mausolus* Five of the seven wonders of the ancient world; *Herodotus and Diodorus Siculus* Greek historians of the fifth and first centuries BCE, respectively.

thereof to immortality as a very memorable miracle. For indeed it is a kind of monstrous miracle, and that of the greatest size for a vessel that this age does yield in any place whatsoever (as I am verily persuaded) under the cope of heaven; pardon me I pray thee (gentle reader) if I am something tedious in discoursing of this huge vessel. For as it was the strangest spectacle that I saw in my travels, so I hope it will not be unpleasant unto thee to read a full description of all the particular circumstances thereof: and for thy better satisfaction I have inserted a true figure[1] thereof in this place (though but in a small form) according to a certain pattern that I brought with me from the city of Frankfurt, where I saw the first type thereof sold. Also I have added an imaginary kind of representation of myself upon the top of the same, in that manner as I stood there with a cup of Rhenish wine in my hand. The room where it stands is wonderful vast (as I said before) and capacious, even almost as big as the fairest hall I have seen in England, and it contains no other thing but the same vessel. It was begun in the year 1589 and ended 1591, one Michael Warner of the city of Landavia[2] being the principal maker of the work. It contains a hundred and two and thirty fuders, three ohms, and as many firtles.[3] These are peculiar names for certain German measures, which I will reduce to our English computation. Every fuder countervails our tun,[4] that is, four hogsheads, and is worth in Heidelberg fifteen pound sterling. So then those hundred two and thirty fuders are worth nineteen hundred and fourscore pounds of our English money. The ohm is a measure whereof six do make a fuder, the three being worth seven pounds ten shillings. The firtle is a measure that countervails six of our pottles:[5] every pottle in Heidelberg is worth twelve pence sterling. So the three firtles containing eighteen pottles, are worth eighteen shillings. The total sum that the wine is worth which this vessel contains, does amount to nineteen hundred fourscore and eight pounds and eight odd shillings. This strange news perhaps will seem utterly incredible to thee at the first:

---

1   *true figure* See the image on the next page, one of five engraved plates included in Coryate's
     travelogue.
2   *Landavia* Landau.
3   *fuders ... firtles* Fuders, ohms, and firtles are German liquid measures.
4   *tun* Large barrel for storing alcoholic drinks.
5   *pottles* English liquid measures, each equal to a half-gallon.

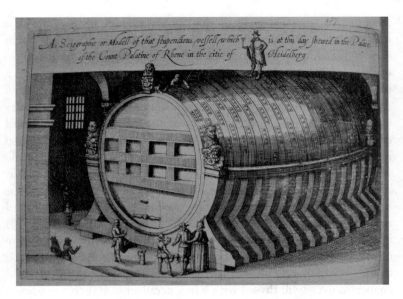

Great Tun of Heidelberg, from *Coryats Crudities.*

but I would have thee believe it. For nothing is more true. More-over thou must consider that this vessel is not compacted of boards as other barrels are, but of solid great beams, in number a hundred and twelve, whereof every one is seven and twenty foot long. Also each end is sixteen feet high, and the belly dimensions, eighteen. It is hooped with wondrous huge hoops of iron (the number whereof is six and twenty) which do contain eleven thousand pound weight. It is supported on each side with ten marvellous great pillars made of timber, and beautified at both the ends and the top with the images of lions, which are the prince's arms, two lions at each end, a fair escutcheon being affixed to every image. The wages that were paid to the workman for his labour, (the prince finding all necessary matter for his work, and allowing him his diet) came to two thousand three hundred and fourscore florins of Brabant,[1] each florin being two shillings of our money, which sum amounts to eleven score and eighteen pounds sterling. When the cellarer[2] draws wine out of the vessel, he

---

1   *Brabant* Region in central Belgium.
2   *cellarer* Household officer responsible for storing and distributing provisions.

ascends two several degrees of wooden stairs made in the form of a ladder which contain seven and twenty steps or rungs as we call them in Somersetshire, and so goes up to the top. About the middle whereof there is a bung-hole or a venting orifice into the which he conveys a pretty instrument of some foot and a half long, made in the form of a spout, wherewith he draws up the wine, and so pours it after a pretty manner into the glass or &c. out of the same instrument. I myself had experience of this matter. For a gentleman of the court accompanied me to the top together with one of the cellarers, and exhilarated me with two sound draughts of Rhenish wine. For that is the wine that it contains. But I advise thee gentle reader whatsoever thou art that intends to travel into Germany, and perhaps to see Heidelberg, and also this vessel before thou come out of the city; I advise thee (I say) if thou does happen to ascend to the top thereof to the end to taste of the wine, that in any case thou drink moderately, and not so much as the sociable Germans will persuade thee unto. For if thou should chance to over-swill thyself with wine, peradventure such a giddiness will benumb thy brain, that thou will scarce find the direct way down from the steep ladder without a very dangerous precipitation. [...] Thus finally I shut up the description of this strange vessel with a certain admirable thing that I heard reported of it in Frankfurt, after my departure from Heidelberg, that the same being full of wine was once drunk out in the space of eight days, at the time of a certain noble meeting of princely gallants at the court.

[...]

I departed from Heidelberg the eight day of September being Thursday about nine of the clock in the morning, and came to the city of Speyer which is twelve miles beyond it, about five of the clock in the afternoon. Betwixt these two cities I passed through a great wood, which by reason of the manifold turnings and windings of the way like a company of voluminous meanders, did so exceedingly perplex me that I got out of the same with no small difficulty. About three miles before I came to Speyer I was ferried over the Rhine in a boat.

My observations of Speyer [...]

I was in the college of the Jesuits who used me very kindly. But one especially above all the rest, whose name was Jonas Keinperger the chief of the Jesuit family, who showed me their library, where I saw a notable company of goodly books. But in one of them I observed a matter that argued the injurious and naughty[1] dealing of the Jesuits. For whereas amongst the rest of their books they had Munster's Cosmography, I looked into it to inform myself something of the antiquities of the city, and by chance turning over some leaves, I found notable places expunged by these critical Aristarches,[2] and demanded of them why they did deface any part of so famous an author's works. They answered me that Munster was a heretic and an apostate, affirming that after he had renounced his monkish religion, he maintained many heretical points in his writings. Wherefore because there were certain matters in his Cosmography that made against the faith of the Catholic Church of Rome, they would not suffer them to remain in the book. How these men and others of diverse papistical orders have dealt with the fathers of the church also, and diverse godly authors of great antiquity by their wicked falsifications, putting out those things that have made against them, and supplying the same with some commentitial forgeries of their own brains, it does evidently appear to the world by the *Index expurgatorius*[3] printed at Geneva and Strasbourg. I found one of those Jesuits so skillful in some of our English histories, that he discoursed unto me of certain ancient matters of old Britain, especially of our kings of Northumberland.[4]

[...]

This city does not embrace that unity of religion that the cities of Strasbourg, Basel, and the other reformed cities of Switzerland [do],

---

1 *naughty* Wicked.
2 *Aristarches* Reference to Aristarchus (c. 216–144 BCE), a Greek textual scholar and librarian of Alexandria, whose name became a byword for the thorough critic.
3 *commentitial* Fictitious; *Index expurgatorius* List of passages in books to be deleted or changed, as stipulated by the Catholic Church.
4 *kings of Northumberland* Kings of the medieval region in northern England known as Northumbria, corresponding to the modern county of Northumberland.

but is distracted into a double religion, Protestant and papistical; the Protestant professing the Lutheran doctrine, being the predominant part, though the cathedral church belongs to the papists in regard their bishop is a papist. For a learned preacher of the city one Nicolaus Frisius that used me very courteously, told me that most of the principal families profess the reformed religion. But there is a kind of murmuring betwixt both parts, though it be so concealed that it breaks not out into any open jars, full liberty of conscience & exercise of religion being permitted to each faction without any contradiction.

[...]

There happened unto me a certain disaster about the midst of my journey betwixt Franckendall[1] and Worms, the like whereof I did not sustain in my whole journey out of England, which was this. I stepped aside into a vineyard in the open field that was but a little distant from the highway, to the end to taste of their grapes wherewith I might something assuage my thirst: hoping that I might as freely have done it there, as I did oftentimes before in many places of Lombardy without any controlment.[2] There I pulled two little clusters of them, and so returned into my way again travelling securely and jovially towards Worms, whose lofty towers I saw near at hand. But there came a German boor upon me (for so are the clowns of the country commonly called) with a halberd in his hand, & in a great fury pulled off very violently my hat from my head (as I have expressed in the frontispiece of my book) looked very fiercely upon me with eyes sparkling fire in a manner, and with his Almanne[3] words which I understood not, swaggered most insolently with me, holding up his halberd in that threatening manner at me, that I continually expected a blow, and was in deadly fear lest he would have made me a prey for the worms before I should ever put my foot in the gallant city of Worms. For it was in vain for me to make any violent resistance, because I had no more weapon than a weak staff, that I brought with me out of Italy. Although I understood not his speeches, yet I gathered

---

1 *Franckendall* Frankenthal.
2 *controlment* Restraint.
3 *halberd* Combination spear and battle-axe; *frontispiece of my book* Engraved title page (page 212, illustration "H"); *Almanne* German.

by his angry gestures that the only cause of his quarrel was for that he saw me come forth of a vineyard (which belike was his master's) with a bunch of grapes in my hand. All this while that he threatened me with these menacing terms I stood before him almost as mute as a Seriphian frog, or an Acanthian grasshopper,[1] scarce opening my mouth once unto him, because I thought that as I did not understand him, so likewise on the other side he did not understand me. At length with my tongue I began to reencounter him, took heart a grace, and so discharged a whole volley of Greek and Latin shot upon him, supposing that it would be an occasion to pacify him somewhat if he did but only thereby conceive that I had a little learning. But the implacable clown

Non magis incepto vultum sermone movetur
Quam si dura silex, aut stet Marpessia cautes.[2]

And was so far from being mitigated with my strange rhetoric, that he was rather much the more exasperated against me. In the end after many bickerings had passed betwixt us, three or four good fellows that came from Worms glanced[3] by, and inquired of me what the quarrel was. I being not able to speak Dutch asked them whether any of the company could speak Latin. Then immediately one replied unto me that he could. Whereupon I discovered unto him the whole circumstance of the matter, and desired him to appease the rage of that inexorable and unpleasant peasant, that he might restore my hat again to me. Then he like a very sociable companion interposed himself betwixt us as a mediator. But first he told me that I had committed a penal trespass in presuming to gather grapes in a vineyard without leave, affirming that the Germans are so exceeding sparing of their grapes, that they are wont to fine any of their own countrymen that they catch in their vineyards without leave, either with purse

---

1 *Seriphian frog ... grasshopper* From the Latin proverbs "Rana Seriphica" (Seriphian frog) and "Acanthia cicada" (Acanthian grasshopper), both of which described silent or unskilled people. In both proverbs frogs and grasshoppers, when moved from their native homes of Seriphos and Acanthus, respectively, ceased to make noise.
2 [Coryate's Note] Aenei. 6. [Latin: At the beginning of his speech her face was no more moved than if she stood as unfeeling stone or Marpesian rocks. The lines refer to Aeneas' encounter with Dido in the underworld.]
3 *glanced* Passed.

or body, much more a stranger. Notwithstanding he promised to do his endeavour to get my hat again, because this should be a warning for me, and for that he conceived that opinion of me that I was a good fellow. And so at last with much ado this controversy was compounded betwixt the cullion[1] and myself, my hat being restored unto me for a small price of redemption, which was twelve of their little coins called fennies, which countervail twenty pence of our English money. But I would counsel thee gentle reader whatsoever thou art that means to travel into Germany, to beware by my example of going into any of their vineyards without leave. For if thou shall happen to be apprehended *in ipso facto* (as I was) by some rustic and barbarous Corydon[2] of the country, thou may perhaps pay a far dearer price for thy grapes than I did, even thy dearest blood.

[…]

I departed from Oppenheim the twelfth day of September being Monday about six of the clock in the morning, and came to the city of Mainz about ten of the clock in the morning, which was ten miles beyond it. It was my hap in this journey betwixt Oppenheim and Mainz to have such a notable companion as I never had before in all my life. For he was both learned and unlearned. Learned because being but a wood-cleaver (for he told me that he was the Jesuits' wood-cleaver of Mainz) he was able to speak Latin. A matter as rare in one of that sordid faculty as to see a white crow or a black swan. Again he was unlearned, because the Latin which he did speak was such incongruous and disjointed stuff, such antipriscianistical eloquence, that I think were grave Cato alive (who for his constant severity was called ἀγέλαστος, because he never or very seldom laughed) he should have more cause to laugh if he should hear this fellow deliver his mind in Latin, than when he saw an ass eat thistles.[3]

---

1 *cullion* Rascal.
2 *in ipso facto* Latin: in the very deed; *Corydon* Generic pastoral name for a rustic.
3 *antipriscianistical* Ungrammatical; *grave Cato* Cato the Elder (234–149 BCE), also known as Cato the Censor, Roman politician; ἀγέλαστος Greek: agelastos, sullen; *ass eat thistles* According to classical anecdotes about Cato the Elder, as ass eating thistles is the only thing that ever made him laugh.

My observations of Moguntia otherwise called Moguntiacum, but commonly
   Mainz [...]

Besides many other things that have greatly graced this city, and made it famous over all Christendom [...] that most incomparably excellent art of printing which was first invented in this city, is not to be esteemed the least, nay rather it deserves to be ranked in an equal dignity with the worthiest matter of the whole city, if not to be preferred before it. For in this city of Mainz was the divine art (to give it an epitheton more than ordinary by reason of the excellency of the invention) of printing first devised by a gentleman or rather a knight of this city one Joannes Cuttenbergius in the year of our lord one thousand four hundred and forty, even in that very year that Frederick the third was inaugurated into the empire; and in the time of their Archbishop Theodoricus who was the sixty-seventh after Crescens[1] the first apostle of the city. Well might that ancient poet write those verses in praise of this noble art that Kirchnerus[2] has cited in his oration of Germany; which I have inserted into my observations:

O Germania muneris repertrix,
Quo non utilius dedit vetustas,
Libros scribere, quae doces, premendo.[3]

For surely if we rightly consider it, we shall find it to be one of the most rare and admirable inventions that ever was since the first foundation of the world was laid. For what I pray can be devised *in rerum natura*[4] more strange than that one man should be able by his

---

1 *Joannes Cuttenbergius* Johann Gutenberg (c. 1400–68), inventor of printing in the west; *Frederick the third* Frederick III (1415–93), Holy Roman Emperor; *Archbishop Theodoricus* Diether von Isenburg (c. 1412–82), Archbishop of Mainz; *Crescens* First Archbishop of Mainz and disciple of St. Paul the Apostle.
2 *Kirchnerus* Kirchner wrote an essay praising travel in Germany that Coryate translated and (in a section omitted from this edition) appended to the beginning of his "observations of High Germany."
3 *O Germania ... premendo* Latin: Discoveress of this gift, O Germany, to whom antiquity gave nothing so useful: to write books by printing, which you teach. The passage is from Filippo Beroaldo's *Varia opuscula* (1513).
4 *in rerum natura* Latin: in the nature of things.

characters composed of tin, brass, & stibium[1] to write more lines in one day than the swiftest scrivener[2] in the world can do in a whole year? According to that old verse

Imprimit una dies quantum vix scribitur anno.[3]

A matter that may seem incredible to the understanding of many men, yet most certainly verified by experience. By virtue of this art are communicated to the public view of the world the monuments of all learned authors that are set abroach out of the sacred treasury of antiquity, and being now freed from that Cimmerian darkness wherein they lurked for the space of many hundred years, and where they did *cum tineis ac blattis rixari*,[4] to the great prejudice of the commonweal of learning, but especially of God's church, are divulged to the common light, and that to the infinite utility of all lovers of the muses and professors of learning. By this art all the liberal sciences are now brought to full ripeness and perfection. Had not this art been invented by the divine providence of God, it was to be feared lest the true studies of all disciplines both divine & human would have suffered a kind of shipwreck, and have been half extinct before this age wherein we breathe. I would to God we would thankfully use this great benefit of our gracious God (as a learned author says) not to the obscuration but the illustration of God's glory, not to disjoin but rather to conjoin the members of Christ's militant church here on earth.

[...]

I was embarked at Mainz the thirteenth of September being Monday, about seven of the clock in the morning, and passed down the goodly river Moenus,[5] which at Mainz does mingle itself with the

---

1 [Coryate's Note] This is a kind of white stone found in silver mines which they use in printing [i.e., antimony.]
2 *scrivener* Scribe.
3 *Imprimit ... anno* Latin: It prints in one day what is with difficulty written in a year.
4 *Cimmerian darkness* Cimmeria was an ancient Nordic European region, its "darkness" proverbial for things unknown and obscure; *cum tineis ... rixari* Latin: with moths and bookworms contend.
5 *Moenus* Main river.

Rhine till I came to a town within four miles of Frankfurt where I arrived, and from thence performed the rest of my journey by land, and came to the city of Frankfurt which is sixteen miles from Mainz, about five of the clock in the afternoon.

[...]

Now I will return again to my liquid journey betwixt Mainz and Frankfurt upon the river Moenus. The bark wherein I was carried contained a strange miscellany of people of sundry nations at that time, whose languages were (I think) a quarter as much confounded as theirs were in ancient times at that famous confusion of Babel.[1] For in this bark there were some few of every principal nation of Christendom travelling towards Frankfurt mart that began the day before. Amongst the rest, one of them was born in the country of Lithuania that adjoins to a part of Poland, a passing sweet scholar, and a traveller that had lately lived in the University of Monachium commonly called Mynichin[2] in Bavaria, a man that yielded singular delight unto me by his variable discourse seasoned with much polite learning.

[...]

My observations of Franckford [...]

This city is commonly called Frankfurt am Main, that is, Frankfurt situate by the river Moenus. [...] There are two things which make this city famous over all Europe. The one the election of the king of the Romans, the other the two noble fairs kept here twice a year, which are called the marts of Frankfurt.

[...]

As for the fair it is esteemed, and so indeed is the richest meeting of any place of Christendom, which continues 14 days together, and

---

1 *Babel* According to Genesis 11, there was a time when all people spoke the same language, and this enabled them to begin to build an incredibly high tower, the Tower of Babel. God stopped the construction and caused them to speak mutually unintelligible languages.
2 *Mynichin* Munich.

is kept in the month of March for the spring, and in September for the autumn. This autumnal mart it was my chance to see. Where I met my thrice-honourable countryman the Earl of Essex, after he had travelled in diverse places of France, Switzerland, and some parts of high Germany. The riches I observed at this mart were most infinite, especially in one place called Under Den Roemer,[1] where the goldsmiths kept their shops, which made the most glorious show that ever I saw in my life, especially some of the city of Nuremberg. This place is divided into diverse other rooms that have a great many partitions assigned unto mercers and such like artificers, for the exposing of their wares. The wealth that I saw here was incredible, so great that it was impossible for a man to conceive it in his mind that has not first seen it with his bodily eyes. The goodliest show of ware that I saw in all Frankfurt saving that of the goldsmiths, was made by an Englishman one Thomas Sackfield a Dorsetshireman, once a servant of my father, who went out of England but in a mean estate, but after he had spent a few years at the Duke of Brunswick's[2] court, he so enriched himself of late, that his glittering show of ware in Frankfurt did far excel all the Dutchmen, French, Italians, or whomsoever else. This place is much frequented during the whole time of the mart with many eminent and princely persons. [...] After this I went to the booksellers' street where I saw such infinite abundance of books, that I greatly admired it. For this street far excels Paul's churchyard in London, Saint James street in Paris, the Merceria of Venice,[3] and all whatsoever else that I saw in my travels. In so much that it seems to be a very epitome of all the principal libraries of Europe. Neither is that street famous for selling books only, and that of all manner of arts and disciplines whatsoever, but also for printing of them. For this city has so flourished within these few years in the art of printing, that it is not inferior in that respect to any city in Christendom, no not to Basel itself which I have before so much commended for the excellency of that art.

---

1   *Under Den Roemer* German: Under the Romans.
2   *Thomas Sackfield* Thomas Sackville, poet, statesman, and author of *Gorboduc* (1561–62), the first English tragedy in blank verse; *Duke of Brunswick* Heinrich Julius (1564–1613), Duke of Brunswick.
3   *Paul's ... Venice* Major sites for booksellers in London, Paris, and Venice.

[...]

The religion of this city is both Protestant and papistical; the Protestants profess Luther's doctrine. The principal church which is dedicated to St. Bartholomew belongs to the papists, most of the other to the Protestants, saving the churches of Monasteries.

I received a special kindness in this city of an English gentleman, with the commemoration of whose name I will finish my observations of Frankfurt, even Mr. Thomas Rowe the eldest son of Sir Henry Rowe,[1] that was Lord Mayor of London about two years since. Truly this gentleman did me such a singular courtesy there, that he has perpetually obliged me unto him all the days of my life.

Thus much of Frankfurt.

[...]

There is a very strange custom observed amongst the Germans as they pass in their boats betwixt Mainz and Cologne, and so likewise betwixt Cologne and the lower parts of the Netherlands. Every man whatsoever he be poor or rich, shall labour hard when it comes to his turn, except he does either by friendship or some small sum of money redeem his labor. For their custom is that the passengers must exercise themselves with oars and rowing *alternis vicibus*, a couple together. So that the master of the boat (who methinks in honesty ought either to do it himself, or to procure some others to do it for him) never rows but when his turn comes. This exercise both for recreation and health sake I confess is very convenient for man. But to be tied unto it by way of a strict necessity when one pays well for his passage, was a thing that did not a little distaste my humour.

[...]

When we were passed Wesel we came to another custom town situate on the same bank of the Rhine, which was the fourth. The name of it is St. Goar,[2] a Protestant town, and it stands in that territory

---

1 *Sir Henry Rowe* Lord Mayor of London in 1607 (d. 1612).
2 *St. Goar* Sankt Goar.

whose inhabitants were in former times called Catti,[1] a very warlike people much mentioned by Cornelius Tacitus and other writers of the Roman histories; but now it has the name of Hassia, which is a landgraviate subject to the renowned prince Maurice the present landgrave[2] of the country. To him does this custom town belong. It has the denomination of St. Goar from a certain holy man called Goarus (for the Latin name of the town is Sanctus Goarus) that came hither out of Aquitaine in the time of the emperor Mauricius,[3] and lived in this place a holy and religious life.

Here I observed a very violent source of the torrent of the Rhine, which comes to pass by means of a swift cataract, that is, a fall of water from some uneven part of the stream. Also I heard that there is a deep gulf, *rapidus vortex*[4] in this place, which with a most incessant greediness swallows down the water by means of the manifold anfracts[5] and intricate windings thereof, which continual drinking up of the water is said to be the natural cause of the great violence of the stream that appears more there than in other places. It is often observed that this place in the time of a raging tempest is so dangerous that no boats dare pass that way, or if any should by force of the storm be driven in against their wills, the passengers do very hardly escape with their lives. This foresaid town of St. Goar does not want the means to make it something memorable as well as the rest of the Rhenish towns, though in quantity it be inferior unto all those that I have already named. For there is one thing in it that does make it much spoken of, whereof I will report a merry and short history. A little within the town gate there hangs an iron collar fastened in the wall with one link, which is made fit to be put upon a man's neck without any manner of hurt to the party that wears it, and they use first to convey it over the head, and so to the neck. This collar does

---

1 [Coryate's Note] From this word comes Cattinelnbogen [Katzenelnbogen] the ancient name of a town in Hassia wherehence the landgrave derives one of his princely titles. [The Catti were an ancient Germanic people. Hassia (now known as Hesse) is a German cultural region; a landgrave is a German prince.]

2 *landgraviate* Province ruled by the landgrave; *Maurice ... landgrave* Maurice, Landgrave of Hesse-Kassel (1572–1632).

3 *Aquitaine* Region in southwestern France; *Mauricius* Flavius Mauricius Tiberius Augustus, Byzantine emperor (c. 539–602).

4 *rapidus vortex* Latin: a swift whirlpool.

5 *anfracts* Meanders.

every stranger and freshman[1] the first time that he passes that way (according to an ancient custom observed amongst them) put upon his neck (at the least as the gentlemen told me that went in my boat) which he must wear so long standing upright against a wall till he has redeemed himself with a competent measure of wine. And at the drinking of it there is as much joviality and merriment as heart can conceive for the incorporating of a fresh novice into the fraternity of boon companions. And from thenceforth he is free from all such manner of exactions as long as he lives. That this is true I know by mine own experience. For I was contented for novelty sake to be their prisoner a little while by wearing of the foresaid collar. This custom does carry some kind of affinity with certain sociable ceremonies that we have in a place of England which are performed by that most reverend Lord Ball of Bagshot in Hampshire, who does with many and indeed more solemn rites invest his brothers of his unhallowed chapel of Basingstone (as all our men of the western parts of England do know by dear experience to the smart of their purses) than these merry burgomasters[2] of Saint Goar use to do.

[...]

This day's journey betwixt the city of Boppard and Uberwinter[3] contained some thirty miles. In this place we solaced ourselves after our tedious labour of rowing as merrily as we could. One merry conceit amongst the rest that I heard in this good company I will here relate. One of my Moguntine associates that was a merry gentleman, and one that had lately been a student in the University of Altorph[4] near the city of Nuremberg, told me as we sat together at supper, that a certain bishop had two kind of wines in his cellar, a better and a worse, that were called by two distinct names, the better *Noli me tangere*, the worse *Utcunque*.[5] And that a certain merry conceited fellow that sat at the bishop's table, having drank once or twice of

1 *freshman* Newcomer.
2 *burgomasters* Town administrators.
3 *Uberwinter* Oberwinter.
4 *Moguntine* Resident of Mainz, from Moguntia, Latin for Mainz; *University of Altorph* University of Altdorf, founded in 1578.
5 *Noli me tangere* Latin: Touch me not; *Utcunque* Latin: Whatever.

the *utcunque*, so much disliked it that he would drink no more of it. Therefore he spoke to one of the bishop's servants that waited at table, to give him a draught of the *Noli me tangere*, & withal pronounced unto him, in the presence of the bishop these two merry Latin verses *ex tempore*.

> *Si das Utcunque, daemon vos tollat utrunque:*
> *Ibis ad astra poli, si fers Me tangere noli.*[1]

With this and such other pleasant conceits we recreated ourselves that night at Uberwinter, and the next morning being Monday and the nineteenth of September, we took boat again about three of the clock, and came to Cologne which was eighteen miles beyond it, about ten of the same morning: our whole journey betwixt Mainz and Cologne was about seventy-eight miles. I observed in a great many places, on both sides of the Rhine, more gallows and wheels betwixt Mainz and Cologne than ever I saw in so short a space in all my life, especially within few miles of Cologne, by reason that the rustic Corydons of the country, which are commonly called the boors and the free-booters (a name that is given unto the lewd murdering villains of the country that live by robbing and spoiling of travellers, being called free-booters, because they have their booty and prey from passengers free, paying nothing for them except they are taken) do commit many notorious robberies near the Rhine, who are such cruel and bloody horseleaches (the very *hyenae & lycanthropi*[2] of Germany) that they seldom rob any man but forthwith they cut his throat. And some of them do afterward escape, by reason of the woods near at hand in which they shelter themselves free from danger. Yet others are sometimes taken, and most cruelly excarnificated and tortured upon these wheels, in that manner that I have before mentioned in some of my observations of France. For I saw the bones of many of them lie upon the wheel, a doleful spectacle for any relenting Christian to behold. And upon those gallows in diverse places I saw murderers hang, partly in chains, and partly without chains. A punishment too

---

1   *Si das ... tangere noli* Latin: If you give "utcunque," a demon take you both: you will go to the stars of heaven only if bringing "noli me tangere."
2   *horseleaches* Aggressively greedy people; *hyenae & lycanthropi* Latin: Hyenas and were-wolves, used here figuratively to describe rapacious people.

good for these cyclopical anthropophagi,[1] these cannibal man-eaters. I have heard that the free-booters do make themselves so strong, that they are not to be taken by the country. For I observed a town about twenty miles on this side Cologne, called Remagen, situate near the Rhine, which some ten years since was miserably ransacked by these free-booters, who banded themselves together in so great a troop as consisted of almost three thousand persons. The town itself they de-faced not, but only took away their goods, to the utter undoing and impoverishment of the inhabitants.

[...]

The end of my observations of some parts of high Germany.

The beginning of my observations of the Netherlands

My observations of Colonia Agrippina commonly called Cologne [...]

The situation of Cologne is very delectable. For it stands in a pleasant and fruitful plain hard by the Rhine, which washes the walls thereof, as it does Basel and Mainz. The compass of it is so great, that I heard it credibly reported a man can hardly go round about it under the space of four hours, which if it be true, it contains in circuit at the least eight of our English miles.

[...]

Their streets and marketplaces are many and very spacious, es-pecially two marketplaces that I took exact notice of above the rest, whereof the one in which they ordinarily sell their necessaries and keep their markets, is a hundred threescore and sixteen paces long, and threescore and three broad. The other where their merchants do meet twice a day which they call in Latin *forum foenarium*,[2] because they use to sell hay in the same, is the fairest that I saw in my whole voyage, saving that of St. Mark's street in Venice. For it is two hundred

---

1   *cyclopical anthropophagi* One-eyed eaters of human flesh.
2   *forum foenarium* Latin: hay market.

and fourscore paces long, and fourscore and four broad. For indeed I meted[1] them both. And this last marketplace is marvellously graced with many sumptuous and stately buildings both at the sides and the ends. Surely the beauty of this marketplace is such by reason of so many magnificent houses including it, that I think if a clown that never saw any fair shows in his life should suddenly arrive there, he would be half amazed with the majesty of the place.

[...]

Here at the conclusion of this history of Cologne I will briefly mention one notable thing that I saw in this city, besides all the rest before mentioned. It was my chance to see the picture of our famous English Jesuit Henry Garnet,[2] publicly exposed to sale in a place of the city, with other things. Whose head was represented in that miraculous figure imprinted in a straw, as our English papists have often reported.[3] A matter that I perceive is very highly honoured by diverse papists beyond the seas. Though I think the truth of it is such, that it may be well ranked amongst the merry tales of Poggius the Florentine.[4]

Thus much of Cologne.

I departed from Cologne in a boat down the Rhine upon a Wednesday being the one and twentieth of September, about two of the clock in the afternoon, after I had made my abode there two days, and came to a certain solitary house nine miles beyond it, situate by the riverside, about eight of the clock at night, being accompanied with four Englishmen whose names were Peter Sage, and James Tower Londoners, William Tassell a Cambridgeshire man. These three had been at Frankfurt mart. The fourth was one Richard Savage a Cheshire man that came then from the University of Minychen in

---

1 *meted* Measured.
2 *Henry Garnet* Henry Garnett (1555–1606), executed for his alleged role in the Gunpowder Plot (1605).
3 *miraculous figure ... reported* Relic associated with Garnett, a husk bearing a drop of blood that resembled his face.
4 *merry tales ... Florentine* Poggio Bracciolini's *Facetiae* (1470), a collection of humorous stories.

Bavaria, where he had spent some time in study. The two latter of these four proceeded in their journey with me till we came to Flushing the farthest town of Zeeland, where I was embarked for England, & there we parted company. Also there was another in our boat, whose company I enjoyed all the way betwixt Mainz and Cologne, that ministered great delight unto me with his elegant learning. His name was Christopher Hagk, born in Koningsperg the metropolitan city of Prussia,[1] and a famous university. Also he was the son and heir of the high consul of the city. A sociable & pleasant gentleman, and one that had been a traveller for the space of a dozen years in the famousest regions of Christendom, as Germany, France, Italy, England, Denmark, Poland, &c.

[...]

When we were a few miles past beyond this town, we glanced by the town of Duisburg situate in Cleveland,[2] also hard by the Rhine. This town is famous for containing the bones of that worthy man Gerardus Mercator born in a town in Flanders called Rupelmunda,[3] who by the universal suffrage of all the learned is esteemed the most excellent cosmographer & mathematician (Ortelius[4] only excepted) that has flourished in the world these thousand years. For he has written such exact and elegant geographical tables as will never suffer his name to be committed to oblivion.

Betwixt Duisburg and the town of Rhine-Bark[5] I observed the lamentable tokens of the Belgian wars, three churches very miserably battered and sacked, which was done by the soldiers of the Grave Maurice.[6] About a mile before I came to Rhine-Bark I saw a certain tower in the town of Dinslaking[7] in the province of Cleveland, the

---

1 *Koningsperg* Königsberg, now Kaliningrad, Russian Federation; *Prussia* Historical region of the southeastern Baltic coast.
2 *Cleveland* Duchy of Cleves.
3 *Gerardus Mercator* Gerard Mercator (1512–94), Dutch geographer and cartographer, famous for the Mercator Projection; *Flanders* Flemish region of Belgium; *Rupelmunda* Rupelmonde.
4 *Ortelius* Abraham Ortelius (1527–98), Flemish cartographer.
5 *Rhine-Bark* Rheinberg.
6 *Grave Maurice* Maurice, Landgrave of Hesse-Kassel.
7 *Dinslaking* Dinslaken.

walls whereof are said to be of such an exceeding thickness that no piece of ordinance is able to pierce it, but it will reverberate the bullet, be it never so great. For I heard it very credibly reported that they are eighteen feet thick. When I came to Rhine-Bark, which is a town belonging to the Archduke Albert,[1] and guarded by a garrison of his soldiers, there happened this accident: our whole company was stayed from passing any farther by certain officers for the space of two hours, to our great terror and amazement, in so much that we could not be suffered to depart till we had been all convened before the governor of the town, who was a Spanish gentleman, a man that used us more graciously than we expected. For after a few terms of examination he gently dismissed us. Here I saw one of their towers most grievously battered with shot, and many of their other buildings, which was done about a dozen years since by the Grave Maurice's soldiers. I heard most tragic news of two Englishmen in this town. For it was reported unto me, that whereas two of them went into the field to fight, the one being slain by the other,[2] he that killed his fellow was condemned by the governor to receive this punishment: to be shot to death by a dozen of his countrymen. And to be first tied to a post or some such thing with a paper pinned upon his breast, having a black mark in the middle. So this was accordingly performed. But the offender was so stout-hearted a fellow that his countrymen were constrained to discharge two or three volleys of shot at him before they could thoroughly dispatch him.

[...]

I arrived at the town of Rees in Cleveland about seven of the clock at night, as I have before said. Of my arrival there I will report one memorable thing. Whereas the gates of the town were locked before we came thither, presently after our arrival we made all the means that might be to be admitted into the town. But we were absolutely denied it a long time. Where upon we went into one of the ships that

---

1   *Archduke Albert* Albert VII (1559–1621), archduke and sovereign ruler of the Netherlands from 1595.

2   *whereas two ... the other* Though it is unclear from this passage whether the murdered English soldier lost a duel to the other or died accidentally due to friendly fire, the punishment meted out seems to suggest the former.

lay at the quay, determining to take a hard lodging there all night upon the bare boards. No sooner were we in the ship but I began to cheer my company as well as I could with consolatory terms, and pronounced a few verses and fragments of verses out of Virgil, tending to an exhortation to patience in calamities, as:

Quicquid erit, superanda omnis fortuna ferendo est.[1]

And,

Per varios casus & tot discrimina rerum tendimus in patriam[2]—

And,

Dabit Deus his quoque finem.[3]

And the same hemistichium[4] that I spoke joyfully unto myself, when with much labour and difficulty I was come to the top of the first Alpine mountain Aigubelette, as I entered into Savoy:

forsan & haec olim meminisse juvabit.[5]

But at last the burgomaster of the town being touched with a certain sympathy of our misery (having himself belike at some time tasted of the like bitter pills of adverse fortune, according to that memorable speech of Dido in Virgil:

Non ignara mali miseris succurrere disco,)[6]

---

1 [Coryate's Note] Aenei. 5. [Latin: Whatever will be, all fortune can be overcome by endurance. Virgil, *Aeneid* 5.710.]
2 [Coryate's Note] Aenei. 1. [Latin: Through various calamities and so many crises we pressed on to our fatherland. Virgil, *Aeneid* 1.204–05.]
3 [Coryate's Note] Ibid. [Latin: God will give us an end to these as well. Virgil, *Aeneid* 1.199.]
4 *hemistichium* Hemistich, or half-line.
5 [Coryate's Note] Ibid. [Latin: One day it will please us to remember even this. Virgil, *Aeneid* 1.203.]
6 *Non ignara ... disco* Latin: not ignorant of misfortune, I learn to help others in misery. Virgil, *Aeneid* 1.630.

was contented that the gates should be opened to admit us into the town, but first he sent two soldiers to us with their muskets charged, to the end to examine us what we were, and so after a few terms of examination they kindly conducted us to our inn, and that to our infinite comfort. For we were all most miserably weather-beaten and very cold, especially I for mine own part, who was almost ready to give up the ghost through cold. But when we came to our inn we were exceedingly refreshed with all things convenient for the comforting of distressed travellers.

[...]

I observed certain things both in this city of Nimmigen[1] and in other towns of the Netherlands, which I could not perceive in any place of high Germany. For it is their custom in the inns to place some few pieces of brown bread hard by the guests' trencher,[2] and a little white loaf or two. In many places also at the beginning of dinner or supper they bring some Martlemas beef (which custom is used also in some places of the Grisons country, as I have before mentioned) and a good pestle[3] of bacon to the table, before they bring any other thing. This I observed at Cologne, Rees, and other places: at the end of the meal they always bring butter. One of their customs I much disliked, that they sit exceeding long at their meals, at the least an hour and a half. And very seldom do they go to supper before seven of the clock. In most places betwixt Cologne and the farther end of the Netherlands even till I came to Vlyshingen commonly called Flushing the farthest town of Zeeland, I observed that they usually drink beer & not Rhenish wine, as in the higher parts of Germany. For they have no wine in their country. This custom also I observed amongst those of Cleveland, Gelderland,[4] and Holland, that whensoever one drinks to another, he shakes his fellow by the hand, and whensoever the men of the country come into an inn to drink, they use to take a tin tankard full of beer in their hands, and sit by it an hour together,

---

1   *Nimmigen* Nijmegen.
2   *trencher* Wooden platter for serving food.
3   *Martlemas beef* Beef from cows slaughtered on 11 November, the feast day of St. Martin, and preserved (through smoking or salting) for the winter; *pestle* Leg.
4   *Gelderland* Province in the central Netherlands.

yea sometimes two whole hours before they will let their tankards go out of their hands.

[...]

I observed another thing also betwixt Gorcom[1] and Dordrecht that moved great compassion in me. For I saw many churches half-drowned, all the upper part of the tower appearing very plainly above the water. There were heretofore fair parishes belonging to these churches, which were utterly defaced with the merciless fury of the angry god Neptune almost two hundred years since, as I will hereafter more particularly declare, so that there is not the least token of them to be seen at this day. Moreover I saw a fair castle drowned a little on this side Dordrecht, which in former times belonged to a nobleman of the country. It was seated in a fair town, which happened to be so overwhelmed with water at the same time, that the sea did so loose his reins of liberty to the destruction of the other towns, that there remains not the least stone thereof to be seen, saving only a part of the foresaid castle that does now belong to the town of Dordrecht, by which they enjoy certain privileges.

My observations of Dordrecht

This city in Latin is called *Dordracum*, but the common word is Dort, and some do call it Dordrecht. It is a very famous, opulent, and flourishing town, and memorable for many things, especially one above the rest the which is worthy the relation. For it is called the maiden city of Holland, (in which respect it may be as properly called parthenopolis, as Naples is in Italy, and Maydenburg[2] in Saxony) and that for these two causes. First, because it was built by a maid, but none of the citizens could tell me either the name of her, or the year of the lord when the foundation was laid. Neither indeed can I find it in any historian that has written of the Hollandish cities. But certain it is that a virgin was the first founder of it. For a monument whereof they have pictured a beautiful virgin in lively colours according to

---

1 *Gorcom* Gorinchem.
2 *parthenopolis* Greek: Maiden city; *Maydenburg* Magdeburg.

the full proportion of her body, over the gate near to their haven at the first entrance into the town, which picture is adorned round about with the arms of the principal families of Holland. Besides, for a farther testimony of this matter they used to stamp the figure of a maid upon one of their coins that is called a doit, whereof eight go to a stiver,[1] and ten stivers do make our English shilling. Secondly, because almighty God has privileged this town with such a special favour and prerogative, as no city or town that I ever read or heard of in all Christendom, saving only Venice. For it was never conquered, though all the circumjacent cities and towns of the whole territory of Holland have at some time or other been expugned[2] by the hostile force.

[...]

But if I should relate how it came to pass that this plot of ground was first converted to an island,

Quis talia fando
Myrmidonum Dolopumve, aut duri miles Ulysses
Temperet a lachrymis?[3]

For indeed it is a most lamentable and tragic matter to be spoken, and such a thing as cannot but move great commiseration. For whereas a part of it was ever joined to the main territory of Brabant, till the year of our lord 1420 it happened that these four foresaid rivers together with a part of the sea, did that very year upon the seventeenth day of April break up their *repagula*,[4] their bounds within the which they did ever soberly contain themselves till then, and made such a woeful inundation in the country, that I never read of the like in Christendom since the general cataclysm in the time of the patriarch Noah. For they overwhelmed sixteen fair towns: some write there were no less than three score and ten of them drowned. And they swallowed

---

1 *doit* Small Dutch coin; *stiver* Dutch silver coin.
2 *expugned* Captured.
3 [Coryate's Note] *Aenei* 2.[6–8.] [Latin: Who could tell such things, if even a Myrmidon or Dolopian or soldier of stern Ulysses could not refrain from tears?]
4 *repagula* Latin: door-bars.

up at the least a hundred thousand persons with all their goods, cattle, and whatsoever else. The pitiful tokens whereof I saw in diverse places of the country thereabout, namely certain towers of churches appearing above the waters, which belonged to those parishes that were frequently inhabited with people till the time of that deluge.

[…]

Having now related some of the principal things of this noble town, I will conclude my observations thereof, partly with mention of their religion, which is the Protestant. For popery is clean exterminated out of the town; and partly with that memorable *elogium* that is commonly attributed unto it by all those that know it well, that it is the very garden of Holland.

[…]

I departed from Dordrecht towards Zeeland in a bark the seven and twentieth of September being Tuesday about noon, and lay the same night in a hard lodging of my bark upon the water, about forty miles beyond it.

[…]

My observations of Vlyshingen commonly called Flushing, but in Latin Flissinga

The situation of this town is very memorable. For it is built in the form of a pitcher, which is slender at both the ends, and wide in the middle. In regard whereof the name of the town is derived from the Dutch word Flessche, which signifies a pitcher. For indeed he that shall rightly consider the form of the building thereof, will say that it does very near represent the fashion of a pitcher. For I for mine own part observed the site of it, and found it very correspondent to the mold of a pitcher, the ends being slender and the middle long. Which is the reason that the inhabitants do present the figure of a pitcher in their flags & banners that are advanced at the tops of the masts in their ships.

[...]

This town is guarded with a garrison of English soldiers, whereof one (who was a gentleman) I saw very martially buried that day that I came into Flushing, with a doleful beating of many drums, and discharging of many volleys of shot. All the companies of soldiers in this town are commanded by that right worshipful and most worthy knight Sir William Browne, who is deputy governor of this town under that right honourable and illustrious Robert Sidney Viscount Lisle.[1]

[...]

I made my abode in Flushing all Friday being the last day of September, and departed therehence in a bark the first day of October being Saturday, about four of the clock in the afternoon, and arrived at the custom house[2] in London the third day of October being Monday, about four of the clock in the afternoon, after I had enjoyed a very pleasant and prosperous gale of wind all the way betwixt Flushing and London.

The distance betwixt Flushing and London is a hundred and twenty miles.

The number of miles betwixt Venice and Flushing: in which account I name only some of the principal cities, as I have done before in the computation of the miles betwixt my native Parish of Odcombe and Venice. For it is needless to name all the particular miles betwixt all the cities and towns I passed through. Because it would be a repetition of that which I have already done.

---

1 *Sir William Browne* Lieutenant Governor of Flushing (d. 1611); *Robert Sidney Viscount Lisle* Robert Sidney (1563–1626), first Earl of Leicester, governor of Vlissingen from 1589, and Viscount Lisle from 1605. He was also the brother of the poet Sir Philip Sidney.
2 *custom house* Office where customs are collected.

Imprimis, betwixt Venice and the inn before mentioned upon
   the top of the mountain Ancone, otherwise called Montane
   de St. Marco, being the farthest bound of the Venetian
   signiory westward.   174
Item, betwixt the inn, and the city of Curia in Rhetia.   76
Item, betwixt Curia and Zurich the metropolitan city
   of Switzerland.   55
Item, betwixt Zurich and Basel.   40
Item, betwixt Basel and Strasbourg.   80
Item, betwixt Strasbourg and Heidelberg.   72
Item, betwixt Heidelberg and Frankfurt.   67
Item, betwixt Frankfurt and Cologne.   92
Item, betwixt Cologne and Nimmigen in Gelderland.   54
Item, betwixt Nimmigin and Dordrecht in Holland.   34
Item, betwixt Dordrecht and Flushing in Zeeland.   53

The total is   797

Again betwixt Flushing and London   120
Again, betwixt London and Odcombe   106
The total betwixt Venice and Odcombe   1023
The total betwixt Odcombe and Venice as I travelled
   over France is (as I have before written)   952
The total of my whole journey forth and back   1975

The cities that I saw in the space of these five months, are five and
forty. Whereof in France five. In Savoy one. In Italy thirteen. In
Rhetia one. In Helvetia three. In some parts of high Germany fifteen.
In the Netherlands seven.

FINIS.

Engraved title page to *Coryats Crudities*.

In Context

A. Paratextual Materials from the 1611 Edition of *Coryats Crudities*

Penned by fifty-eight individuals including Ben Jonson and John Donne, the "Panegyricke Verses" that open *Coryats Crudities* offer a humorous verse miscellany made up of mock encomiastic poems (poems of praise) written in a variety of languages and literary forms. Together they amount to an elaborate joke on Coryate, employing a proto-burlesque mode to poke fun at the traveler's mock-heroic journey. It seems Coryate himself commissioned some of the material collected in the "Verses," though most of the poems came to him unsolicited after word got out about the invitation to ridicule Coryate in verse (for Coryate's account of the genesis of the "Panegyricke Verses," see "An Introduction to the ensuing verses" below). Some of the most damning statements about Coryate in the "Panegyricke Verses" are qualified by printed marginal notes, which often supply clarifying and/or defensive glosses of the panegyrists' witty lines. There is a strong probability these printed marginal notes were written by Coryate himself.

Many of the poems refer to the engraved title page at the beginning of *Crudities* (reproduced on page 212), which depicts several of Coryate's escapades during his five-month European tour. The most prominent references to the engraved title page are found in Laurence Whitaker's "Certain opening and drawing distiches" and Ben Jonson's "Charms to unlock the mystery of the Crudities," both of which consist of satirical couplets keyed to the labeled title-page vignettes. Jonson's "Charms" accompany two other pieces he wrote for *Crudities*, a "character" of Coryate and an acrostic on his name. Collected here as well are six of the dozens of "Panegyricke Verses" originally printed in *Crudities*, including a particularly famous contribution by John Donne.

1. Laurence Whitaker, "Certain opening and drawing distiches, to be applied as mollifying cataplasms to the tumors, carnosities, or difficult pimples full of matter appearing in the author's front, conflated of stiptike and glutinous vapours[1] arising out of the Crudities: the heads whereof are particularly pricked and pointed out by letters for the reader's better understanding"

A

First, th'author here glutteth sea, haddock & whiting[2]
With spewing, and after the world with his writing.

Or,

Ye haddocks twixt Dover and Calais,[3] speak Greek;
For Tom filled your maws with it in Whitsun[4] week.

B

Though our author for's venery[5] felt no whip's smart,
Yet see here he rides in a Picardy cart.[6]

C

This horse pictur'd shows, that our Tatter-de-mallian[7]
Did ride the French hackneys,[8] and lie with th'Italian.

---

1   *Laurence Whitaker* English politician (1577/78–1654) and a friend of Coryate's; *distiches* Couplets; *cataplasms* Poultices; *tumors, carnosities* Swellings, skin growths; *author's front* Engraved title page of *Coryats Crudities*. Also a pun ("front" = "face" and "frontispiece"); *conflated of stiptike and glutinous vapours* Composed of tissue-contracting, sticky vapors.
2   *whiting* Common British whitefish.
3   [marginal note] Imperat. [*Imperatur*, Latin: it is ordered.]
4   [marginal note] Viz., anno 1608, when he began to travel. [Whitsun week occurs before Whitsunday (i.e., Pentecost), which is held on the seventh Sunday after Easter.]
5   *venery* Sexual indulgence.
6   *Picardy cart* Wheeled method of transport in France's Picardy region.
7   [marginal note] A word that in the Helvetian tongue signifies a ragged traveller. [Helvetian is a Latinate term meaning Swiss.]
8   *hackneys* Common horses.

Or,

Our author in France rode on horse without stirrup,
And in Italy bathed himself in their syrup.[1]

Or,

His love to strange horses he sorteth out prettily,[2]
He rides them in France, and lies with them in Italy.

D

He has crossed sea and land, now the clouds (says the text)
Of th'air he is climbing; 'ware Tom, fire[3] is next.

E

Here to his land-frigate he's ferried by Charon,[4]
He boards[5] her; a service a hot and a rare one.

Or,

Here to a touch-hole[6] he's row'd by his gondolier,
That fires his linstock,[7] and empties his bandolier.[8]

---

1   *syrup* Referring to illustration "M" on the engraved title page, which depicts Coryate sleeping at the feet of horses in a Bergamo stable. "Syrup" is used figuratively here to refer to horse urine.
2   *sorteth out prettily* Provides attractively.
3   [marginal note] The four elements.
4   *land-frigate* Prostitute. Literally speaking, a frigate is a boat, especially a warship; *Charon* Driver of the boat that ferries souls to the classical Underworld; here, he is invoked figuratively in reference to the gondolier.
5   *boards* Engages sexually.
6   *touch-hole* Cannon-hole used for igniting explosive charges.
7   *linstock* Long staff holding a match at its end, used to light cannons.
8   [marginal note] That is, the beauty of her countenance, and sweet smatches of her lips did enflame his tongue with a divine and fiery enthusiasm, and emptied the bandolier of his conceits, & inventions, for that time. [A bandolier is a belt holding ammunition. The sexual double meaning of this couplet is fairly obvious, regardless of the marginal note's deflective gloss.]

F

Here his frigate shoots eggs at him[1] empty of chickens,
Because she had made his purse empty of chicquins.[2]

Or,

Here she pelts him with eggs, he says, of rosewater,[3]
But trust him not reader, 'twas some other matter.

G

In vain here does Coryate pipe[4] and dispute,
His wench was, Jews will not be caught with his flute.[5]

Or,

Thy courtesan clipped[6] thee, ware Tom, I advise thee,
And fly from the Jews, lest they circumcise thee.

H

He longs for sweet grapes, but going to steal 'em,
He findeth sour grasps[7] and gripes from a Dutch skelum.[8]

---

1 *shoots eggs at him* Throws eggs at him. This episode does not occur in the prose travelogue of *Coryats Crudities*, suggesting that it was a) invented to humorous effect for the purpose of embellishing the engraved title page, or b) it really happened but was left out of the prose travelogue, and the news spread orally.

2 *chicquins* Chequins, or Italian gold coins.

3 *eggs … rosewater* Presumably egg-shaped objects containing rosewater, not literal eggs.

4 *pipe* Talk loudly.

5 *flute* With the double meaning of a) the means through which Coryate might lead the Jews to convert, and b) Coryate's penis (with an additional pun on the previous line's "pipe," meaning flute). The Jews and prostitute are mentioned in the same line because Coryate encountered both during his stay in Venice.

6 *clipped* A pun: "clipped" can mean "fleeced, stripped of money," but also "embraced."

7 *sour grasps* Unpleasant grasps, with a pun on "sour grapes," referring to Coryate's encounter with the boor in the German vineyard.

8 [marginal note] A rascal in Dutch.

Or,

Here is the combat our author may glory at,
With halberd the boor lays on, and with Greek Coryat.[1]

I

Here is his trophy victoriously dight[2]
With case,[3] shoes, and stockings, and lice put to flight.

Or,

See here his poor case, his shoes clouted with cunning,[4]
His stockings strong-smelling, and lice away running.

Or,

See our louse-bitten traveller's ragged device,[5]
Of case, shoes, and stockings, and cannibal lice.

Or,

This gibbet[6] the false case and hose does requite,
That harbour'd the vermin that their master did bite.

K

This should be his picture, 'tis rather his emblem,[7]
For by (K)[8] it notes him, though 't little resemble[9] him.

---

1   *halberd* Combination spear and battle-axe; *with Greek Coryat* Not knowing what to do
    in his encounter with the German boor, Coryate "discharged a whole volley of Greek and
    Latin shot upon him, supposing that it would be an occasion to pacify him somewhat" (see
    page 191).
2   *dight* Arranged.
3   *case* Clothing.
4   *clouted with cunning* Skillfully patched.
5   *device* Emblematic design.
6   *gibbet* Gallows.
7   *emblem* Allegorical drawing.
8   [marginal note] As being the first letter of his name in Greek.
9   [marginal note] But you differ in opinion (Mr. Laurence) from all my other friends that
    have compared together the counterfeited and the living figure.

Or,

This picture unlike him, shows he's not come home as
He went, but chang'd, and turn'd travelling Thomas.

Or,

This picture unlike him, shows he's not himself,
But chang'd since he proved a travelling elf.[1]

Or,

Know reader, the notes and contents of this book,
Are not to be guessed by th'author's carv'd[2] look.

L

These be the three countries with the cornucopia,
That make him as famous, as More his *Utopia*.[3]

Or,

Here France gives him scabs, Venice a hot sun,[4]
And Germany spews on him out of her tun.[5]

M

The horse he bestrid till he mounted his chair
Does kindly bestride him at Bergamo fair.[6]

---

1   *elf* Poor creature.
2   *carv'd* Engraved, i.e., referring to the image on the engraved title page, which would have
    been incised in a copper plate.
3   *Utopia* Thomas More's *Utopia* (1516).
4   *scabs* Syphilis; *hot sun* Sexual experience or prostitute, with heat and "sun" used figurative-
    ly.
5   *tun* Large vessel for wine, with specific reference to the Great Tun of Heidelberg, which
    Coryate describes in his travelogue.
6   *Bergamo fair* Week-long fair in Bergamo, which Coryate describes in the prose travelogue.

Or,

He courted a wench, but penance for his game o[1]
He does by lying with horses at Bergamo.

Or,

The Italian horse more than French his love feels,
For he rode on the one, and lay at th'others heels.

N

Most politic Thomas, now thou are no fol[2] I see,
For wanting no money, thou beggest in policy.[3]

LAURENCE WHITAKER.

2. Ben Jonson,[4] "Here follow certain other verses, as charms to unlock the mystery of the Crudities"

A

Here, like Arion,[5] our Coryate does draw
All sorts of fish with music of his maw.

B

Here, not up Holborn,[6] but down a steep hill,
He's carried 'twixt Montreil and Abbeville.

---

1   *game o* "O" has been added both to complete the rhyme and Italianize the English word "game."
2   [marginal note] The French word for a fool.
3   *beggest in policy* To avoid having to give money to country beggars near Baden-Baden, Germany, Coryate turns the tables and begs from them. His begging is a shrewd tactic, not a necessity for survival, thus begging in policy. The strategy works, as the beggars leave Coryate alone.
4   *Ben Jonson* English poet and dramatist (1572–1637).
5   *Arion* Greek lyric poet who, after being kidnapped by pirates, attracted dolphins to his boat with hymns sung to Apollo; after flinging himself into the sea he was rescued by one of the dolphins.
6   *Holborn* Holborn Hill, London.

C

A horse here is saddled, but no Tom him to back,
It should rather have been Tom that a horse did lack.

D

Here up the Alps (not so plain as to Dunstable)[1]
He's carried like a cripple, from constable to constable.[2]

E

A punk[3] here pelts him with eggs. How so?
For he did but kiss her, and so let her go.

F

Religiously here be bids, row from the stews,[4]
He will expiate this sin with converting the Jews.

G

And there, while he gives the zealous bravado,[5]
A Rabbi confutes him with the bastinado.[6]

H

Here, by a boor[7] too, he's like to be beaten,
For grapes he had gather'd before they were eaten.

---

1 *not so ... Dunstable* Not as plain as Dunstable, whose proverbial plainness is a reference to the Dunstable Way/Road, known for its straight and even-leveled path.
2 *constable to constable* Coryate encountered different constables in the cities and towns which he visited.
3 *punk* Prostitute.
4 *stews* Red-light district.
5 *gives the zealous bravado* Speaks vehemently and boastfully against [Judaism].
6 *bastinado* Cudgel.
7 *boor* Country peasant.

I

Old hat here, torn hose, with shoes full of gravel,
And louse-dropping case, are in the arms[1] of his travel.

K

Here, finer than coming from his punk you him see,
F.[2] shows what he was, K. what he will be.

L

Here France, and Italy both to him shed
Their horns,[3] and Germany pukes on his head.

M

And here he disdain'd not, in a foreign land,
To lie at livery,[4] while the horses did stand.

N

But here, neither trusting his hands, nor his legs,
Being in fear to be robbed, he most learnedly begs.

BEN JONSON.

---

1   *arms* Coat-of-arms.
2   [marginal note] Not meaning by F. and K. as the vulgar may peevishly and wittingly mistake, but that he was then coming from his courtesan a freshman, and now having seen their fashions, and written a description of them, he will shortly be reputed a knowing, proper, and well traveled scholar, as by his starched beard and printed ruff may be as properly insinuated. [The "F ... K" joke and many other jokes in the Jonson and Whitaker verses poke fun at Coryate's visit to and description of the Venetian courtesans.]
3   *horns* Cornucopiae.
4   *To lie at livery* To be stabled, as a horse, but also a literal reference to Coryate lying underneath horses while sleeping at Bergamo.

3. Ben Jonson, "Character of the famous Odcombian, or rather Polytopian,[1] Thomas the Coryate"

The Character of the Famous Odcombian, or rather Polytopian Thomas the Coryate Traveller, and Gentleman Author of these Quinque-mestrial[2] Crudities. Done by a charitable friend, that thinks it necessary, by this time, you should understand the maker as well as the work

He is an engine, wholly consisting of extremes, a head, fingers, and toes. For what his industrious toes have trod, his ready fingers have written, his subtle head dictating. He was set a going for Venice the fourteenth of May, anno 1608 and returned home (of himself)[3] the third of October following, being wound up for five months, or thereabouts: his peises two for one.[4] Since, by virtue of those weights[5] he has been conveniently able to visit town and country, fairs and markets, to all places, and all societies a spectacle grateful, above that of Nineveh, or the city of Norwich;[6] and his is now become the better motion, by having this his book his interpreter: which yet has expressed his purse more than him, as we the rest of his commenders have done, so unmercifully charging the press with his praise.[7] But to that gale, he sets up all sails.[8] He will bear paper (which is cloth) enough.[9] He has ever since the first design of printing hereof, been à

---

1   *Character* Satirical prose character sketch of a type or profession, modeled on the characters of Theophrastus (c. 371–c. 287 BCE); *Polytopian* Well-traveled, literally "many-placed."
2   *Quinque-mestrial* Five-month-long (Coryate traveled in Europe for five months).
3   *of himself* By himself.
4   *peises two for one* "Peises" are weights used in clock movements. The image draws on the metaphor of Coryate as an "engine" or clock, and presents the peises as a guarantee that Coryate will return safely from his travels ("two for one" means Coryate would receive double his initial investment if he returned to England alive).
5   *weights* I.e., peises. These extra "weights" enabled Coryate to travel quickly around Europe.
6   *Nineveh … Norwich* Nineveh, an ancient Assyrian city, was associated with pride in the Old Testament and destroyed in the seventh century BCE. Norwich was the terminus of William Kemp's dancing journey from London to Norfolk, a spectacle described in *Nine Days' Wonder* (1599).
7   *motion* Mechanism, machine (but with a pun on "motion" as puppet or puppet-show); *expressed his purse* Displayed its great cost (Coryate underwrote the publication of *Crudities*); *commenders … praise* Contributors to the "Panegyricke Verses"—including Jonson—wrote so many commendatory verses that the book's production cost increased dramatically. To "charge" the press is to overload it.
8   *sails* With a pun on "sales." In other words, Coryate sells books ("sets up all sails") thanks to the advertising "gale" of commendatory verses.
9   *He will bear … enough* Coryate will have enough paper (figured as the canvas cloth used for sails) to sell copies of his book, the handmade paper of which is literally made out of recycled rag cloth.

Deliciis to the court; but served there in his own clothes, and at his own costs: where he has not been costive of acquaintance to any, from the palatine to the plebian;[1] which popularity of his (it is thought by some of his Odcombians) may hurt him. But he free from all other symptoms of aspiring, will easily outcarry that; it being a motley and no perfect ambition: the rather, because when he should have been taken up for the place (though he hastily prevented it with a tender of himself) he conditioned to have no office of charge or nearness cast upon him, as a remora[2] of his future travail; for to that he is irrecoverably addicted. The word travail affects him in a wain-ox, or a pack-horse.[3] A carrier[4] will carry him from any company that has not been abroad, because he is a species of a traveller. But a Dutch-post[5] doth ravish him. The mere superscription[6] of a letter from Zurich sets him up like a top: Basel or Heidelberg makes him spin. And at seeing the word Frankfurt, or Venice, though but on the title of a book, he is ready to break doublet, crack elbows,[7] and overflow the room with his murmur. He is a mad Greek, no less than a merry,[8] and will buy his eggs,[9] his puddings, his gingerbread, yea cobble his shoes in the Attic dialect, and would make it a matter of conscience to speak other, were he trusted alone in a room with an andiron of state.[10] The greatest Politic that advances into Paul's[11] he will quit, to

---

1 à Deliciis to the court Court-favorite; costive of acquaintance Reluctantly sociable; palatine to the plebian Aristocrat to the commoner.

2 motley Diversely composed, imperfect; taken up for the place Given a position at court; tender of himself Formal offer of himself; conditioned Negotiated; office of charge or nearness Burdensome position that requires one to stay close to home; remora Impediment (the remora, a type of suckerfish, was once believed to retard the progress of ships).

3 The word travail ... pack-horse The word "travel" makes Coryate excited even over banal journeys via ox-cart (a "wain" is a cart) or pack-horse.

4 carrier Bearer of letters and messages.

5 But a Dutch-post Just a Dutch-post, a small sailing vessel bearing letters from the Low Countries.

6 superscription Address.

7 break doublet, crack elbows Tear clothing, slap elbows.

8 mad Greek, no less than a merry "Mad" and "merry" were common qualifiers of "Greek" in Coryate's England; both terms were used to refer to revelers and merry companions.

9 [marginal note] I mean when he travelled. A thing that I know he scorned to do since he came home. [Coryate clearly disdained grocery shopping, as evinced in his remarks on Venetian lords shopping at the farmer's market.]

10 buy his eggs ... Attic dialect Conduct his everyday affairs in the Athenian dialect of the Greek language; make it ... other Esteem it a grave offense to speak in another language; andiron of state Pillar of state.

11 Politic ... Paul's Politician who walks in St. Paul's Churchyard. "Politic" references the ridiculous traveler Sir Politic Would-be from Ben Jonson's comedy Volpone (1606).

go talk with the Grecian that begs there—such is his humility—and doth grieve inwardly he was not born that countryman for that purpose.[1] You shall perceive a vein or thread of Greek run through his whole discourse, and another of Latin, but that is the coarser. He is a great and bold carpenter of words, or (to express him in one like his own) a logodaedale:[2] which voice, when he hears, 'tis doubtful whether he will more love at the first, or envy after, that it was not his own. All his phrase is the same with his manner and haviour, such as if they were studied to make mourners merry: but the body of his discourse able to break impostumes, remove the stone,[3] open the passage from the bladder, and undo the very knots of the gout; to cure even where physic has turned her back, and nature hung down her head for shame, being not only the antidote to resist sadness, but the preservative to keep you in mirth, a life and a day. A man might undo the college that would practise with only him.[4] And there is no man but to enjoy his company, would neglect anything but business. It is thought he lives more by letting out[5] of air, than drawing in; and feared, his belly will exhibit a bill in Chancery against his mouth for talking away his meals.[6] He is always tongue-major of the company, and if ever the perpetual motion[7] be to be hoped for, it is from thence. He will ask, how you do? Where you have been? How is it? If you have travelled? How you like his book? with, what news? and be guilty of a thousand such courteous impertinences in an hour, rather than want the humanity of vexing you. To conclude this ample traveller in some bounds you shall best know him by this: he is frequent

---

1   [marginal note] Not to beg, but to talk Greek the better with the natural Grecians.

2   *logodaedale* Literally, "word craftsman," i.e., one who is crafty in words. The word is "like his own" because of its Greek etymology (Coryate is a frequent coiner of new English words from Greek roots).

3   *impostumes* Abcesses; *the stone* Gall- or kidney-stones.

4   *A man might … only him* Since Coryate's writing (described as an "antidote" and "preservative" in the previous sentences) is exceptionally effective at healing the sick, medical doctors practicing at a college would not have any work—they would be "undone" by a lack of patients.

5   [marginal note] I mean in the foreparts, not the hinder.

6   *his belly … his meals* His stomach will sue his mouth for denying him meals (by talking).

7   *tongue-major* Most loquacious person; *perpetual motion* Abstract goal of perpetual motion, but also with a specific reference to the machine displayed in King James I's Eltham Palace in 1607, purportedly with the ability to achieve perpetual motion (a phenomenon proved impossible by later scientific developments).

at all sorts of free tables, where though he might sit as a guest, he will rather be served in as a dish, and is loath to have anything of himself kept cold against the next day. To give the non-ultra of him in a word, he is so substantive[1] an author as will stand by himself without the need of his book to be joined with him.

Here ends the Character, attended with a Characterisme[2] Acrostic

4. Ben Jonson, "To the Right Noble Tom, Tell-Troth, of his Travails, the Coryate of Odcombe, and his Book now going to travel"

T rie and trust Roger,[3] was the word, but now
H onest Tom Tell-Troth puts down Roger, how?
O f travel he discourses so at large,
M arry he sets it out at his own charge;[4]
A nd therein (which is worth his valour too)
S hows he dares more than Paul's Churchyard[5] durst do.

C ome forth thou bonny[6] bouncing book then, daughter
O f Tom of Odcombe that odd jovial author,
R ather his son I should have call'd thee, why?
Y es thou were born out of his travelling thigh[7]
A s well as from his brains,[8] and claimest thereby
T o be his Bacchus as his Pallas: be
E ver his thighs Male then, and his brains She.

Ben. Jonson.

---

1 *non-ultra* Concluding summary; *substantive* Having substance, independent.
2 *Characterisme* Characterization.
3 *Trie and trust Roger* Tested and thus trustworthy man.
4 *sets ... charge* Personally underwrites the publication of his travelogue.
5 *Paul's Churchyard* Central location for London booksellers/stationers. Jonson implies that London stationers would not dare take on the expense of printing *Coryats Crudities*.
6 *bonny* Comely (with a secondary meaning of "big").
7 *born out of his travelling thigh* As Bacchus was born from the thigh of Jupiter. Jupiter, Bacchus's father, was forced to reveal his true form to his lover Semele, destroying her when he appeared as bolts of lightning. Semele was pregnant with Bacchus at the time, and Jupiter sewed the unborn child into his thigh for the remainder of his gestation period.
8 *from his brains* As Pallas Athena was born from Jupiter's head. Jupiter slept with the goddess Metis and impregnated her with Pallas Athena; but when he learned the child would be stronger than he, Jupiter swallowed Metis whole. Pallas Athena would later spring from Jupiter's head, full-grown and fully armed.

5. Thomas Coryate, "An Introduction to the ensuing Verses"

I here present unto thee (gentle reader) the encomiastic and panegyric verses of some of the worthiest spirits of this kingdom, composed by persons of eminent quality and mark, as well for dignity as excellency of wit; such as have vouchsafed to descend so low as to dignify and illustrate my lucubrations without any demerit of theirs[1] (I do ingenuously confess) with the singular fruits of their elegant inventions, which they have expressed in the best and most learned languages of the world, two only excepted which are the Welsh[2] and Irish. But in that I exhibit unto thy view such a great multitude of verses as no book whatsoever printed in England these hundred years had the like written in praise thereof; ascribe it not I entreat thee to any ambitious humour of me, as that I should crave to obtrude[3] so many to the world in praise of my book. For I can assure thee I solicited not half those worthy wights[4] for these verses that I now divulge; a great part of them being sent unto me voluntarily from diverse of my friends, from whom I expected no such courtesy. At last when I saw the multitude of them to increase to so great a number, I resolved to put above a thousand of them into an *Index expurgatorius*,[5] and to detain them from the press. Whereupon the Prince's Highness (who has most graciously deigned to be the *Hyperaspist*[6] and *Moecenas* of my book) understanding that I meant to suppress so many, gave me a strict and express commandment to print all those verses which I had read to his Highness. Since then that inevitable necessity has been imposed upon me, I have here communicated that copious rhapsody[7]

---

1   [Coryate's Note] Mistake me not reader. I refer this word to the word lucubrations. [Lucubrations are studies, meditations.]

2   [Coryate's Note] Ironia. [Welsh is indeed represented in the "Panegyricke Verses" (poems by Hugh Holland and Richard Hughes); this note, and the sentence it is appended to, both mockingly deride the notion that Welsh might be considered one of "the best and most learned languages of the world."]

3   *obtrude* Proffer intrusively.

4   *wights* People, especially unlucky ones; here the contributors to the "Panegyricke Verses."

5   *Index expurgatorius* List of passages in books to be deleted or changed, as stipulated by the Catholic Church.

6   [Coryate's Note] You shall understand the meaning of this word in a marginal note upon the verses immediately ensuing. [As Coryate explains in a marginal note to a commendatory poem not included in the present edition, "Hyperaspist" means "shield above" in Greek.]

7   *rhapsody* Literary medley.

of poems to the world that my learned friends have bountifully bestowed upon me; wherein many of them are disposed to glance at me with their free and merry jests, for which I desire thee (courteous reader) to suspend thy censure of me till thou has read over my whole book.

6. Selected "Panegyricke Verses" from *Coryats Crudities*

a. John Donne, "Incipit Joannes Donne"[1]

Oh to what height will love of greatness drive
Thy leavened spirit, sesqui-superlative?[2]
Venice vast lake[3] thou had seen, would seek then
Some vaster thing, and found a courtesan.
That inland sea having discovered well,
A cellar-gulf,[4] where one might sail to hell
From Heidelberg, thou longed to see; And thou
This book, greater than all, produces now,
Infinite work, which does so far extend,
That none can study it to any end.[5]
Tis no one thing; it is not fruit, nor root;
Nor poorly limited[6] with head or foot.
If man be therefore man, because he can
Reason, and laugh, thy book does half make man.
One half being made, thy modesty was such,
That thou on th'other half[7] would never touch.
When will thou be at full, great lunatic?[8]
Not till thou exceed the world? Can thou be like

---

1   *Incipit* Latin: he begins;   *Joannes Donne* John Donne (1572–1631), English poet and clergyman. This is one of the very few of his poems that Donne allowed to be printed in his lifetime.

2   *leavened* Inflated; *sesqui-superlative* Extremely superlative ("sesqui" literally means "one-and-a-half times").

3   *Venice vast lake* Venetian lagoon, part of the Adriatic Sea.

4   *cellar-gulf* Great Tun of Heidelberg ("cellar" because the tun was held in a wine cellar, "gulf" because of the enormous volume of wine contained in the tun).

5   *end* Purpose or conclusion.

6   *poorly limited* Piteously bounded.

7   *th'other half* Reason.

8   *lunatic* With a pun on the etymological root luna (moon), to which "be at full" also refers.

A prosperous nose-born wen,[1] which sometime grows
To be far greater than the mother-nose?
Go then; and as to thee, when thou did go,
Munster did towns, and Gesner[2] authors show,
Mount now to Gallo-Belgicus;[3] Appear
As deep a statesman, as a gazetteer.[4]
Homely and familiarly, when thou come back,
Talk of Will Conqueror, and Prester Jack.[5]
Go bashful man, lest here thou blush to look
Upon the progress of thy glorious book.
To which both Indies sacrifices send;[6]
The west send gold, which thou did freely spend,
(Meaning to see't no more) upon the press.[7]
The east sends hither her deliciousness;
And thy leaves must embrace what comes from thence,[8]
The myrrh, the pepper, and the frankincense.
This magnifies thy leaves; but if they stoop
To neighbor wares,[9] when merchants do unhoop

---

1   *nose-born wen* Nose-wart.

2   *Munster* Sebastian Münster, whose *Cosmographia universalis* (1544) Coryate drew upon
    extensively in his description of Germany;   *Gesner* Conrad Gessner (1516–65), whose
    Bibliotheca universalis (1545) was a bibliography listing and describing thousands of books.

3   *Gallo-Belgicus Mercurius gallobelgicus* (1588–1638), a German printed newsletter.

4   *gazetteer* Newspaper journalist. To "appear as deep a statesman as a gazetteer," then, is to
    have a shallow understanding of politics and statecraft.

5   *Will Conqueror, and Prester Jack* William I (c. 1027–87), also called William the Conqueror,
    King of England and leader of the Norman invasion (1066). Prester John was a legendary
    Christian king of Africa whom many European explorers and diplomats attempted (un-
    successfully) to discover on their travels. The implication is that Coryate would be lying
    (or delivering old news) if he came home telling tall tales of long-dead kings and legendary
    monarchs.

6   *both Indies sacrifices send*   In the metaphor introduced by this phrase, both the West In-
    dies (Caribbean and South America) and East Indies (Southeast Asia) send "sacrifices" to
    Coryate's book: "gold" from the West Indies becomes English money pledged by patrons in
    support of the book's production, while spices from the East Indies are wrapped in the paper
    making up *Crudities*.

7   *thou did freely ... upon the press* Coryate paid for the printing of *Crudities* partially with
    money earned from a bet he made with Joseph Starre of Yeovil, linen draper (and probably
    also from English patronage, figured here as "the west" who "send gold").

8   *And thy leaves ... thence* Your paper [from *Crudities*] will be recycled as wrapping for eastern
    drugs and spices.

9   *but if they stoop ... wares* If the paper from *Crudities* were used to wrap a lesser kind of
    consumer good ("neighbor wares" to the eastern spices).

Voluminous barrels, if thy leaves do then
Convey these wares in parcels unto men,
If for vast tomes of currants, and of figs,
Of medicinal, and aromatic twigs,[1]
Thy leaves a better method do provide,
Divide to pounds, and ounces subdivide;[2]
If they stoop lower yet, and vent our wares,
Home-manufactures, to thick[3] popular fairs,
If omnipregnant[4] there, upon warm stalls
They hatch all wares for which the buyer calls,
Then thus thy leaves we justly may commend,
That they all kind of matter comprehend.
Thus thou, by means which th'Ancients never took,
A pandect[5] makes, and universal book.
The bravest heroes,[6] for public good
Scattered in diverse lands, their limbs and blood.
Worst malefactors, to whom men are prize,
Do public good, cut in anatomies;[7]
So will thy book in pieces: for a Lord
Which casts at portescues, and all the board,
Provide whole books;[8] each leaf enough will be
For friends to pass time, and keep company.
Can all carouse[9] up thee? No: thou must fit
Measures; and fill out for the half-pint wit.[10]
Some shall wrap pills, and save a friends life so,

---

1   *vast tomes ... twigs* Vast amounts of currants, figs, etc., with a joke on the large size of *Crudities* (its paper capable of wrapping quite a lot of fruit, drugs, and spices).
2   *Divide ... subdivide* The paper from *Crudities* can be used to help divide medicinal substances into smaller amounts.
3   *Home-manufactures* English-made goods; *thick* Crowded.
4   *omnipregnant* Capable of producing anything.
5   *pandect* Encyclopedic treatise.
6   *bravest heroes* Soldiers and fighters (who lose their lives in foreign wars to protect their homeland).
7   *Worst malefactors ... cut in anatomies* Criminals who hunt men for sport can become useful to society when their bodies are dissected.
8   *for a Lord ... whole books* Give entire copies of *Crudities* to gaming Lords, who will need the paper to record gambling debts owed in portegues, or Portuguese gold coins.
9   *carouse* Drink.
10 *fit ... half-pint wit* Coryate (figured here as variously sized alcoholic drinks) must accommodate the differing wits and tastes of his readers.

Some shall stop muskets,[1] and so kill a foe.
Thou shall not ease the critics of next age
So much, at once their hunger to assuage.[2]
Nor shall wit-pirates hope to find thee lie
All in one bottom, in one library.[3]
Some leaves may paste strings there in other books,[4]
And so one may, which on another looks,
Pilfer, alas, a little wit from you,
But hardly much;[5] and yet, I think this true;
As Sybil's was, your book is mystical,
For every piece is as much worth as all.[6]
Therefore mine impotency I confess;
The healths[7] which my brain bears, must be far less;
Thy giant wit o'erthrows me, I am gone;
And rather than read all, I would read none.

---

1 *stop muskets* Furnish paper wadding for musket charges.
2 *their hunger to assuage* Because the leaves of *Crudities* will be wrapping paper for foodstuffs.
3 *wit-pirates ... one library* Plagiarists will not be able to find a complete copy of *Crudities* in any one library (its leaves having been recycled for so many diverse uses).
4 *Some leaves ... other books* Pages from *Crudities* will be used as pastedown endpapers in other printed books (these were papers affixed to the inside covers of books to protect the exposed sewing bands of the binding structure).
5 [marginal note] I mean from one page which shall paste strings in a book. [That is, a page from *Crudities* used as a pastedown endpaper. "A little wit" has a playful double meaning here: little because it comprises the material from only a single page of *Crudities*, or little because there is little wit in *Crudities* to begin with.]
6 *As Sybil's ... all* Reference to the Sibylline Books of prophecies, which the Sibyl of Cumae (a mythical Roman prophetess) offered for sale to Tarquinius Superbus, king of Rome. After Tarquinius refused the initial asking price, the Sibyl burned three of the nine books; she then demanded the initial price for the remaining six. Tarquinius's second refusal led to three more burned volumes, and in the end the obstinate king paid the full initial amount for the last three books. Just as three Sibylline Books cost the same as nine, each page of *Crudities* is as valuable as the whole book. Donne's statement can be interpreted two ways: the pages and book are either valuable or worthless.
7 *healths* Toasts, drinks. Donne means his brain cannot handle Coryate's "full-pint wit" and must only imbibe in small quantities.

b. John Donne, "In eundem Macaronicon"[1]

As many perfect Linguists as these two Distichs will make,
So many sensible Statesmen will be made by this, your book.
For my honour it is enough to be understood here; for I leave
The honour of being believed by no one, gladly, to you.[2]

In eundem Macaronicon.

Qvot, dos hæc, Linguists perfetti, Disticha fairont,
     Tot cuerdos States-men, hic liure fara tuus.
Es sat a my l'honneur estre hic inteso; Car I leaue
     L'honra, de personne nestre creduto, tibi.

Explicit Ioannes Donne.

John Donne, "In eundem Macaronicon" ("a Macaronic on the same").

---

1 *In eundem Macaronicon* Latin and Greek: a Macaronic on the same [subject]. This poem
  is an example of macaronic verse, a form originating in early sixteenth-century Italy that
  blends words and forms from vernacular languages with Latin for playful effect. The name
  derives from the Italian word *maccaroni*, formerly denoting cheaply made flour dumplings.
  Donne's macaronic verse includes Latin, English, French, Italian, and Spanish; see the fac-
  simile also included here. Translation by Roger Kuin.
2 *As many ... to you* The poem's two couplets will give its readers an impressive command of
  languages, just as Coryate's travel writing will create "sensible statesmen" among his audiences (both are tongue-in-cheek statements, as the lines are made up of blended languages
  and Coryate's book intentionally eschews matters of foreign government). To Donne, it
  would be enough for his readers simply to understand his poem's meaning, but Coryate
  must persuade his audiences to believe his unbelievable travel account.

c. Laurence Whitaker, "Sonnet composè en rime à la Marotte"[1]

Sonnet composed in Marotian rhyme,[2] adapted to the style of the book's Author;[3] made in praise of that Heroic Odcombian Giant, named not Pantagruel but Pantacrane,[4] i.e. neither fish, flesh nor good red herring but all Crane,[5] served up here in a Gallimaufry, hash, or Capirotade,[6] to have its destined place in the Library of St Victor's Abbey in Paris,[7] between Beardape's *Of baboons and monkeys* and Fartblower's *Of the Nobility of Tripes*;[8] and to be known as *Coryats Capirotade*, or, *The Apodemistichopezology of the Odcombe-Yeovilian of Somers(o)t*[9] in &c.

---

1 *Sonnet composè ... Marotte* French: Sonnet composed in Marotian rhyme. Translation by Roger Kuin, with minimal edits by Philip Palmer.

2 [marginal note] Known according to the style of Clement Marot the old French poet. [Anne Lake Prescott, in *Imagining Rabelais in Renaissance England* (Yale, 1998), points out that the marginal note "deliberately misidentif[ies]" the original French "à la Marotte" because "a *marotte* was a fool's scepter" (72). Clément Marot (c. 1496–1544) was also a French poet.]

3 *the book's Author* Thomas Coryate.

4 *Pantagruel* Gigantic character in the comic literary satire *Gargantua and Pantagruel* (1532–35), written by François Rabelais; *Pantacrane* Pun on "Pantagruel" (the original French is "Pantagrue"; "grue" means crane in French).

5 *neither fish ... red herring* Proverbial for "neither one nor the other" (red herring is a cured fish); *all Crane* Literal meaning of "Pantacrane" in previous line. The original French reads "tout Grue."

6 *Gallimaufry* Dish comprising various bits of food; *hash* Dish of finely chopped meat; *Capirotade* Meat and cheese hash.

7 *Library of St Victor's Abbey in Paris* Fictional library in Book Two, Chapter Seven of Rabelais's *Gargantua and Pantagruel*, whose catalog contains dozens of satirically titled fake books.

8 *between Beardape's ... Tripes* Reference to two of the fake books in Rabelais's catalog of the Library of St. Victor's Abbey. Since Rabelais lists thirty books shelved between these two volumes in his catalog of the Abbey library, the line is also a joke on the extremely large width of *Coryats Crudities*.

9 *The Apodemistichopezology* Invented portmanteau word comprising several Greek words/roots, including *apodemica* (Greek: travel), *demistich* (Greek: half-line), *pezos* (Greek: walking on foot), and *logy* (Greek: the study of). Combined together the word means something like "The Study of Foot-Travel in Half-Lines"; *Odcombe-Yeovilian* A person from the region of Odcombe and Yeovil: Coryate was born and raised in the village of Odcombe, which is a little under four miles from the town of Yeovil; *Somers(o)t* Pun on Somerset, Coryate's home county, and "sot," meaning "fool."

If this land's spacious meads and forests cool
(In which was bred this precious prating fool[1])
Or Switzerland, or lands 'neath German sun,
could but provide some sweet companion
of spirit similar and like estate[2]
to him, that old Deucalion, once great,
and Pyrrha would in them now be reborn:
for from their downflung pebbles nought was born
but mass of men and hence a world made new:[3]
But of the stones where Badger[4] here once threw
His glance (on bridges and on gallows high,
Church towers, or statues that do Justice try[5])
At once is born a great and horrid tome[6]
Of grand discourses, that has now become
The anvil of our wit,[7] a world of folly,
Pleasure for those whom gout makes melancholy.
Shut up, Rab'lais, now downcast be the pride
Of your great Sausages, who kindly tried
Your Giant[8] to receive in th'Isle of Wild:[9]
For Odcombe's Giant, stones and stumps beguiled
The time,[10] and spoke; even the nutmeg dry
In this work entertained him, tastefully.[11]

---

1 [marginal note] That is to say, a traveler, of the Greek word, βαδιζειν. [Greek: *badizein*, to walk. The original French word is "Badin."]

2 *estate* Condition.

3 *that old Deucalion ... made new* Reference to the myth of Deucalion and Pyrrha, a married couple who were the sole survivors of a catastrophic flood sent by Zeus. After the flood the Titan Themis instructed them to throw stones, which transformed into a new generation of human beings.

4 [marginal note] A certain animal that has strong and sharp eyesight. [The original French "nostre Blaireau" literally translates to "our Badger," referring to Thomas Coryate.]

5 *statues that do Justice try* Statues depicting Justice holding scales.

6 *great and horrid tome* *Coryats Crudities*, which in its original edition ran to over 900 pages.

7 *has now ... our wit* I.e., *Coryats Crudities* has become an anvil upon which the wits of the mock panegyrists are shaped.

8 [marginal note] Pantagruel.

9 [marginal note] An island also named by Rabelais. [Reference to *Gargantua and Pantagruel* 4.35, where Pantagruel encounters an island of animate sausages.]

10 *stumps* Tree stumps; *beguiled ... time* Helped pass the time.

11 *even the nutmeg ... tastefully* Even the spices Coryate encountered during his travels kept him company ("tastefully" being a pun on the flavor of nutmeg).

But why such interlocutors?[1] Poor fool,
His crest-proud[2] head inspired in him this rule:
That, knowing not the tongues of men abroad,[3]
On stumps and stones he'd spend his passion's hoard.[4]

d. Hugh Holland, "To Topographical Typographical[5] Thomas"

I sing the man, I sing the woeful case,[6]
The shirt, the shoes, the shanks that served to trace
Seven countries wide, the greater was his pain,
That two to one[7] he ever came again,
Yet two for one he came: O muse, O maid,
(If maid or muse) say what has so beraid[8]
This silly soul,[9] and drove him to such labours,
As had his hide been only made for tabors?[10]
Recount my girl, what did he with the French,
Before he courted the Venetian wench?
How could he leave his well-boiled beer, & scape,
To drink the raw blood of the German grape?
Wherewith his watery teeth being set on edge,

---

1   *such interlocutors* That is, the stones, stumps, and plants.

2   *crest-proud* Having a figurative rooster's comb (or "crest"), symbolic of pride.

3   *knowing not ... abroad* Not understanding foreign languages.

4   *On stumps ... hoard* Coryate spent all of this time abroad describing trees, plants, and stone monuments.

5   *Hugh Holland* English poet (1563–1633) and friend of Coryate's; *Typographical* Related to printing.

6   *I sing the man* Parody of the opening phrase of Virgil's *Aeneid*: Arma virumque cano (Latin: I sing of arms and the man); *case* Misfortunate instance (but with a pun on "case" meaning clothing).

7   *two to one* Before embarking on his journey through Europe, Coryate made a bet with the linen draper Joseph Starre. Coryate deposited an initial sum of £40 with Starre before he left: if he died on the journey Starre could keep the money, but if he returned to England Starre would owe Coryate 200 marks (around £133). Holland's "two to one" and "two for one," then, are inaccurate descriptions of the bet; 3.3 to 1 would be more accurate (though unsuited for the poem's meter).

8   *beraid* Besmirched.

9   [marginal note] *Insignem pietate virum*. [Latin: A man distinguished in piety. "Silly" could mean both weak and pious.]

10   *tabors* Drums.

He nigh had lost of teeth his double hedge.[1]
At home much did he suffer, much abroad,
And never once (poor ass)[2] did cast his load,
Yet further went than Scaracalasino,[3]
And after littered lay at Bergamo.
This usage did he bear abroad uncivil,[4]
At home too was he born not far from Yeovil.
In Odcombe parish yet famous with his cradle,
A chick he hatched was of an egg unaddle.[5]
Whence a young cockerel he was sent for knowledge
To Winchester, and planted in the college:[6]
Not there to prove a goose (for he is none)
But that he might with other cocks come on.[7]
Where lo a dwarf in stature he so pliant
Grew in the Greek, that he became a giant,
Pronouncing than Demosthenes each letter
More plain, and reading all than Homer better,
This prince of poets, that of rhetoricians.[8]
His Latin too deserves more praise than Priscian's[9]
For Coryate lives, and Priscian he is dead,
No marvel; Coryate brake so oft his head.
Now when in Greek and Latin he could gravel[10]
His school fellows, forsooth he needs will travel;

---

1   [marginal note] ἕρκος ὀδόντων. *Hom.* [Greek: barrier of teeth, an emblem of epic terseness, which is a heroic quality in Homer's *Iliad*.]
2   [marginal note] Note reader that a traveller must have the back of an ass, the mouth of a sow, the eye of a hawk, a merchant's ear, &c. [These are references to popular sayings.]
3   *Scaracalasino* Scaricalasino, nickname for Monghidoro, Italy, a town at the top of a steep hill.
4   *This usage ... uncivil* Coryate tolerated the "uncivil usage" of having to sleep in a Bergamo horse-stable.
5   *unaddle* Not rotten.
6   *Winchester ... college* Coryate attended Winchester College, an elite boy's school in Hampshire, England.
7   *with other cocks come on* Coryate acted not as a foolish or silly goose, but as a headstrong rooster, "a young cockerel."
8   *This prince ... rhetoricians* Homer is the prince of poets, Demosthenes of rhetoricians.
9   *Priscian* Latin grammarian (sixth century CE).
10 *gravel* Confound (in debate).

Not for bare language, but (his charges earning
On the by) on the main, for real learning.
Be Basel proof and Zurich too, and Frankfurt,
As thou in print may see, if thou him thank for't.
What would he with more tongues? He has enough,
That which he has is fine neat-leather tough:[1]
And yet at Calais to confound the mass
Some say he spake the tongue of Balaam's ass.[2]
And others, that with Sampson's ass's jawbone[3]
He slew whole hosts: so is he rough and rawbone.[4]
T'were but a frump[5] to name the ass's back,
Each common traveller bears thereon his pack:
I therefore leave the ass for fear he doubt,
Or others for him, that I should him flout.
But as the serpent (not the goose) that hisses,
So is he wise, and equaled with Ulysses;
Who towns of many men has seen & manners:[6]
The more was he beholding to the tanners.[7]
If he had but one only pair of shoes,
Then how much leather think ye could he lose?

    He has seen Paris garden and the lions,
And Paris garden of all France, and Lyons,
With all the towns that lie twixt this and Venice,
Where (howbeit some say he played at tennis)
He more prevailed against the 'xcoriate[8] Jews,

---

1 *fine neat-leather tough* Tough as fine calf-leather.

2 *Balaam's ass* Donkey miraculously given the power of speech in Numbers 22. In the story the donkey can see an angel invisible to Balaam; when the donkey tries to avoid the angel Balaam curses it and demands it move in the direction he desires. The donkey is then given the power to speak and tells Balaam about the angel.

3 *Sampson's ass's jawbone* Weapon with which Sampson slew hordes of Philistines in Judges 15.

4 *rawbone* Large-framed, intimidating.

5 frump Jeer.

6 *Ulysses ... manners* Cf. Homer's *Odyssey* 1.4: "Many cities did he visit, and many were the nations with whose manners and customs he was acquainted"; *Ulysses* Odysseus, mythical Greek hero-trickster and protagonist of Homer's *Odyssey*.

7 *tanners* Craftsmen who prepare and tan animal hides for leather-making.

8 *'xcoriate* Excoriated, or flayed (with a reference to circumcision).

Than Broughton[1] could, or twenty more such Hughs,
And yet but for one petty poor misprision,[2]
He was nigh made one of the circumcision.
But holla, that's a part that must be privy;[3]
Now go we to the town of learned Livy.[4]
Where being before licentiate,[5] he proceeded
To beg like a poor Paduan, when he needed.
Then through Vicenza and Brescia does he go
Among the Cogleons,[6] those of Bergamo.
Who made him lie in litter like a villain:[7]
Then views he, in his case of fustian, Milan.
(Not Milan fustian though) yet such a trophy[8]
As might become a soldan or a sophie.[9]
Which in his frontispiece he doth extol,[10]
Like those of Marius in Rome's Capitol.[11]
And well the case was lined with powdered ermine,[12]
Though others think it was some stranger vermin.
Now should I tell his travels with the Dutch,
But that my muse does fear to drink too much.
For, if the water of poor Hippocrene[13]
Does make her drunk, what will the wine of Rhene?

---

1   *Broughton* Hugh Broughton (1549–1612), English consul to Venice in the late sixteenth century.

2   *misprision* Misunderstanding.

3   *privy* Private.

4   *town of learned Livy* Padua, birthplace of Titus Livius (59 BCE–17 CE), Roman historian whose writings were an important source for Elizabethan writers including Shakespeare.

5   *licentiate* Permitted.

6   *Cogleons* Cogleones, plural of an Italian surname.

7   *villain* Rustic.

8   *Milan fustian* Milanese cloth; *trophy* Memorial of military victory, here referring to Coryate's clothing displayed on the engraved title page (illustration "I").

9   *soldan or a sophie* Turkish rulers. This comment creates a bathetic effect (anticlimactic juxtaposition of the trivial and serious) because "a trophy" that "might become a soldan or sophie" would be opulent and Coryate's "trophy"—ragged and riddled with lice—is anything but.

10   *frontispiece … extol* On the engraved title page it is displayed (see illustration "I").

11   *those of Marius … Capitol* Public monuments commemorating the military victories of Gaius Marius (c. 157–86 BCE).

12   *powdered ermine* Spotted weasel fur.

13   *Hippocrene* Fountain of the Muses.

Both Heidelberg I pass, and the great hogshead,
Which he bestrid himself, like a great hogs-head.
Who list[1] the pains or pleasure take to look,
Shall this and more find printed in the book.
Whose merits here I will not further raise:
That were my friend to sell, and not to praise.
Perhaps I know some that have seen the Turk,
Yet would be whipped ere they wrote such a work.
But what a volume here will rise anon,
When he has seen both Turk and Prester John?[2]
Enough: yet in his Crudities behoof,[3]
This will I say: it is a book of proof.
Wherein himself appears (I will be plain)
No fool in print, nor yet a knave in grain.[4]

e. John Hoskins, "Incipit Joannes Hoskins"[5]

Also there is this tune added to the verses, and pricked[6] according to
the form of Music to be sung by those that are so disposed. [...]

Admired Coryate, who like a Porcupine
Dost shew prodigious[7] things to thy countrymen.
As that beast when he kills doth use his own darts,[8]
So do thy pretty quills make holes in our hearts.[9]
That beast lives of other company destitute,[10]

---

1   *list* Desires.
2   *Turk and Prester John* Referring to the Middle Eastern travels upon which Coryate was soon
    to embark.
3   *behoof* Benefit.
4   *No fool ... grain* Coryate did not humiliate himself in print with *Crudities*, nor is he an
    inveterate knave.
5   *Joannes Hoskins* John Hoskins (1566–1638), poet and judge who, along with many con-
    tributors to the "Paneygricke Verses," participated in sociable meetings at the Mitre Tavern
    (London) with Coryate and others.
6   *pricked* Set down with marks or "pricks," as in the writing of music, with a pun on the
    porcupine's pricking spines.
7   *shew* Show; *prodigious* Amazing.
8   *darts* Quills or spines. It was formerly believed that porcupines could shoot their quills over
    short distances to incapacitate prey.
9   *thy pretty quills ... hearts* Your clever writing [denoted by "quills"] affects our hearts.
10 *That beast ... destitute* Porcupines are solitary animals.

So wentest thou alone every way absolute.
That beast creepth afoote, *nec absque pennis*,[1]
So didst thou trot a journey hence to Venice.
Live long foe to thy foe fierce as a Porcupine,
Live long friend to thy friend kind as a Porcupine.
Henceforth add to thy crest[2] an armed *Histrix*,[3]
Since thy carriage hath resembled his tricks.[4]

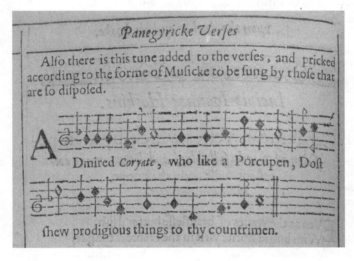

Opening lines of Hoskins's poem on Coryate, set to music.

---

1 *nec absque pennis* Latin: and without wings.
2 *crest* Coat-of-arms.
3 *Histrix* Greek: porcupine. It is "armed" (with a pun on the meaning of crest as "coat-of-arms") with quills.
4 *carriage* Conduct or behavior; *his tricks* With a pun on "Histrix."

f. John Dones, "Incipit Joannes Dones"[1]

Lo here's a man, worthy indeed to travel,
Fat[2] Libyan plains, strangest China's gravel.
For Europe well hath seen him stir his stumps:[3]
Turning his double shoes to simple pumps.[4]
And for relation,[5] look he doth afford
Almost for every step he took a word;
What had he done had he ere hugged th'Ocean[6]
With swimming Drake or famous Magellan?[7]
And kis'd that unturn'd cheek[8] of our old mother,[9]
Since so our Europe's world he can discover?[10]
It's not that French[11] which made his Gyant[12] see
Those uncouth islands where words frozen be,
Till by the thaw next year they're voiced again;[13]
Whose *Papagauts*, *Andoûilets*,[14] and that train

---

1   *Joannes Dones* Perhaps John Donne, poet (see the poem above titled "Incipit Joannes
    Donne"). Scholars have argued both for and against Donne's authorship of the poem.
2   *Fat* Fertile.
3   *stir his stumps* Walk quickly.
4   *double shoes* Double-soled shoes; *simple pumps* Single-soled shoes with low heels.
5   *relation* Account of travel.
6   *ere* Rather; *hugged th'Ocean* Sailed on the sea.
7   *Drake* Sir Francis Drake (1540–96), English explorer and pirate; *Magellan* Ferdinand
    Magellan (1480–1521), Portuguese explorer. Both figures are known for their early circum-
    navigations.
8   [marginal note] *Terra incognita.* [Latin: unknown land.]
9   *our old mother* Mother Earth, i.e., Earth.
10 *Since ... discover?* Since therefore he can explore Europe. Coryate did not "hug th'Ocean"
    like Drake or Magellan but instead traveled in Europe.
11 [marginal note] *Rablais.* [The French writer François Rabelais.]
12 [marginal note] *Pantagruel.*
13 *Those uncouth islands ... again* Beginning of an extended allusion to episodes from Rabe-
    lais's *Gargantua and Pantagruel*. In Chapters 55–56 of Book Four, Pantagruel finds words
    frozen in the Arctic ice during his travels.
14 *Papagauts, Andoûilets* French: popehawks, sausages. References to episodes in Rabelais's
    Gargantua and Pantagruel: in Chapter Three of Book Five, Pantagruel and company arrive
    at the Ringing Island and see the popehawk, which is a thinly veiled satirical stand-in for
    the Roman Catholic Pope; the travelers land at Savage Island in Chapter 35 of Book Four,
    where they encounter a civilization of animate sausages.

Should be such matter for a Pope to curse[1]
As he would make;[2] make! makes ten times worse,[3]
And yet so pleasing as shall laughter move:
And be his vain,[4] his gain, his praise, his love.
　　Sit not still then, keeping fame's trump[5] unblown:
But get thee Coryate to some land unknown.
From whence proclaim thy wisdom with those wonders,
Rarer than summer's snows, or winter's thunders.
And take this praise of that th'ast[6] done already:
Tis pity ere thy flow should have an eddy.[7]

Woodcut of Coryate's shoes, by Henry Peacham (1578–c. 1644), English emblematist, included in *Coryats Crudities*.

1　*Pope to curse*　The Pope would be angry reading Rabelais, especially the episode of the popehawk.
2　*As he would make*　That is, literary "matter" written by Rabelais.
3　*makes ten times worse*　That is, Coryate's writing is ten times "worse" than Rabelais's. The line can be construed as an insult (if the reader sympathizes with the Pope and hates Rabelais) or a compliment (if the reader finds Rabelais's satire clever and entertaining).
4　*be his vain*　Satisfy his (Coryate's) vanity.
5　*trump*　Trumpet.
6　*th'ast*　Elision of "thou hast."
7　*thy flow should have an eddy*　Your "flow" (of writing) should have an interruption. An eddy runs against the main current.

B. Materials from *Coryats Crambe* (1611)

Coryats Crambe (London, 1611) contains all the material Coryate could not fit into *Crudities*, and is thus less a sequel or follow-up volume than an appendix to his travelogue. *Crambe* features additional "Panegyricke Verses" that arrived too late to be printed in *Crudities*, as well as several prose texts relating to the early production, circulation, and reception of the volume. These prose texts include dedicatory orations to members of the British royal family to whom Coryate presented deluxe copies of *Crudities*, two of which—orations to Prince Henry Frederick and King James I—are collected here.

1. "Certain verses written upon *Coryats Crudities*, which should have been printed with the other panegyric lines, but then were upon some occasions omitted, and now communicated to the world"

a. Ben Jonson, "Incipit Ben. Jonson"

To the London reader, on the Odcombian writer, Polytopian Thomas the traveller.

Whoever he be, would write a story at
The height,[1] let him learn of Mr. Tom Coryate;
Who, because his matter in all should be meet,[2]
To his strength, hath measured it out with his feet.[3]
And that, say philosophers, is the best model.
Yet who could have hit on't but the wise noddle[4]
Of our Odcombian, that literate elf?
To line out no stride, but passed by himself?
And allow you for each particular mile,

---

1   *height* Highest point.
2   *meet* Well-suited.
3   *hath measured ... feet* Coryate has determined the book's content by physically measuring it with traveled footsteps.
4   *noddle* Head.

By the scale of his book, a yard of his style?[1]
Which, unto all ages, for his will be known,
Since he treads in no other man's steps but his own.
And that you may see he most luckily meant
To write it with the self same spirit he went,
He says to the world, let any man mend it,
In five months he went it, in five months he penned it.
But who will believe this, that chances to look
The map of his journey, and sees in his book,
France, Savoy, Italy, and Helvetia,
The low countries, Germany and Rhetia
There named to be travelled? For this our Tom saith:
Pies on't, you have his historical faith.[2]
Each leaf of his journal, and line does unlock,
The truth of his heart there, and tells what a clock
He went out at each place, and at what he came in,
How long he did stay, at what sign he did inn.
Besides he tried ship, cart, wagon, and chair
Horse, foot, and all but flying in the air:
And therefore however the travelling nation,
Or builders of story have oft imputation
Of lying,[3] he fears so much the reproof
Of his foot, or his pen, his brain or his hoof,
That he dares to inform you, but somewhat meticulous
How scabbed, how ragged, and how pediculous[4]
He was in his travail, how like to be beaten,
For grapes he had gathered, before they were eaten.
How fain for his venery he was to cry (*Tergum o*)[5]
And lay in straw with the horses at Bergamo,
How well, and how often his shoes too were mended,
That sacred to Odcombe are now there suspended,

---

1   *scale … style* Each line of text in *Crudities* metaphorically corresponds to a specific physical
    distance traveled by Coryate; the "scale of his book" equates one mile traveled to one "yard"
    of Coryate's prose style.
2   *Pies on't* Pox on it (an exclamation of irritation); *historical faith* Credibility as a historian.
3   *travelling nation … lying* A popular saying in the period was that "travelers lied by
    authority."
4   *pediculous* Lousy (i.e., full of lice).
5   *fain for his venery* Gladly for his sexual pleasure; *Tergum o* Latin: Oh, [my] back!

I mean that one pair, wherewith he so hobbled
From Venice to Flushing, were not they well cobbled?
Yes. And thanks God in his pistle[1] or his book
How many learned men he has drawn with his hook
Of Latin and Greek, to his friendship. And seven
He there does protest he saw of the eleven.[2]
Nay more in his wardrobe, if you will laugh at a
Jest, he says, *Item* one suit of black taffeta[3]
Except a doublet, and bought of the Jews:
So that not them, his scabs, lice, or the stews,
Or anything else that another should hide,
Does he once dissemble, but tells he did ride
In a cart twixt Montreil and Abbeville.
And being at Flushing enforced to feel
Some want, they say in a sort he did crave:[4]
I writ he only his tail there did wave;[5]
Which he not denies. Now being so free,
Poor Tom have we cause to suspect just thee?[6]
No: as I first said, who would write a story at
The height, let him learn of Mr. Tom Coryate.

Explicit Ben. Jonson

[...]

---

1 *pistle* Epistle, i.e., Coryate's "Epistle to the Reader."
2 *And seven ... eleven* Coryate claims he visited seven of the eleven European scholar-correspondents mentioned in *Crudities*.
3 *Item one suit* This phrasing mimics formulaic language used in wills, inventories, and other enumerative genres; *black taffeta* Black silk.
4 *crave* Desire.
5 *I writ ... did wave* I wrote only that Coryate acted obsequiously like a dog (but with a possible double meaning of "waved his penis there," i.e., had sex in Italy with a Venetian courtesan).
6 *just thee* Only you or equitable you.

b. Hugh Holland, "Incipit Hugo Hollandus"[1]

The same hand again to the Idiot's[2] readers

Upon five principal harangues of the Odcombian orator, and prose-poet *Coryate* the Crude, *Hugonis Hollandi Carmen trimtrammetrum kimcamiasticum sive coxcomiasticum Odcomiasticumque*[3]

In speech there are eight parts (quotes he)[4]
But here in five not one I see:
So are they wove, and with that art
(O monstrous skill!) part within parts.
And yet his tongue that was the shuttle,[5]
In every point is not so subtle,
But you may see him here in gross,[6]
As well as Cheap or Charing Cross.[7]
Now he that cannot hear his sound,
In study is or sleep profound:
Or has his ears pawned to the pillory,[8]
Or lost their use with great artillery.

---

1   *Incipit Hugo Hollandus* Hugh Holland's second poem on Coryate was canceled during the printing of *Crambe*, but the original leaf survives in two copies.
2   [marginal note] In the dative not the genitive case, (that were more than the fustian case) from which he was miraculously and oraculously delivered. [Dative and genitive are cases of Latin nouns, used for indirect objects and possessives, respectively. A fustian case is a coarse cloth shirt. The note suggests that rather than "to the Idiot's," "to the Idiots" is the correct reading, which would mean that it is the mock commenders, not Coryate, who are idiots. Reading "Idiot's" in the genitive case is "more than the fustian case" because it would call Coryate an idiot directly, rather than only implying it through the example of his "fustian case" (i.e., Coryate would be an idiot to go on a journey with just one shirt).]
3   *harangues* Speeches (i.e., Coryate's presentation speeches to the royal family); *Hugonis ... Odcomiasticumque* Latin: The absurd, awkward, or coxcombiastic and Odcombiastic song of Hugh Holland.
4   [marginal note] The patron of our lusty Juventus, *viz William Lilly*. [William Lily (1468?–1522/23) was an English grammarian and author of a popular grammatical textbook. Lily was the "patron of our lusty Juventus" (i.e., patron of our youth) because of his ubiquity in early modern elementary education.]
5   *shuttle* Weaving instrument.
6   *in gross* In a general way.
7   *Cheap or Charing Cross* Eastcheap and Charing Cross, both places in London.
8   *pawned to the pillory* Nailed to the pillory, a wooden frame on a post with openings for the head and hands—a device designed for public punishment and humiliation.

He is so loud, and makes more noise
Than any of the Roaring Boys.[1]
Your taste will tell you he is fresh,[2]
(Though he be neither fish nor flesh)[3]
For here is not a dram of salt[4]
And yet no nose can find a fault.[5]
Nay, every noddy-nose[6] may well
His fragrant flowers of rhetoric smell:
Whereof who does not like the scent,
Let him make trial by his vent.[7]
As he is seen, heard, tasted, felt:
So easily may he be smelt.
Yet none can touch[8] him to the quick,
Yea if one do he will not kick.
Which shows (what ere before did pass
Twixt him and me)[9] he is no ass;[10]
For asses[11] used to feed on thistles:
But he writes Greek and Latin pistles,[12]
And here orations five has printed
(Who would have thought he had so stinted?)[13]

---

1   *Roaring Boys* Riotous bands of drunken gentlemen, common in seventeenth-century London.
2   [marginal note] New out in print.
3   [marginal note] Which is but part of the body, and the body part of him.
4   [marginal note] For salt serves to keep from tainting and putrefaction.
5   *no nose ... fault* Coryate doesn't smell bad.
6   *noddy-nose* Fool's nose.
7   [marginal note] The great vent and sale of his books. [This line includes a pun on "vent" meaning to break wind.]
8   [marginal note] He will not easily be moved to choler.
9   *what ere before ... him and me* Reference to the poem Hugh Holland wrote for Coryate in *Crudities*.
10 [marginal note] If need be I can bring my compurgators that in my former rhymes to the *Crudities* I meant the word ass, and not the thing ass. ["Compurgators" are witnesses. Holland references the line from his poem in *Crudities*: "I therefore leave the ass for fear he doubt."]
11 [marginal note] M.T.C. is welcome to all sorts of free tables. Vide the Character before the *Crudities*. ["M.T.C." is an abbreviation for "Mr. Thomas Coryate." Holland references Ben Jonson's "Character of the famous Odcombian, or rather Polytopian, Thomas the Coryate."]
12 *pistles* Letters.
13 *stinted* Limited [himself].

Five with the senses just in number,
Your understanding not to cumber,
And could (but that he would be thrifty)
As well as five, have printed fifty.
These are his second fruits and mellow;
Which prove his first fruits had a fellow.
But as all firster fruit be raw,
And fill with *Crudities* the maw,[1]
So are the later, without question,
More ripe, and make more quick digestion.
To stay you therefore from that Banquet,[2]
Where Tom was tossed as in a blanket,[3]
These dainties[4] he has served in since
To close your stomachs like a quince.[5]

Explicit Hugo Hollandus.

[…]

2. Thomas Coryate, "Certain orations pronounced by the author of the Crudities, to the King, Queen, Prince, Lady Elizabeth, and the Duke of York, at the delivery of his book to each of them"

This oration following was pronounced to the Prince in the Privy
Chamber at S. James[6] upon Easter Monday last, between six and sev-
en of the clock in the afternoon.

---

1 *fill with Crudities the maw* Fill the mouth with raw food. In addition to being the title of
   Coryate's travelogue, "crudities" are also raw or indigestible pieces of food.
2 [marginal note] Whereunto M.T.C. was lately bid to his own cost, but (a pies on't) all is
   now well again. [This reference is to *The Odcombian Banquet* (1611), a pirated edition of
   the "Panegyricke Verses" from *Crudities*. When Holland writes Coryate "was lately bid to
   his own cost" to "attend" the banquet, he means that Coryate lost money to the Banquet
   (because it negatively impacted sales of *Crudities*).]
3 *tossed as in a blanket* Agitated.
4 *dainties* Literally, delicacies; here, figuratively referring to *Coryats Crambe*.
5 *close … quince* Fill your stomachs as though you had eaten a quince.
6 *Privy Chamber at S. James* Private room reserved for the royal family at St. James's Palace,
   Westminster.

Most scintillant Phosphorus or our British Trinacria, even as the crystalline dew, that is exhaled up into the air out of the caverns & spongy pores of the succulent Earth, does by his distillation descend, and disperse itself again upon the spacious superficies of his mother Earth, and so consequently fecundate[1] the same with his bountiful irrigation: So I a poor vapour composed of drops, partly natural, partly literal, partly experimental, having had my generation within the liquid walls of this far-decantated island, being drawn up by the strength of my hungry and high-reaching desire of travel, and as it were craned up with the whirling wheel[2] of my longing appetite to survey exotic regions, have been hoisted to the altitude of the remote climates of France, Savoy, Italy, Rhetia; Helvetia, Alemannie, and the Netherlands; and being there in a manner involved for a time in the sweaty and humid clouds of industry capital, digital, and pedestrial, did distend the bottle of my brain with the most delectable liquor of observation, which I now vent and shower down upon the young and tender plants sprouting out of the same earth from the which like a poor[3] mushroom I first ascended. With this May dew of my Crude collections (May I well call it, because in May I first undertook my journey) I have now filled this new-laid eggshell, not doubting of the like effect in your highness the radiant sun of our English hemisphere, that the great Phoebean lamp has over a natural eggshell produced by a checkling hen, and filled with the pearly juice of the watery clouds, which is to elevate it to a far more eminent height than its own desert can mount it unto, and so by your gracious irradiation[4] to make it conspicuous and illustrious. Yes, (which is more) I wish that by the auspicious obumbration of your princely wings, this sense-less shell may prove a lively bird, whose bill with length & strength

---

1   *scintillant Phosphorus* Sparkling Phosphorous, or the morning star (predawn planet Venus); *British Trinacria* British Sicily; *distillation* Condensation; *superficies* Surfaces; *fecundate* Impregnate.

2   *experimental* Based on experience, experienced; *far-decantated* Well-known (literally "far-sung"); *craned up ... wheel* Hoisted up by the rotating wheel (a reference to the proverbial wheel of fortune).

3   *industry ... pedestrial* Labors of the head, fingers, and feet; *distend ... brain* Stretch out the leather bottle of my brain; *vent* Pour; *poor* Lowly.

4   *May dew* Dew gathered in May or on May Day specifically; this dew was believed to have medicinal value; *new-laid eggshell* This phrase begins an extended book as egg/bird meta-phor; *great Phoebean lamp* Sun; *checkling* Merry; *irradiation* Shining.

may reach and peck the very mountains of Arabia, and these nestle, increase and engender, and so breed more birds of the same feather that may in future time be presented as novelties unto your heroical[1] protection. In the meantime receive into your indulgent hand (I most humbly beseech your Highness) this tender feathered Red-breast.[2] Let his cage be your Highness's study, his perch your princely hand, by the support whereof, he may learn to chirp and sing so loud, that the sweetness of his notes may yield a delectable resonancy *Ultra Garamantas & Indos.*[3]

Dixi[4]

To the King in the chamber of presence at Royston[5] the second day of April being Tuesday, about eleven of the clock in the morning.

It were no marvel if the like should happen unto me (most invincible monarch of this thrice-renowned Albion, and the refulgent carbuncle[6] of Christendom) speaking unto your most excellent majesty that did once to Demosthenes that thunder-bolt of Athens, when he spake to Philip King of Macedon, even to be as mute as a Seriphian frog, or an Acanthian grasshopper;[7] since the very characters imprinted in the forehead of a king are able to appall the most confident

---

1   *auspicious obumbration* Favorable overshadowing; *nestle* Make nests; *more birds ... feather* More travelogues like *Crudities*; *heroical* Grand, heroic.

2   [Coryate's Note] Because the book was bound in crimson velvet. [Reference to the copy of *Crudities* Coryate presented to Prince Henry: it was bound in red velvet and its printing mistakes were hand-corrected by Coryate himself.]

3   *Ultra Garamantas & Indos* Latin: Beyond the Indies.

4   *Dixi* Latin: I said (meant to signify the end of the speech).

5   *chamber ... Royston* Room in James I's palace at Royston (Hertfordshire) used for meeting visitors.

6   *Albion* Britain; *refulgent carbuncle* Shining gem.

7   *Demosthenes ... Macedon* Ancient Greek orator Demosthenes (384–322 BCE) had several political confrontations with Philip of Macedon (382–336 BCE) over the fate of Athens; Demosthenes's tenacity in these arguments earned him the epithet "thunder-bolt of Athens." Here Coryate notes an instance when Demosthenes was silent before the king and could not speak; *Seriphian frog ... grasshopper* From the Latin proverbs "Rana Seriphica" (Seriphian frog) and "Acanthia cicada" (Acanthian grasshopper), both of which describe silent or unskilled people. In both proverbs frogs and grasshoppers, when moved from their native homes of Seriphos and Acanthus, respectively, ceased to make noise.

orator that ever spake, much more myself the meanest orator in your majesty's kingdom, whom if I should compare to a frog at having crawled many leagues by water, or to a grasshopper, as having hopped many miles by land, why should I wonder if by the gracious aspect of your resplendent excellency, words, speeches, and orations should be drawn from me, since by the very inarticulate sound of Amphion's harp, stocks and stones, mountains and valleys were said to dance lavoltoes and roundelays?[1] But what talk I of airy speeches? Why do I mention expatiating orations? The Persians (as the ancient historians do make us believe) were wont to present their kings with real gifts and anniversary oblations.[2] I being no Persian born, but intending ere long by the propitious indulgence of the celestial powers to be borne upon Persian ground, do offer unto your majesty a far-grown but a home-spun present, made indeed of coarse wool, but plucked from the backs of the glorious palaces, the lofty cloud-threatening towers and decrepit mountains of France, Savoy, Italy, Rhetia, Helvetia, Ale-mannie, and the Netherlands; spun into a thread by the wheel of my brain the spindle of my pen, and the oil of my industry in my native cell of Odcombe in the county of Somerset, and now woven into a piece of raw cloth in the printer's press of the most famigerated[3] city of London. The lists[4] of this cloth are the verses at both the ends of my book. In the beginning whereof some of the most singular and selected wits of your majesty's triangular monarchy do combat in the lists of Helicon and Parnassus;[5] and in the end my father's ghost alone doth diverberate the enthusiastic air of Pierian poesy.[6] But I glory not so much in imitating the Persian vassals, as in following the trace of our English merchants, who returning from foreign and remote

---

1 *appall* Make pale; *Amphion's harp* Amphion was the mythical son of Zeus and founder of the city of Thebes. His harp's music charmed the stones to move autonomously and form a wall around the city; *lavoltoes* Lively dances of Italian origin; *roundelays* Round dances.

2 *oblations* Gifts.

3 *famigerated* Well known abroad.

4 *lists* Borders, edges.

5 *triangular monarchy* Three-part monarchy of England, Scotland, and Wales; *lists of Helicon and Parnassus* Poetic competitions (literally the tournaments of the Muses; both Helicon and Parnassus are mountains sacred to the Muses).

6 *in the end ... poesy* Reference to the Latin poems of Coryate's father George Coryate (d. 1607), which are collected at the end of *Crudities*; *diverberate* Cleave in two; *Pierian poesy* Poetry of Pieria, the traditional home of the Muses in Greece.

navigations, do bring home in their vessels many uncouth[1] and transmarine commodities; but herein I differ from them. For they bring home their rarities in their ships. But I have brought home my ship and her far-fetched lading in myself. My ship (my dread sovereign) is my book, which I brought home swimming in the liquid ocean of my brain. She is now rigged, and trimmed, and ready to hoist sail; your majesty's favour will be unto it both like a pleasant gale of wind in the poop to make it bear sail, and like a well-fenced dock and secure haven of tranquility, where she may ride at anchor in a Halcedonian calm, and shoot off her ordinance against the critical pirates and malignant Zoiles[2] that scour the surging seas of this vast universe.

Dixi

---

1   *uncouth* Unknown.
2   *poop* Poop deck, located at a ship's stern; *Halcedonian* Tranquil; *Zoiles* Critics, in reference to Zoilus (fourth century BCE), a Greek critic known for being harsh.

C. Additional Materials from Other Sources

There are no manuscript drafts of *Coryats Crudities* extant today, but two handwritten texts relating to the composition and early reception of the travelogue have survived. The first is an autograph letter to the administrator Sir Michael Hicks (1543–1612), in which Coryate implores Hicks to help him gain the official approval he needs to have *Crudities* printed. A portion of the letter details the long hours Coryate spent in Venice writing up his travel observations. This letter was bound into the back of the specially bound copy of *Crudities* Coryate presented to Prince Henry Frederick (British Library G.6750). The second text collected here is a poem entitled "On Thomas Coriat," which circulated widely in seventeenth-century Oxford University circles in manuscript form but was never printed.

1. Thomas Coryate, letter to Sir Michael Hicks, 15 November 1610

To the right worthy Sir Michael Hicks Knight give these with all speed

Right worshipful and generous Sir

Though I fear I shall incur your reprehension for presuming to write unto your worship: yet I hope that superficial acquaintance which I had with you lately at Mr. Ingram's[1] (where it pleased you after a very debonair and courteous manner to take notice of me) will in some sort dispense with my boldness. I write unto you partly by way of deprecation for my error committed at that time at Mr. Ingram's table, which I beseech you to impute not to any voluntary malapertness of mine but rather to the merry prompting of that jovial blackbearded gentleman that sat next unto me who you know is so much given to his παρρησια and liberty of speech that sometimes

---

1   *Mr. Ingram*   Sir Arthur Ingram (c. 1571–1642), English politician.

he will not stick *amicissimum quempiam perstringere*[1] even to glance with some exquisite strain of wit at the dearest friend he has: partly also for that I am so bold to insinuate myself unto you with a suit whereunto if it shall please you to condescend not only I myself shall be obliged unto you for it in the straightest bond of true observance till I (after the fatal dissolution of my body and soul), but perhaps many notable members of our commonwealth may render no small thanks unto you for the same. Therefore, without any long introductions, to discover unto you the sum of the matter, it is thus; having travelled about 2 years since in these seven famous countries France, Savoy, Italy, Rhetia commonly called the Grisons' country, Helvetia alias Switzerland, some parts of high Germany, and the Netherlands, I was disposed to turn my microcosm (a phrase that a certain learned gentleman not long since used of me) into eyes, I mean to pry into all things of chiefest remark that were obvious unto my eyes in every place where I travelled, in so much that by my incessant industry and Herculean toil I wrote so many observations in the foresaid countries, as have filled very near 4 quires[2] of paper, having in the space of 5 months surveyed 47 cities. And this my itinerary I have concealed so long that it seemed *cum tineis ac blattis rixari* (as elegant Angelus Politianus writes of certain of his books in an epistle to Laurentius Medici Duke of Florence[3]) determining indeed rather, *Thetidi aut Veneris eas largiri marito* than to evulge[4] them to the light of my country before the consummation of my future travels, which I think will be very near 10 years hence. But some of my dear friends especially a certain learned gentleman one Mr. Laurence Whitaker hath used

---

1 *deprecation* Supplication; *malapertness* Presumption; παρρησια Greek: parresia, license of tongue; *amicissimum quempiam perstringere* Latin: to touch closely any dearest friend.

2 *quires* In paper-manufacturing or stationery, a quantity of sheets of paper: twenty-four or twenty-five sheets, depending on country of origin.

3 *cum tineis ... rixari* Latin: to dispute with moths and bookworms; *Laurentius ... Florence* Lorenzo de' Medici (1449–92), ruler of Florence. In the first letter of Book I of Poliziano's *Letters*, he writes that his handwritten correspondence has "cum blattis et tineis rixabantur." Here Poliziano does not refer to specific "books," as Coryate suggests, but to his letters. Coryate incorrectly identifies the addressee of Poliziano's letter, which is written to Piero II de' Medici (1472–1503), not Lorenzo de' Medici (Piero's father).

4 *Thetidi ... marito* Latin: to grant them as a gift either to Thetis [Greek sea goddess] or to Venus' spouse [Vulcan, Roman god of fire] (i.e., to cast into the sea or flames); *evulge* Make public.

such importunity of persuasions unto me, who amongst other things alleged that excellent proverbial verse

$$\Pi o\lambda\lambda\grave{a}\ \mu\varepsilon\tau a\xi\grave{v}\ \pi\acute{\varepsilon}\lambda\varepsilon\iota\ \kappa v\lambda\iota\kappa o\varsigma\ \kappa a\grave{\iota}\ \chi\varepsilon\iota\lambda\varepsilon o\varsigma\ \check{a}\kappa\rho o v^{1}$$

that I have confidently resolved by God's gracious permission to imprint the observations of my past travels for the benefit of my travelling countrymen before I go abroad again. For which cause determining to dedicate them to the Prince I went lately to his Highness pronounced an oration unto him before a great assembly of courtiers and withal presented unto him my journal, who so graciously accepted it that he has promised to entertain the dedication thereof. Since which time I have laboured very much about the licensing of my book that it might be printed, first with the late Archbishop of Canterbury,[2] whose sudden death hath much defeated my designment. After that with some of the high commissioners and the Bishop of London,[3] of whom I cannot get an approbation seeing it is not in their power to allow any books to be printed (as they affirm) but theological, so that the whole scope of my suit unto your worship does tend unto this, that you would vouchsafe to intercede for me unto my Lord Treasurer[4] that it would please his Lordship to give order it may be printed in London with some expedition. The Prince not only approving yea applauding it together with all those elected flowers of gentility that flourish in his Princely court, but also earnestly expecting it, especially since there is not as much as one line contained in my whole journal that makes against our state or any foreign Prince confederate with us, or against religion or good manners, my book containing principally the most remarkable antiquities of those cities that I have described yea and so many of them that I hope you will pardon me though I think that no man of our nation since the incarnation of Christ has observed more for the time in the foresaid countries. Which I hope you would not hold to be unlikely if you did but know what intolerable pains I took in my travels both by day and night, care affording myself 2 hours rest sometimes of the whole 24

---

1 $\Pi o\lambda\lambda\grave{a}$ ... $\check{a}\kappa\rho o v$ Greek: Many things often slip twixt cup and lip.
2 *Archbishop of Canterbury* Richard Bancroft (c. 1544–1610).
3 *Bishop of London* George Abbot (1562–1633).
4 *Lord Treasurer* Robert Cecil (1563–1612), first earl of Salisbury.

in the city of Venice by reason of my continual writing. Whereupon diverse Englishmen that lay in the same house with me observing my extreme watchings wherewith I did grievously excruciate[1] my body instantly desired me to pity myself and not to kill myself with my inordinate labours. To conclude, if it shall please your worship to gratify me in this my earnest supplication you will add unto me the very spurs of diligence and give me wonderful encouragement to observe such things in my future travels as I doubt not but shall be acceptable to the King and Queen themselves and all their royal children as also to the greatest peers and nobles of this kingdom, in hope whereof I will commend your worship to the gracious clientele of the omnipotent Jehovah.

From my chamber in Bowe Lane[2] this 15th November 1610

your worship's most suppliant beadsman[3]

Thomas Coryate

2. Anonymous, "On Tom Coriat"

Tom coming near the Italian coast
Of all his journeys past began to boast
   For travel was his fate:

He could not give himself to ease,
A greater journey than all these,
   His heels did meditate.[4]

I fear not these proud rocks said he
Alps Apennines what e'er they be:
   I fear nor wind, nor weather.

---

1   *watchings* States of wakefulness; *excruciate* Torture.
2   *Bowe Lane* Historical London street running north-south, located east of St. Paul's Cathedral.
3   *beadsman* Petitioner.
4   *meditate* Consider.

To those proud mountains will I go
And try whether heaven yea, or no,
    Be worth the coming thither.

Thus lifting up his heels aloft
He for good luck the Gods besought,
    In taming of that rock,

With resolution stout & brave
As swift as did that cripple knave,
    That stole Paul's weathercock.[1]

He had not passed half a mile
His dauntless courage 'gan to quail[2]
    And erst he back did look,

It's not for naught, that men do talk[3]
'Fore God (quoth he) a vengeance walk[4]
    As ere I undertook.

His feet were so bedecked[5] with corns
That he did seem to tread on thorns
    At each step which he tread,

His laziness did think it fit,
Therefore a little down to sit
    To view the works of God.

---

1   *that cripple ... weathercock* Story about a disabled man who climbed St. Paul's Cathedral to
    steal the silver weathercock from its steeple; the money he received for selling the weather-
    cock, combined with a lifetime of earnings from begging, enabled the man to build a Lon-
    don gate that would be named Cripplegate in his honor.
2   *quail* Fail.
3   *talk* Talk of the difficulty of climbing the Alps.
4   *vengeance walk* Difficult hike.
5   *bedecked* Ornamented.

Then he began the state to chide
Because they never did provide
    Some pretty odd device,[1]

To pluck up such as weary were
As for himself he did not care,
    And mount them in a trice.[2]

Up to the top at length he got
With very much ado God wot[3]
    And eagerly desired,

That mighty Jove would take the pains
To dash out the unworthy brains
    That offered to be tired.

What pin-clouts, or what sparrow-bills
Could overcome these mighty hills
    Had not Tom. Cor: done it?[4]

Had any wager then been laid
Upon his heels, or on his head,
    He certainly had won it.

His feet were chafed, & through some chink
Crept into heaven a vengeance stink[5]
    Which bred no simple odds,[6]

---

1   *pretty odd device* Clever rare contraption.
2   *To pluck ... trice* To hoist up weary travelers in an instant, a convenience Coryate forbore (not true in the prose travelogue, where he pays two men to carry him to the top in a sedan chair).
3   *wot* Knows.
4   *pin-clouts* Pins for patching together rags; *sparrow-bills* Little iron nails, sometimes used to mend shoes; *What pin-clouts ... done it?* What travelers could climb the Alps if Coryate hadn't already done it? (The pin-clouts and sparrow-bills represent travelers, who would use both objects to mend their typically ragged clothing.)
5   *vengeance stink* Great stink.
6   *bred no simple odds* Caused not an insignificant conflict.

It made Jove rise up from his seat
Whiles he sat merry at his meat
    With all the *Minor* Gods.

Jove swore in verse, Jove swore in prose
And whilst he swore he held his nose
    And verily did think,

That *Ganymede* had let a scape[1]
And mixt it with the juice of grape
    And gave it him to drink,

I verily am of an opinion
(Quoth he) that you have played the minion[2]
    But with a modest[3] face,

(Quoth he)[4] I have no such vile quality
But tis the stink of some mortality[5]
    That is about this place,

But *Venus* knew of all this quarrel
And left the Gods in equal parle[6]
    And wot you why?

Venus did look amongst her smocks[7]
For some old rags to make him socks
    His feet stunk out of cry.[8]

---

1   *Ganymede ... scape* Ganymede (Jupiter's cupbearer) had broken wind.
2   *Quoth he* Said Jupiter; *minion* Underling, understood in a derogatory sense.
3   *modest* Without impropriety. Jupiter believes Ganymede is acting impudently despite the "modest" look on his face.
4   *Quoth he* Said Ganymede.
5   *stink of some mortality* Human stench.
6   *parle* Debate.
7   *smocks* Women's undergarments.
8   *out of cry* Beyond measure.

Permissions Acknowledgments

"Coryats crudities; hastily gobled vp in five moneths trauells..."
Folger STC 5808. Courtesy of the Folger Shakespeare Library.

"Thomas Coriate traueller for the English vvits..." Folger STC
5811. Courtesy of the Folger Shakespeare Library.

From the Publisher

A name never says it all, but the word "Broadview" expresses a good deal of the philosophy behind our company. We are open to a broad range of academic approaches and political viewpoints. We pay attention to the broad impact book publishing and book printing has in the wider world; we began using recycled stock more than a decade ago, and for some years now we have used 100% recycled paper for most titles. Our publishing program is internationally oriented and broad-ranging. Our individual titles often appeal to a broad readership too; many are of interest as much to general readers as to academics and students.

Founded in 1985, Broadview remains a fully independent company owned by its shareholders—not an imprint or subsidiary of a larger multinational.

For the most accurate information on our books (including information on pricing, editions, and formats) please visit our website at www.broadviewpress.com. Our print books and ebooks are also available for sale on our site.

On the Broadview website we also offer several goods that are not books—among them the Broadview coffee mug, the Broadview beer stein (inscribed with a line from Geoffrey Chaucer's *Canterbury Tales*), the Broadview fridge magnets (your choice of philosophical or literary), and a range of T-shirts (made from combinations of hemp, bamboo, and/or high-quality pima cotton, with no child labor, sweatshop labor, or environmental degradation involved in their manufacture).

All these goods are available through the "merchandise" section of the Broadview website. When you buy Broadview goods you can support other goods too.

broadview press
www.broadviewpress.com

The interior of this book is printed on 100% recycled paper.